CAPE COD MODERN

CAPE COD MODERN

Midcentury Architecture and Community on the Outer Cape

Peter McMahon and Christine Cipriani

Foreword by Kenneth Frampton
New Photographs by Raimund Koch
New Drawings by Thomas Dalmas

Metropolis Books

CONTENTS

Hayden Walling, Lechay Studio, Wellfleet (1959)

ACKNOWLEDGMENTS

This book is, in part, a result of the Cape Cod Modern House Trust project to gather and archive documentation of Cape Cod modernism, and we thank the past and present members of the trust's board of directors for their support at every stage. We are equally grateful for the generous support of the Graham Foundation for Advanced Studies in the Fine Arts.

We could not have told this story without the cooperation and enthusiasm of the designers, and the late designers' families, friends, and clients, who generously shared their recollections, insights, photographs, and other source material: Michael Baldwin, Sarah Baldwin, Sara Barrett and the Wilkinson family, Charlotte Borsody, Tamas Breuer, Paul Brodeur, Bethany Bultman, Ivan Chermayeff, Peter Chermayeff, Rudd Falconer, Nathaniel Gardiner, Harvey Geiger, Noa Hall, Lee Halprin, Gilly Hatch and the Hatch family, Hayden Herrera, Nathaniel Hesse, Charles Jencks, Ati Gropius Johansen, Avis Kaeselau, Julie Kepes, Paul Krueger, Jenny Lion, Nick Macdonald, Steven Matheson, Norman McGrath, Hattula Moholy-Nagy, Florence Phillips, Sue Porter, Blair Resika, Susan Saarinen, Ben Schawinsky, Maurice K. Smith, Eleanor Stefani, Katherine Stillman, Christopher Walling, Gloria Watts, Peter Watts, Tom Weidlinger, John Taylor "Ike" Williams, Helen Miranda Wilson, Guy Wolff, and the Zehnder family.

For kindly sharing insights or research in their areas of expertise, or otherwise supporting our work, we thank Tulay Atak, Bob Bailey, Richard Boonisar, Linda Brown, Bill Burke, Brad Collins, Malachi Connolly, Mary Daniels, Leona Rust Egan, Amy Finstein, David Fixler, Bob Hayden, K. Michael Hays, Victoria Kennedy, Silvia Kolbowski, Duks Koschitz, Bill Lyons, Alyssa Moquin, Alan Powers (whose monograph on Serge Chermayeff was invaluable), and Helen Purcell. We also appreciate the assistance

of Leslie Edwards at the Cranbrook Archives; Jason Escalante at the Avery Architectural & Fine Arts Library, Columbia University; Teresa Harris at the Marcel Breuer Digital Archive, Bird Library, Syracuse University; Johanna Kasubowski and Ardys Kozbial at the Frances Loeb Library, Harvard Graduate School of Design; Barbara Kennedy at the Wellfleet Historical Society; Hope Morrill, formerly at the National Park Service; and Sally Zimmerman at Historic New England.

Special thanks to Diana Murphy, our publisher at Metropolis Books, whose passion for this project runs deep and has been immensely gratifying. For reading all or part of the manuscript and sending comments that sharpened and improved the book, we are deeply grateful to Cammie McAtee, Edward Ford, Isabelle Hyman, and our copy editor, Anne Thompson. Kenneth Frampton has been enthusiastic about our work at every stage, from research to finished book. We thank Thom Dalmas for his essential drawings, and those volunteers, students, and instructors who contributed surveys and preliminary drawings. Photographer Raimund Koch's talent is matched only by his work ethic, and we thank him for his commitment to getting the shot. Rita Jules designed the beautiful book we all wanted.

Peter McMahon: I thank my sister, Ellen McMahon, for her support and counsel, and my mother, Alice Annand McMahon, for early aesthetic immersion.

Christine Cipriani: I thank my husband, Al Velella, for making my work on this project possible in more ways than words can express; my parents, Cory and Barbara Cipriani, for encouragement and loving child care during spells of research and writing; and Tera Kemp, Amy Caldwell, and Trisha Gura for friendship and wisdom.

FOREWORD

KENNETH FRAMPTON

This painstakingly researched and beautifully written study of what has hitherto been a virtually unknown strain in the evolution of modern architectural culture in North America is the fruit of seven years of research on the part of its two authors, the designer and preservationist Peter McMahon and the writer and editor Christine Cipriani. The book is illustrated by more than 200 archival photographs, and greatly enriched by some 70 recent color shots of surviving houses by the distinguished photographer Raimund Koch, as well as by the meticulous drawings of Thomas Dalmas. This is an extraordinarily exhaustive study not only of a rich trove of modern vacation homes built on the Outer Cape between 1938 and 1977, but also of a peculiarly hybrid culture that, partly European and partly American in origin, gave rise to a fertile intellectual, artistic, and political milieu, which was as much about experimental modes of living and radical thought as it was about a responsive and progressive architectural culture.

In four thematic chapters, the authors outline the four phases of building on the Outer Cape, beginning with a survey of the first four centuries of an unselfconscious vernacular. Despite its well-burnished New England look today, the Outer Cape, with its infertile soil, scrub oaks, and storm-battered pitch pines, had been something of an outback, accessible only by rail or by a meandering local road, prior to the construction of Route 6 in the 1950s. Fishing was the primary mode of livelihood until its decline in the late nineteenth century. Around the turn of the century, painters began to frequent Provincetown, attracted by its light and its picturesque harbor. With the advent of World War I and the consequent inaccessibility of Paris, they were to be joined by the summer migration of the New York art and literary scene to Cape Cod. The decline of fishing as a way of life would be followed not only by the expansion of the art colony in Provincetown but also by a brief spell of railroad tourism before the rise in mass ownership of the automobile over the first half of the twentieth century, which enabled the adventurous to explore the scrubland of the Outer Cape for the first time.

In the second chapter, the authors focus on the "Brahmin Bohemians," documenting both their artistic initiatives and their unconventional modus vivendi. The first of that generation was the 20-year-old Harvard undergraduate Jack Phillips, the progeny of an American elite family going back to the seventeenth century. By the time he inherited land on the Cape, he was already a nonconformist with strong artistic leanings, which eventually induced him in 1938 to erect his audacious dune studio on the edge of the ocean. This large timber shed, which would subsequently be used as both a studio and a rendezvous for dance parties, had two unabashedly modern aspects — its abstract, slightly mono-pitched clapboarded form and its outsized full-height window facing out over the sea. Phillips was joined in Wellfleet in the late '30s by two other autodidact artist/builders coming from elite backgrounds — Jack Hall and Hayden Walling, both of whom designed modern vacation homes for others while they themselves preferred to live in adapted vintage houses.

The only professional architect among these builders was Bostonian art patron Nathaniel Saltonstall, whose legacy in Wellfleet is an unequivocally modern, deftly planned cottage settlement of 1949, now known as The Colony.

By the early 1940s, modernism had arrived on the Cape, for around this time Phillips met the Bauhaus émigrés Walter Gropius and Marcel Breuer, and, at some remove, the architect and designer Serge Chermayeff, who had recently left Great Britain. As the authors note, upon their arrival in the States, the Bauhauslers elected to take their first vacation on a tiny peninsula off of Cape Cod, and this happenstance points the way to the third chapter, entitled "Community and Privacy: The Europeans." This era saw the piecemeal proliferation of the modern vacation cottage, which, despite the émigré respect for the local vernacular, was nonetheless characterized by a number of invariably modern features, such as a simple orthogonal, economically modular structure elevated clear of the ground so as to adapt to the varying contours of the site, and covered by a flat or slightly pitched roof. Chermayeff was the first architect among this group to summer regularly on the Cape, and after renting a cottage from Phillips in the early '40s, he purchased the site and erected a modular, mono-pitched timber-framed house and studio on it, slightly raised off the ground and enlivened by brightly colored side panels reminiscent of nautical flags.

In 1944, at Chermayeff's urging, Breuer bought a plot of land nearby, on which he built, in 1949, a house for his family's occupation. This led to Breuer's invention of his prototypical long house, conceived from the outset as a lightweight, modular timber-framed struc-

Walter and Ise Gropius visiting the Chermayeff family in Wellfleet, ca. late 1950s

ture elevated clear of the ground on widely spaced timber posts, plus an external porch cantilevered from the main frame. This single-story prism of the house itself was divided into zones for sleeping and living, with a freestanding fireplace situated on the axis of the living volume at one end. This generous space, plus the adjacent screened-in porch, afforded a particularly open and liberative environment.

Breuer's designs for vacation houses on the Outer Cape, even when elaborated into two parallel prisms or expanded across a central entry deck, as in the Scott and Wise houses, were variations on the same theme, as was the small house that he designed for György and Juliet Kepes. One figure to move away from Breuer's long house model was the brilliant Hungarian structural engineer Paul Weidlinger, whose three-bedroom house with a square plan was poised on a platform built on top of a wire-cable-braced timber framework.

By the time one reaches the last chapter of this study, devoted to late modernism, it is possible to see this book as a record of the spontaneous evolution of a fragile subset of modern architecture in America, touching on the comings and goings of an unending stream of artists, writers, scientists, and politicos who were active on the Outer Cape from the mid-'30s to the 1970s. Over this period, the towns of Wellfleet, Truro, and Provincetown were populated in the summer by a wide spectrum of an East Coast elite, ranging from the radical editor of the *Partisan Review*, Dwight Macdonald, accompanied by Edmund Wilson and Mary McCarthy, to such leftist gurus as Howard Zinn and Noam Chomsky, and interspersed here and there with creative mavericks like Bernard Rudofsky, Costantino Nivola, and Saul Steinberg, and even with an occasional prestigious figure from the Kennedy circle, such as the historian Arthur Schlesinger, Jr.

Within the late modern swan song of this account, two figures emerge with particular prominence. The first of these was the young Cambridge protégé of Josep Lluís Sert, the tyro-architect Paul Krueger, who would be given the task of realizing Le Corbusier's Carpenter Center for the Visual Arts at Harvard in the early 1960s. The second was Charles Jencks, the son of the pianist and atonal composer Gardner Jencks — who in 1939 built a totally traditional house and studio overlooking the bay separating the Outer Cape from the mainland. Charles Jencks, who by the mid-'70s had become the world-renowned theorist of architectural postmodernism, staked out his own claim to a vacation site on the Cape in 1970, initially by acquiring a number of barrack huts that had been combined by the ubiquitous Phillips, and then by building his own ironically elaborated "decorated shed" to serve as a studio.

Krueger's brand of late modernism would embody a particularly heroic cultural statement, inasmuch as his strikingly original Mark House, built in 1966 on a sloping site in Truro, was a 12-foot-wide timber house modeled on a typical duplex within Le Corbusier's Unité d'Habitation in Marseille of 1952. Through an ingenious adaptation from concrete to wood, Krueger was able to combine the tectonic of a Provincetown fisherman's shack with a dwelling type whose ultimate form derived from a Carthusian monastic cell. The result still projects from a heather-covered hill as a massive vertical prism in wood held in place against the gale-force winds and even hurricanes by wire cable stays on either side of its megaron form. Still standing after nearly 50 years and occupied by its original clients, it testifies today like a flag flying in the breeze to the ineffable durability of the tradition of the Cape Cod modern house.

PROLOGUE

Walter Gropius was tired.

As founder of the legendary Bauhaus design school in Germany, and architect of the school's landmark glass-skinned building in Dessau (1926), Gropius had become almost larger than life in the international design world. When political pressures made the Bauhaus increasingly challenging to operate, he had decamped to Berlin and then London, but political, economic, and cultural conditions in the 1930s all crippled his attempts to change the course of European building. Architecture schools in America, in contrast, were hungry for change. In 1936, Gropius accepted a lifetime professorship at Harvard's new Graduate School of Design, and in early 1937 he and his wife, Ise, moved to the United States, where they ricocheted from one welcome event to another in Cambridge and New York — "63 parties," Gropius moaned in a letter, while Ise put the number at 57.[1]

Ready to regroup and experience the New World on their own terms, the couple rented a house for the summer on Planting Island, in Marion, Massachusetts, near the base of Cape Cod — "a marvelous piece of earth," Gropius wrote to his London colleague Maxwell Fry. They now hosted a festive reunion of Bauhaus masters, students, and colleagues who had recently fled the troubles abroad. The first to arrive were Marcel Breuer — the young star architect and furniture designer who would soon join Gropius at Harvard — and the Austrian graphic designer Herbert Bayer. Next came the Hungarian artist and photographer László Moholy-Nagy and the Swiss-born painter Xanti

Schawinsky, and finally the German museum curator Alexander Dorner and his wife, Ella. Warmed by shared memories of an earlier trip to Switzerland, the group now happily feasted, bathed in the brisk waters of Buzzards Bay, and planned their futures on a new continent, all sensing they were on the cusp of a momentous new phase in their lives. The trip sealed Breuer's decision to stay in the United States. He wrote to a friend within a week, "Here at the seaside with the Gropiuses I am having a magnificent time; America has above all taken me by pleasant surprise." Dorner dubbed their Massachusetts idyll the Summer Bauhaus.[2]

The flight of Europe's avant-garde during the buildup to World War II would permanently transform American architecture and design. Gropius and Breuer, teaching a modified version of the Bauhaus curriculum at Harvard, nurtured a generation of modernists who would dominate American architecture for decades: Edward Larrabee Barnes, Philip Johnson, I. M. Pei, Paul Rudolph, and Edward Durell Stone, to name just a few. Schawinsky taught with Bauhaus master Josef Albers at Black Mountain College, in North Carolina; Moholy-Nagy became the first director of the New Bauhaus in Chicago, founded in 1937; and Bayer secured work at New York's Museum of Modern Art, helping to curate the watershed 1938 exhibition *Bauhaus 1919–1928*.

Yet even as they moved on, the group never lost its connection to Cape Cod. Several members returned, when they had the means, to travel farther up the peninsula, rent cabins, buy land, and design their ideal summer homes. And although Gropius himself never

View of Northeast Pond from the deck of Charlie Zehnder's Kugel/Gips House, Wellfleet (1970)

Top: Walter and Ise Gropius on beach. *Left*: At the end of their first summer in Massachusetts, the Bauhauslers sent this postcard to an architect friend in Budapest. Written by Marcel Breuer, it said, "For the time being we have flooded the U.S.A.," and was signed by Herbert Bayer, Breuer, Gropius, and Xanti Schawinsky.

put down roots on the Cape, he was often present as both houseguest and ineffable influence on the course of twentieth-century design.

Around the time the Summer Bauhaus convened, a young Boston Brahmin named John C. "Jack" Phillips received an inheritance: 800 acres of what was then considered a bug-infested wasteland on the dangerous Outer Cape shore. After a few years in France studying art — not architecture — Phillips settled in Wellfleet and designed the area's first modern house and studio.

In 1944, he sold land to the British architect Serge Chermayeff, and soon, through social ties, Breuer, the multitalented artists György and Juliet Kepes, the structural engineer Paul Weidlinger and his wife, Madeleine, and the Finnish architect Olav Hammarström and his wife, the textile designer Marianne Strengell, had bought plots nearby. Within a few years, the woods were thick with designers from central and northern Europe and gentlemen artist-woodsmen like Phillips. A few stayed year-round, but most made annual

Gropius (center, with hat) in the summer of 1937 on Planting Island, at the base of Cape Cod, flanked by Schawinsky, Bayer, Breuer (mostly hidden), and Mary Coss, imitating the classical sculpture *Laocoön and His Sons*. Coss would soon become curator of architecture at the Museum of Modern Art, New York, where she worked on exhibitions with Alvar Aalto and others, and in 1944 she married Edward Larrabee Barnes.

retreats from their professional homes, making Wellfleet a sudden junction of intellectual currents from New York, Boston, Cambridge, and the country's top schools of architecture and design. In a town best known for its oysters, freshwater ponds, and dual shorelines — sunrise on the ocean, sunset on the bay — avant-garde homes began to appear amid the pitch pines and sand dunes. Three decades later, there were about a hundred modern houses of interest here.

While outer Cape Cod's contributions to twentieth-century art, theater, and literature are well known, its profusion of midcentury architecture has gone mostly unnoticed. Ironically, this was somewhat deliberate. These modern houses are the opposite of monumental, often comprising less than a thousand square feet. Most are hidden in the woods. Even so, most are introverted on the approach, peering at guests from high ribbon windows while bursting open to the landscape in back. Their designers initially had no clients; they built for themselves and their families, or for friends sympathetic to their goals. Their summer homes were laboratories,

thought experiments, places to revisit problems and work through ideas without spending much money.

These modernists were not iconoclasts, exactly: they took cues from colonial cottages and fishing shacks, including the classic pitched-roof cottage now known universally as a Cape. Borrowing from traditional materials (such as cedar siding), methods, and precepts, they fashioned basic lumberyard materials into new designs that solved genuine problems. Whereas earlier builders set Capes in vales and hollows for shelter from the elements, many modernists built on mounds — and lifted their houses on pilings — to leave the land untouched while capturing light, breezes, and views. By the 1960s, younger architects were collaborating with the masters, establishing their own practices, and evolving the new vernacular as the aims and forms of modern architecture itself widened beyond their origins. The result of this ferment is a body of work unlike any other, a regional modernism that fused Bauhaus ideals and postwar innovations with the building traditions of Cape Cod fishing towns.

Bauhaus colleagues Schawinsky, László Moholy-Nagy, and Bayer at Planting Island, Massachusetts, 1937

Many of these designers came of age around World War II, when building commissions were few. They earned a living in either academia or carpentry. Out of both necessity and ideology, they wanted to create affordable housing for a growing population. Accordingly, on the Cape, they used inexpensive, off-the-shelf materials such as plate glass and Homasote, the first and only construction material made of recycled paper. Some designers, like their thrifty colonial forebears, used salvaged materials; and some used no glazed windows at all, only screens. The results were almost temporary in their construction. Cottage decor was informal — walls were hung with original artwork by owners' friends, and rooms could be stocked with butterfly or Windsor chairs, whatever was affordable and functional. Kitchens were small and utilitarian, an afterthought to the indoor-outdoor gathering space.

This ad hoc, improvisational quality is what sets Cape Cod modernism apart from other regional adaptations of the modern movement. Many of these houses were thrown together with whatever materials were handy, from eighteenth-century bricks and beams to entire abandoned structures such as army barracks or a water tower. If the property held an old house or cabin, most designers simply grafted a modern house onto it, forming a permanent hybrid. Because most designed their first Cape Cod house for themselves, they relished the freedom to take risks and sometimes to fail — as one architect did with a magnificent fireplace that filled his living room with smoke. And, like the traditional Cape, the modern houses were repeatedly modified and enlarged to suit their owners' changing needs and means.

Ultimately, it was the designers' talented guests and clients who made their community a destination: the Gropiuses, who stayed early and often with the Breuers and Chermayeffs; three generations of the Saarinen family; Florence and Hans Knoll; Surrealist painter Max Ernst and his wife, art collector Peggy Guggenheim; *New Yorker* cartoonist Saul Steinberg and writer Dwight Macdonald; historian Arthur Schlesinger, Jr.; and countless others. Many designers worked until 4 or 5 p.m., then repaired to one another's houses for martinis, salami, and Triscuits. And in the quiet summers of the 1940s, their Saturday-night bonfires on Newcomb Hollow Beach led to more love affairs than will ever be documented.

———

Modernism is fundamentally essentialism: a quest to find the inherent qualities and possibilities of spaces, materials, colors, and light, and use them to design elegant solutions without historical reference or quotation. Building on the revolutionary Bauhaus philosophy, which married those essentials to skilled craftsmanship and affordable modes of production, the modern movement in architecture blended two seemingly disparate strands. One embraced mass production, new materials, and new construction technologies, and aimed to dazzle with previously impossible feats of engineering — to express the spirit of a new machine age. The other celebrated authentic, preindustrial, handmade goods and methods. What the two have in common is functionality without bourgeois pretense.

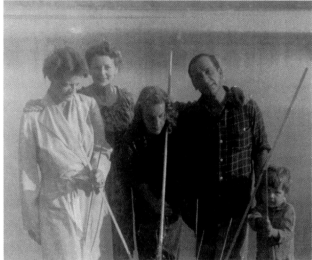

Photographs taken on Ryder Pond, Truro, ca. 1945. *Left*: Gropius, Schawinsky's assistant, and Schawinsky. *Right*: Irene Schawinsky, Ise Gropius, Schawinsky's assistant, Schawinsky, and son Ben

In the 1920s, Breuer won international fame for furniture made of bent tubular steel hung with hand-wrought cane or leather; 20 years later, on Cape Cod, his cottage for the Kepeses (1949) achieved a similar effect with unfinished plywood and pine, factory-made plate-glass windows, hand-thrown ceramics, and handwoven grass-cloth floor mats.

Today, technology and handicraft are reuniting in areas such as small-scale prefabricated housing, humanitarian design activism, and intricate, digitally enabled architectural forms. Many in the design world are focused on reducing the human footprint through renewable energy, minimal dwellings, nomadic structures, even treehouses — versions of the same ideals that drove the Cape Cod modernists and, in many ways, their colonial predecessors.

The modernists' work on the Outer Cape, once experimental, is now historic. In 1959, U.S. senators Leverett Saltonstall and John F. Kennedy sponsored legislation to create the Cape Cod National Seashore, a narrow, 40-mile strip of 44,600 acres along the peninsula's coast. Gambling that the legislation would not pass, developers and waterfront-property owners began frantically building in the dunes; in 1961, President Kennedy signed the bill into law. For houses erected during the legislative lull between 1959 and 1961, the government generally bought out the owners at market value and gave them a 25-year lease, at the end of which the structures would be demolished and the land would revert to its natural state. As it happened,

many houses went into administrative limbo, vacant but still standing, becoming sad shells of a cultural moment that had passed. By 2003, thanks to the work of a handful of preservationists, seashore officials had an inkling that at least half a dozen of its modern buildings were historically significant. The nonprofit Cape Cod Modern House Trust, founded in 2007, has since acquired long-term leases on three important modern homes within the seashore's boundaries — the Kugel/Gips House, the Hatch House, and the Weidlinger House — and, one by one, restored them.

From the Summer Bauhaus onward, the Cape's modern designers enjoyed a lifestyle based on communion with nature, solitary creativity, and shared festivity. Their houses captured this ethos with their blurring of indoors and outdoors, their secluded studios, and their outdoor party spaces. The group did serious work on the Cape, and exchanged ideas while walking in the woods or boating on a pond. Despite their cosmopolitan backgrounds, a surprising number, including Breuer, are buried by their homes in this quiet place. Their work is now threatened by the passage of time in an unforgiving climate, its transience a poignant testament to their sensitive, sparing designs.

Notes

1. Pearlman, *Inventing American Modernism*, 71–73, 251 n. 113; Reginald Isaacs, *Walter Gropius: Der Mensch und sein Werk* (Berlin: Mann Verlag, 1983), vol. 2, 854. Quotation translated by Ati Gropius Johansen and Stefanie Werner.
2. Hyman, *Marcel Breuer, Architect*, 95; Isaacs, 854–55.

ARCHITECTURE ON THE EDGE
FOUR HUNDRED YEARS OF
BUILDING FOR THE MOMENT

Like a sparkling wine, the Cape was made under pressure — the fierce double pressure of natural forces and human energy.

— KATHARINE SMITH AND EDITH SHAY

People here have been nourished by beauty and change and danger.

— MARY HEATON VORSE

Five thousand years from now, Cape Cod will be gone.

Humans were late arrivals to this rugged curl of land south of Boston, and we came just in time. The Cape was dragged into being just eighteen thousand years ago, near the end of the most recent Ice Age. The northward retreat of the giant Laurentide Ice Sheet left a graceful, arm-shaped edge of sand, gravel, clay, and rock surrounded by rising salt water. The highest ridge of that pile of debris, the glacial moraine, now forms a topographical backbone down the Cape, surrounded by outwash plains that slope westward into Cape Cod Bay. Lingering ice boulders, standing firm as meltwaters deposited land around them, eventually melted into deep puddles known as kettle ponds — now some of the loveliest, most secluded settings on outer Cape Cod.

Since that time, Atlantic waves and currents have been pounding the Cape's outer shore in oblique, wind-blown patterns, steadily eroding the beach and pushing enough sand northward to create all of Provincetown and its harbor. Even the otherworldly dunes of the Province Lands, cherished by generations of painters,

writers, and photographers, are a flash in the pan of geological time: formed by the displacement of sandy points south, they were woodlands just a few hundred years ago. Humanity's appetite for lumber scraped them into bare dunes, which had to be manually replanted to keep the drifting sand from smothering Provincetown. The land is in endless flux.

And the sea has never stopped rising.

Architecture on Cape Cod has always been imbued with this sense of impermanence. Every type of building here — domestic, commercial, maritime, holiday — has an element of the ephemeral. Buildings near the water were often set on pilings, or stilts, to avoid being crushed or soaked by the weather; in a storm, water, snow, or sand would swirl under and around the building rather than drift against it. In the twentieth century, attitudes toward the shore began to shift from fear to excitement, and many fish houses, dune shacks, and lifesaving stations were repurposed and prized by creative people for their very closeness to nature. Many were, in turn, poetically lost to the sea.

Cape Cod's most famous house type, the snug, harmonious Cape, was built to last. It was an English house — simple, practical, and handsome. A Cape was not easily ruined — but it could be moved. When the ocean encroached on a neighborhood, or business called from the harbor, owners would lift, roll, and float these steadfast abodes from one part of town to another. Complicating their pedigrees, many early houses were built or expanded with recycled lumber from different times and places. Go back far enough

Looking south at Paul Krueger's Mark House, Truro (1966)

Clay cliffs, Truro. Erosion has shaped Cape Cod's shoreline in ways both scenic and destructive.

Nauset Light Beach, Eastham

and the bones of every house on Cape Cod hold multiple stories. An old building may be historic, but it probably isn't original to one period.

When the modernists arrive, they will build on these traditions of enterprise, flexibility, and economy, often consciously borrowing elements of Cape Cod's vernaculars that typify modern ideals. Wampanoag wetus, classic Capes, dune shacks, huts of refuge, and maritime sheds on pilings were all framed structures with a skin. They wore their locally available, often second-hand materials honestly, achieving a handsome profile with little or no adornment. They sat lightly on the land, with little or no foundational footprint, and were sited to interact with nature in the most respectful way — sometimes to their benefit, sometimes to their detriment. And they were often designed and built by the user, with no professional intermediary.

———————————

Yet the modernists were hardly the first to incorporate elements of Cape Cod's earlier building types. The seventeenth-century colonists had not been architectural innovators; their villages resembled those of rural Britain, with only gradual concessions to local climate and custom. And at the very beginning, the settlers simply copied what they saw in front of them: the Wampanoag wetu, a domed hut.

The Outer Cape has been occupied, on and off, for at least 5,000 years. Members of the Wampanoag tribes, including the Nausets and Pamets, traditionally lived in wetus — imprecisely called wigwams by British explorers — made of resilient cedar saplings covered with mats of bark or reeds. Wetus were arched and elongated, rather like a loaf of bread, and their construction made them highly adaptable. To build one, tribesmen and -women bent and joined a framework of saplings, lashing them together at crossing points with withes (flexible willow branches) or bark strips. Women then sheathed the frame in 6- to 9-foot-long bark strips, lapping them like shingles; in summer, they used mats woven of reeds or grass. Inside the wetu, another, more decorative layer of mats provided extra protection.

Stripped of their bark or reed walls, these Outer Cape wetus reveal their hybrid ancestry: Wampanoag frames bookended by English doors and chimneys.

A central fire pit served as a furnace and stove, and mats could be adjusted over a hole in the roof for draft and smoke control. Wetus were watertight, and said to be warmer in winter than the colonists' homes.

Most of New England's tribes were settlers, not nomads. Because each new move meant clearing trees by stone ax, the Wampanoag positioned their villages carefully and maintained them for generations. In choosing a site, they looked for a place easily cleared, with a height both strategic and scenic, a nearby hill or evergreen grove for shelter from the north wind, a source of firewood, and sources of water for drinking, fishing, and travel. When they ventured out on hunting and fishing trips — which sometimes doubled as beach vacations — they often built a temporary wetu on the new site. The entire skin of such a wetu could be pulled after use and the frame left bare for the group's next visit.[1]

Desperate for shelter, the first English settlers copied the Wampanoag wetu and made it their own with two modifications: a framed wooden door in lieu of a hanging mat, and a fireplace with a chimney instead of a smoke hole.[2] With its watertight yet portable sheathing, the wetu was an object lesson in sustainable construction. It became the first in a chain of building types that would lend their best aspects to new arrivals.

Cape Cod's leading contribution to world architecture is more than just a style. By the mid-twentieth

The Bound Brook Island area of northern Wellfleet in the early twentieth century. In 1953, the eighteenth-century Cape in the background, the Joel Atwood House, became the home of self-taught designer-builder Jack Hall.

century, it had become a prototype. The extraordinary consistency of the Cape silhouette initially reflected adherence to Old World building traditions, overlaid with a New World Puritan ethos of economic modesty.[3] Three hundred years later, it symbolized easy mass production in postwar suburbs. And Cape Cod's modernists respected this particular precursor, sometimes to the point of living in one.

Beloved for its handsome proportions and antique charm, the Cape has always been, from top to bottom, a utilitarian house. Designed, as a local saying went, with a "short hoist and a long peak," the Cape was well suited to the harsh coastal climate of New England — the low, 7-foot ceilings of the main floor conserved heat indoors, and the steeply pitched roof resisted snow accumulation. The squat profile assumed a useful crouch against the wind, and Cape Cod builders sited the house for natural shelter in a hollow or on low

ground. (In the 1850s, Henry David Thoreau wrote that such homes were almost "concealed entirely, as much as if they had been swallowed up in the earth.") The roof pitch reflected the earlier use of thatch in both England and the colonies, but it persisted long after thatch gave way to shingles, relaxing only gradually and finding its angle of repose at around 45 degrees. On the exterior, settlers adapted to their new climate by covering what was probably a Tudor-style half-timbered facade with shingles and/or clapboards.[4] Indoors, however, the early Cape clearly expressed its structure with a network of slightly irregular oak or chestnut beams.

The original, seventeenth-century Cape was a medieval English–style thatched-roof cottage modified with New World materials. When colonists first settled Cape Cod, in the 1630s, dense forests of cedar, oak, and other hardwoods extended to the water's edge. The earliest Capes were framed with posts and beams of

As fine an example of the Cape as still stands, the Joel Atwood House was built around 1730 and later extended. It was Hall's home for the second half of the twentieth century.

hand-hewn oak or chestnut, set on a wooden sill over an 8- or 12-inch fieldstone foundation, with only a small, cylindrical root or "beanpot" cellar below grade. Settlers covered their exterior walls and roofs with sheathing — a skin of planks applied to the frame — and clad them in hand-cut, lapped cedar shingles (also called shakes) or, less commonly, clapboards. Because the scarcity of lime made plaster expensive, they filled their walls with clay or brick.[5]

The house was anchored by a massive, central stone chimney, which fanned out to provide two ground-floor hearths including the large fireplace and brick-domed oven of the main living space, known as the keeping room. The chimney bulged and narrowed as it rose from the foundation, exiting the roof as a compressed rectangular box. When an early Cape burns down or is demolished, you can see the organic, undulating shape of this masonry as it twists and slopes outward and

upward in the course of its various functions. The stair to the upper floor normally wound hard up against the chimney, so steep and slim that today it feels more like a ship's ladder. The flexibility of the Cape plan allowed owners to add windows, dormers, bathrooms, closets, and ultimately entire ells, or additions, to the house without affecting its basic form. Two smaller plans, the half Cape and three-quarter Cape, lent themselves to a sort of modular construction: as a family grew in size and fortune, one house could be expanded or two combined to form a classic or even larger Cape.

It was Yale president Timothy Dwight who gave the house its nickname after noting its popularity throughout Cape Cod in 1800. On the peninsula itself, the Cape remained the style of choice until the mid-nineteenth century, when Victorians and Greek Revivals appeared. In the 1920s, swelling waves of tourists inspired a zeal for historic preservation, and the Cape cottage and

The Cape house plan was endlessly flexible. The silhouette best known today is the full Cape (right), but smaller forms included the half cape (left) and three-quarter Cape (middle).

other colonial styles began to make a comeback. During the Great Depression, the federal government seized on the Cape as a prototype for affordable single-family housing, and the resulting plans offered by the Federal Housing Administration (FHA) were embraced nationwide for their rare combination of appeal and economy. At the same time, in 1937, the Works Project Administration (WPA) added a Cape Cod book to its Federal Writers' Project series of travel guides. The author, Josef Berger, included a disquisition on Capes that now reads like a modernist manifesto:

Cape Cod's main contribution to the architecture of homes is simplicity. The principle seems to be, roughly, that the looks of a house are not enhanced by any "gadget" or trick which does not in some way add to its function as a shelter; and conversely, if the need for shelter is perfectly fulfilled, and the structure best designed to meet the elements where it stands, its looks will take care of themselves — will be good looks.[6]

Writers Katharine Smith and Edith Shay, in their Depression-era guidebook *Down the Cape,* go one step further and hold up the Cape as an embodiment of democratic principles born in a Puritan context. Smith, married to the novelist John Dos Passos, and Shay, wife of the bookseller and publisher Frank Shay, were members of the Outer Cape's progressive arts community. Their vision of the house, like Berger's, contains a modern ideal: in this case, equal opportunity through simple, affordable housing.

Cape Cod houses are wooden witness of the idea of severe doctrine combined with a stiff-necked belief in the civil and political rights of the individual. They seem frail but are sturdy, look small but are larger than they look, they are plainly built out of plain materials, and their chief beauty is their proportion. [They] have about them a democratic equality which is part of their early American charm, and the virtues of thrift, neatness and independence are built up visibly in the solid frames of hewn oak, hand-split shingles, careful construction and detail.[7]

Although Capes are often admired for their harmonious proportions, their builders usually prized function over form. This was especially true when a house was expanded; the floor plan of a renovated Cape often meandered erratically. Half and three-quarter Capes were asymmetrical from the start, and even a full Cape might have an off-center chimney. About the only ornament applied to early Capes was a bit of chamfering on the main interior structural beams. Architectural historian Hugh Morrison wrote in the 1950s that "the Colonial builder's primary concern was with the need to be filled, the materials to be used, and the shaping of them into a sound and workmanlike structure. . . . He shaped his rooms according to need [and] let structure express itself, he used his materials frankly as they came."[8]

After World War II, the work of developer William Levitt — creator of Long Island's Levittown and other planned suburbs — spread the Cape across the American landscape. Thanks to its simple plans and lines,

The Solomon Howes House, built in 1800 on Queen Anne Road in Chatham, is a rare Cape with an original bow or "ship's bottom" roof. To achieve this profile, the roof timbers were painstakingly shaped to evoke a ship's hull.

the house was readily mass-produced, so Levitt delivered thousands of copies partially prefabricated and devised an assembly-line system for speedy construction on-site.[9] The resulting swaths of suburban uniformity, and their descendants nationwide, made Levitt a bête noire in the design world. And yet, considering the proven efficacy of the Cape Cod house plan, Levittown actually embodied a Bauhaus ideal: affordable reproductions of useful design for the common household.

———————

Despite their durability, which helped thousands of English settlers find their feet and raise their families in a challenging new world, even Capes and other premodern area houses were not locked in place. Over the centuries, whole neighborhoods of them have traveled from land to sea and back. Houses were raised off their meager foundations using screw jacks with 6-foot handles; at that point, some were pulled, winched, or rolled overland by oxen or horses, some were reportedly mounted on beams and skidded over icy ground like sleds, and others were floated across bays and harbors to their new destinations. Other houses were "flaked" — dismembered like fish — and their carefully numbered parts carted off and reassembled.[10]

In her 1942 memoir *Time and the Town*, Provincetown journalist Mary Heaton Vorse credits a centuries-old fishing tradition for the town's architectural fluidity:

In the mid-nineteenth century, the entire population of the fishing village on Long Point—the sandy spit of land that rims Provincetown's harbor—moved to the mainland, houses and all.

...When the Winslows bought a piece of property near us and went to build a new house there, the question was what to do with the old house. The carpenter was a Provincetown man and he was not for a moment perplexed. He rolled the old house out into the bay and there he anchored it. A storm came up and for two days the distracted house rocked and curtsied. Its shutters and doors blew open and the blank windows and the yawning door looked like a doleful screaming mouth.

One day Tony Avellar shouted to me, "Want to come and tow a house over to Beach Point?"

He hitched his gas boat to the house and slowly we chugged and bobbed across the Bay, where men rolled the house across the beach, and there it became a garage.[11]

Across the Outer Cape, entire villages moved when threatened by shifting economics or shorelines. Over the course of the nineteenth century, the populations of Provincetown's Long Point and Wellfleet's Bound Brook, Griffin, and Billingsgate islands all nudged their houses from coastal sites to what is now the town center, near the harbor. Through the nineteenth century, it was the rare house in Wellfleet that had stood unaltered since its construction. Most had been either moved or expanded — with parts recycled from yet another house or a ship.

Running quite literally through Cape Cod's architecture from the seventeenth to the mid-twentieth centuries is salvage, or the use of recycled materials in construction. Raised in a resource-poor environment with a Puritan underpinning of thrift, Cape Codders "never throw anything away," wrote Berger in his WPA guidebook. Because of the scarcity of milled lumber and the labor intensity of carving post-and-beam timbers by hand, builders often reused wood from old houses or scavenged milled wood from ships. Wrecks along the Atlantic coast were, sadly, a renewable source until the twentieth century, with some two disasters every winter month at the height of the Age of Sail. Timbers and other parts of doomed vessels appear in every type of building on the Cape, including barns, windmills, huts of refuge, Province Lands dune

In most places when a man builds a house he builds it and there it stands, practically unchanged, keeping the same form in which it began, and almost invariably in the same place.... [But] Provincetown men are not landsmen.... Provincetowners have spent so much of their time on the sea in ships that they look upon houses as a sort of land ship or a species of houseboat and therefore not subject to the laws of houses.

Every man who owns a boat or a vessel overhauls it, alters it, tinkers with it. That is why all Provincetown people tinker with their houses and keep adding to them perpetually ... and why the houses do not stay upon their foundations after the fashion of those in other towns but go wandering up roadways or sandy dunes.

In search of lumber and other salvage, wreckers picked clean the bones of wrecked ships. This one, the schooner *Fortuna*, was destroyed in 1894 near Peaked Hill Bars, at the treacherous northern tip of Cape Cod.

The *Jason*, carrying jute from Calcutta to Boston in 1893, met its end off Cape Cod. The ship's remnants washed or were pulled onshore, where they gradually became construction timber.

A classic Cape Cod salt works in East Dennis, 1892

Windmills pumped seawater into the salt works, their hand-hewn members forming the kind of ad hoc, functional structure and renewable energy source that would inspire twentieth-century designers.

shacks, and the 1805 Federal-style Wellfleet house that now holds the restaurant Winslow's Tavern. Thoreau noted the practice in Truro: "The objects around us, the make-shifts of fishermen ashore, often made us look down to see if we were standing on terra firma," he wrote in *Cape Cod* (1865). "In the wells everywhere a block and tackle were used to raise the bucket, instead of a windlass, and by almost every house was laid up a spar or a plank or two full of auger-holes, saved from a wreck. . . . The light-house keeper, who was having his barn shingled, told me casually that he had made three thousand good shingles for that purpose out of a mast."[12]

Cape Cod's salt works, with their giant evaporation vats, were another source of lumber until they faded from use in the mid-nineteenth century. Settlers had initially made salt by boiling seawater in wood-fired kettles, a grossly inefficient practice that helped to decimate the Cape's woodlands. Starting in the late eighteenth century, saltmakers built windmills to pump seawater into hundreds of long wooden troughs, equipped the troughs with movable hipped roofs in case of rain, and waited for the sun and breeze to do their work. As Berger noted, salt took its toll on this wood: "The heavy timbers of old houses on the Cape are of two kinds — those that will 'take paint' and those that won't. And those that won't are usually 'salt-works timbers.'" Salted wood had a telltale woolly texture and quickly rusted carpenters' tools and nails, but it was too cheap and plentiful to throw away.[13]

All of this moving, melding, recycling, and rebuilding, with components from different places and periods, can make it hard even for historians to establish the age and ancestry of an older Cape Cod house. And, as we have seen, the recycling habit sometimes extended to entire houses themselves. In the twentieth century, modern architects would uphold the traditions of salvage and economy by repurposing building types, appropriating industrial elements for residential use, and drawing on the new resource of manufactured recycled materials.

This Cape Codder practiced architectural salvage by inhabiting an upturned dory.

Cape Cod's eastern shore is the most dramatic coast in New England. For many of its 40 miles, a sheer wall of clay-spattered, grass-whiskered dunes — "as steep a slope as sand could lie on," marveled Thoreau — reflects the sounds of the surf on empty sand. A walk on this windy stretch has a bracing effect that will inspire encomiums as long as it stands above water. Thoreau was the first eminent writer to probe its spirituality, calling it "the true Atlantic House, where the ocean is land-lord as well as sea-lord, and comes ashore without a wharf for the landing." Returning to Concord with the roar of the waves in his ears, Thoreau knew the scene would never grow stale: "The keeper of the light, with one or more of his family," he had observed in Truro, "walks out to the edge of the bank after every meal to look off, just as if they had not lived there all their days." The editor and World War I veteran Henry Beston, who spent much of 1925 in a self-designed dune shack near Eastham, was no less humbled, writing in *The Outermost House*: "In that hollow of space and brightness, in that ceaseless travail of wind and sand and ocean, the world one sees is still the world unharassed of man, a place of the instancy and eternity of creation and the noble ritual of the burning year."[14]

Yet all who engage with this terrain know that the love is unrequited. The late Beston could not have been

Taken around 1900, this photograph likely shows a surviving "hut of refuge," built in the late eighteenth century to shelter ship-wrecked sailors.

Henry Beston's memoir, *The Outermost House* (1928), set on Nauset Beach, is a classic work of nature writing. This rare photograph shows the house, which Beston named the Fo'c'sle, on its original site, before it was moved upland for protection and eventually washed away in 1978.

surprised to know that his house, even after it was moved to a safer site, was washed out to sea in the Blizzard of '78. "You can't make friends with the Great Beach," wrote Smith and Shay in *Down the Cape*. "You can love it and live on it; it can become part of your life,

but it holds itself aloof and the few traces of man's presence seem of no more consequence than piles of driftwood." Even Thoreau admitted, "It is a wild, rank place, and there is no flattery in it."[15]

In a perspective utterly foreign to our own, locals used to call this the Back Shore, or Backside, as if the entire Outer Cape were mentally turned toward the mainland. During the Age of Sail the ocean was as much foe as friend to Cape Cod, giving and taking life with equal vigor. The few houses near the coast were little help to shipwrecked sailors blinded by the dead of night or a violent nor'easter. With the Coast Guard far in the future, the Massachusetts Humane Society was founded in 1785 to bring a measure of hope to men cast overboard in a storm. Eventually, society volunteers would build and man boathouses, but their first projects were "huts of refuge" — tiny beach shacks where survivors could huddle until conditions improved. The first hut went up in 1794 in North Truro, but "it was built in an improper manner" and sited on

The former Peaked Hill Bars life-saving station, where Eugene O'Neill wrote several plays in the 1920s, lost its footing in the winter of 1931. Undaunted, like a sort of literary obelisk, the chimney—added by the station's previous owner, Mabel Dodge—stood proud.[19]

too bare a dune, wrote James Freeman, a Unitarian minister and member of the Humane Society, in 1802. "The strong winds blew the sand from its foundation, and the weight of the chimney brought it to the ground; so that in January of the present year it was entirely demolished." The hut collapsed six weeks before a ship ran aground right beside it.[16]

Fortunately, by 1802 there were six new huts between Monomoy, south of Chatham, and Race Point, in Provincetown. Freeman set out to document their whereabouts, and distributed his findings in a pamphlet so sailors would have a sense of where to stumble in a storm. He also described the huts' design: "Each hut stands on piles, is eight feet long, eight feet wide, and seven feet high; a sliding door is on the south, a sliding shutter on the west, and a pole, rising fifteen feet above the top of the building, on the east. Within, it is supplied either with straw or hay; and is farther accommodated with a bench." By 1804, the hut at Nauset Beach had already saved three lives. After their

schooner burned and their lifeboat capsized, wrote historian Henry Kittredge, one "Captain Schott and his two men spent a tolerably comfortable night in this shelter, buried in straw and listening to the fourteen-foot surf which pounded the beach outside."[17]

The volunteers who maintained the huts sometimes fell down on their duties. Thoreau, who was transfixed by the hut he encountered on the beach near Wellfleet, found that "there were some stones and some loose wads of wool on the floor, and an empty fire-place at the further end; but it was not supplied with matches, or straw, or hay, that we could see, nor 'accommodated with a bench.' . . . This, then, is what charity hides! Virtues antique and far away with ever a rusty nail over the latch."[18] But in the late nineteenth century, the Humane Society was succeeded by the U.S. Life-Saving Service, which built new stations to hold lifeboats, gear, and dormitories for trained rescue workers. One station stood near Provincetown at Peaked Hill Bars, a deadly morass of shifting sand bars at the Cape's northern tip.

Long known as Euphoria, this 12-by-16-foot shack built in 1930 was occupied for several decades by the New York writer Hazel Hawthorne Werner, a descendant of Nathaniel Hawthorne. Over the years, Provincetown's dune shacks have sheltered artists and writers including Edmund Wilson, John Dos Passos, Tennessee Williams, Mark Rothko, and Norman Mailer.

When the Peaked Hill Bars station was decommissioned in 1914 due to its fast-eroding position, a New York art patron, Sam Lewisohn, bought it for his friend Mabel Dodge, the Greenwich Village salonista. Dodge had the station's walls and ceilings painted white, her signature decorating scheme, and the floor painted blue, and she furnished the rooms with rush mats, Italian pottery, striped pillows, and two couches that had belonged to Isadora Duncan. In 1919, Eugene O'Neill's father bought the station as a wedding present for the young playwright and his second wife. The otherwise depressive O'Neill, himself a former seaman, wrote contentedly here for six summers. Despite (or because of) its inaccessibility — playwright Susan Glaspell called the walk from town a "thrilling struggle" — the house became an occasional gathering

place for New York literati. The building was essentially a Cape designed with extra depth, to accommodate boats, and topped with a watchtower. The critic Edmund Wilson, who rented it in the late 1920s, remembered its "wide square rooms decorated in the colors of the landscape — the light but vivid yellows and blues of the sand and the sky and . . . the living room, with its set of big plates each one pictured with a different kind of fish." By 1931, storm surf had pounded the station's sandy perch to oblivion, and the building broke free of its chimney and fell into the sea.[20]

Out in the Province Lands, the untamed sweep of sand at the tip of the Cape, a series of dune shacks not much larger than lifesaving huts are among the world's most romantic examples of the genre. Built in the early twentieth century by life-saving servicemen with

This gabled shack, now called Tasha after the family that inherited it, was occupied for decades by the poet Harry Kemp. Measuring just 8 by 12 feet, it was initially a hen house at the nearby Peaked Hill Bars life-saving station.[23]

time — and often wood from wrecked ships — on their hands, they were sometimes used as love nests for the builders and their wives or girlfriends. All are clad in cedar but their designs vary widely, from classic gabled cottages to tiny square boxes with shed roofs (pitched in one direction) that give them a proto-modern silhouette. To this day the shacks have no indoor plumbing, no electricity, and no way to keep the sand out. They have drawn artists and writers for almost a century.

Poet Cynthia Huntington, who in the 1990s spent three summers in the shack called Euphoria, reminds us in her memoir, *The Salt House*, how lovingly these architectural oddities have to be maintained. "Uneven and raw, wobbly, frequently of eccentric design, they seem unlikely candidates to have endured the ravages of wind and time," she reflects, "yet perhaps a dozen or so still remain in use, continually patched and mended, shingled, shored up, and shoveled out." For better and worse, life on stilts at the continent's edge is an ongoing dance with the elements: "The shack rocks gently in wind. Set up on wood pilings against the second dune, it lets the wind under it, gently lifting. . . . In the high

bunk, I feel the shack sway like a boat at anchor." Yet these structures have enjoyed longer lives than their waterfront neighbors. In 2012, all nineteen of the remaining shacks and the 1,950-acre sandbox that is their backyard — collectively called the Dune Shacks of the Peaked Hill Bars Historic District — were added to the National Register of Historic Places.[21]

The naturalist Robert Finch was wandering these dunes in the early 1960s when he stumbled, unwittingly, on the gabled hut that had belonged to Harry Kemp, self-styled Poet of the Dunes from the late 1920s to 1959.[22] Finch's description of the abandoned shack's interior captures the essence of the twentieth-century artists' retreat on outer Cape Cod.

Against one wall were two bunk beds, each covered with real bearskin blankets. On another wall a series of rough bookshelves supported an extensive and remarkably eclectic library.

There were esoteric works by Swedenborg and Kierkegaard, a volume of Beethoven sonatas, a large poetry collection (including first editions

Oyster Houses, Wellfleet, Mass.

Wholesale oyster, clam, and scallop houses hover on pilings above Wellfleet Harbor. In a classic Cape Cod architectural dance, the scallop house, right, became a blacksmith's shop and was later moved to South Wellfleet, while Higgins Shellfish, left, was moved across the street in 1959 to form part of the Captain Higgins restaurant, now called Pearl.[25]

of Sandburg and Frost), a novel done completely in woodcuts, and cheap nineteenth-century editions of Hawthorne and Dickens. But there were also dozens of paperback science-fiction novels and westerns. . . .

On the floor were scattered piles of oversized 78 rpm records, mostly classical and operatic selections on old and obscure labels. I picked one up, an original Caruso recording dated 1916. . . . Sand had seeped in through the cracks in the windows and walls and had formed a thin layer over everything on the floor, including the records.[24]

This melding of urban high culture and total rusticity is key to understanding modern architects' later interactions with Cape Cod's terrain. Kemp's house functioned as a tiny capsule of civilization that absorbed the wild without disturbing it. To say that

these shacks have small footprints is almost absurd; their plans are more like paw prints. With their light touch on the land, their reverence for the surrounding environment, and their emphasis on the inner life, the shacks can be seen as honorary progenitors to the modern homes a few miles south.

———————

In the Outer Cape's harbors, commercial buildings were often set on pilings for dual access to boats and docks, and they, too, evolved in function from purely mercantile to social to artistic. Shellfishermen would gather here to unload, shuck, and sell oysters, clams, and scallops and to share news and gossip. Wellfleet's Everett Higgins Shellfish Shop became a gathering spot known informally as the Spit and Chatter Club, where proprietor Captain Higgins sold clams and oysters, gave haircuts, and fed the pot-bellied stove. A *Cape Codder* reporter wrote in 1984, "Before the days of television, all the local news, politics, social happenings and the hilarious doings of the 'foreigners' emanated from the Spit and Chatter Club. The membership, of course, was closed. One had to be a lifelong resident of Wellfleet, wear hip boots folded down, carry a quahaug rake, play checkers, be fluent in local profanity and clam up when customers came to buy shellfish."[26] When a shack's pilings started to buckle after years of abuse by water and salty winds, the fishermen simply braced them diagonally with 2-by-4 scraps and went on their way. This, too, will recur in modernist work: simple, spontaneous fixes to problems of program or climate.

A short walk from Captain Higgins's shellfish shack was Wellfleet's legendary Chequessett Inn, built at the end of a 400-foot-long wharf in the bay. Designed to make guests feel as if they were at sea, it was the first significant work of local architecture that purposely engaged with, rather than evaded, its perilous surroundings. The banana magnate Lorenzo Dow Baker, who founded the company that later became Chiquita, opened the resort in 1902 to fan the flames of upmarket tourism: as elegant a building as ever sat on a pier in New England, it comprised 62 guest rooms on four stories, a sweeping boardwalk, a parking area, and massive outdoor rocking chairs built to withstand coastal winds. "The Chequessett Inn is built upon a site unique among hotels in New England," boasted its brochure, "on the end of a spacious pier directly over the water. . . . Our guests are sensible of the exhilarating conditions of a sea voyage with absolute exemption from its dangers."[27] The exemption lasted but 32 years: in 1934, a violent storm destroyed the inn from below, slamming ice floes against its pilings until the building collapsed. Reconstruction was impossible during the Great Depression, and by the end of World War II, the touristic landscape had changed. The stumps of the great inn's piers are still visible at low tide.

Even as the Chequessett Inn embodied the brief age of the grand resort on outer Cape Cod, another salt-soaked gathering place of its time embodied something new: modern artists repurposing a traditional building.

This 1962 photograph shows the bracings of an oyster house at the end of its life in Wellfleet's Duck Creek.

At land's end in Provincetown, the once-thriving fishing industry and associated trades — rigging, blacksmithing, cooperage, storage, salt, and so on — had dwindled with the rise of power boats and refrigeration. In 1912, the last "banker" sailed from Provincetown to Newfoundland's Grand Banks, and Provincetown's picturesque nineteenth-century wharves were soon sitting idle. Within a few years they became plein-air scenes and studio sites for Provincetown's many art students, who had been gathering since Charles Hawthorne, inspired by the area's clear, brilliant light, opened the Cape Cod School of Art in 1899. Several accomplished painters, including Charles Demuth, Edwin Dickinson, Marsden Hartley, Ross Moffett, and Ambrose Webster, were now working in Provincetown, representing a rough duality of academic and modern styles that would duke it out for years in local galleries. By 1916, the town had five art schools, and so many art students that the first annual ball of the Provincetown Art Association drew 800 people in costume. Provincetown was "probably the biggest art colony in the world," said the *Boston Globe*, and the new denizens were "unconventional": the women wore "smocks of such various hues that when you see a crowd of them painting on a wharf they look like a sort of human flower garden."[28]

New York journalist and labor activist Mary Heaton Vorse was among the first outsiders to make Provincetown her second home, in 1907, and she wasted no time in cajoling friends to join her. In the summers of 1915 and 1916, with Europe submerged in the horrors of World War I, much of Greenwich Village found its way to Provincetown rather than Paris. In 1915, Vorse and her husband, Joe O'Brien, bought Provincetown's 75-year-old Lewis Wharf, where a gabled fish house wobbled gently on its aging pilings. Vorse and O'Brien rented the second story of the building to Bror Nordfeldt for his Modern Art School, and the first floor to painter Margaret Steele. Among the couple's close-knit, mostly New York–based friends were playwrights whose realistic work was eschewed by New York's theater producers. Led by George Cram "Jig" Cook, who was suffused with the ideal of communal creative effort, the group began to stage its own plays at the waterfront rental home of two of its members. Later that summer, Vorse offered her fish house as a theater.[29]

The first bills on Lewis Wharf featured two premieres: Cook's *Change Your Style*, a comedy about the tensions between Provincetown's traditional and modern art schools, and Wilbur Daniel Steele's *Contemporaries*, a raw drama about the politics of homelessness in New York. With performances 30 feet above the surf and 100 feet out in the bay, the enthusiasts briefly achieved their dream of a community-run theater that gave voice to new American plays and playwrights. In her memoir *Time and the Town*, Vorse wrote a heartfelt account of the transformation of the smelly old building, where seats were made of "planks put on sawhorses and kegs."

Our wharf, with the fishhouse on the end, was conveniently at hand to serve as a theater. The fishhouse . . . had a dark weathered look, and around the piles the waves always lapped except at extreme low tide. There was a huge door on rollers at the side and another at the end which made it possible to use the bay as a backdrop. The planks were wide and one could look through the cracks at the water. The color of the big beams and planks was rich with age.

We dragged out the boats and nets which still stood there. We all made contributions to buy lumber for seats and fittings. We made the seats of planks put on sawhorses and kegs. . . . Out of these odds and ends we made a theater, which was to have such unsuspected and far-reaching effects beyond the borders of Provincetown.

The night for the first performance came. Four people stood in the wings with lamps in their hands to light the stage. Lanterns with tin reflectors were placed before the stage like old footlights. Four people stood beside the lamp bearers with shovels and sand in case of fire, and with these lights the fishhouse took on depth and mystery. . . .

I sat in the audience on the hard bench, watching the performance, hardly believing what we had done. The audience was full of enthusiastic people — a creative audience. In spite of its raining in torrents, everyone had come down the dark wharf lighted here and there by a lantern.[30]

The following year, in 1916, the players themselves renovated the fish house to make it more versatile as a theater. That summer's playbill included the debut of 27-year-old Eugene O'Neill, newly arrived from New York, where he had heard about the experimental winds blowing at the end of the Cape. O'Neill's *Bound East for Cardiff* is set in the crew's quarters of a ship at sea. By all accounts, the audience at the premiere was spellbound: as O'Neill's phenomenal talent was revealed in this nautical drama informed by his own experience, the surf swished below, an evening fog appeared as if on cue, and the Long Point foghorn brayed. "The tide was in," remembered Susan Glaspell, who was married to Cook, "and it washed under us and around, spraying through the holes in the floor, giving us the rhythm and the flavor of the sea." As for the old

In the years before the car made families mobile, tourists were lured to the Cape by full-service resorts. Wellfleet's Chequessett Inn, promising a nautical experience on its bayside pier (off Mayo Beach, near the bend in Kendrick Avenue), was among the first Cape Cod buildings to treat its risky surroundings as an asset.

THE INN. LOOKING WEST

pier, "It is not merely figurative language to say the old wharf shook with applause."[31]

Provincetown's summer of 1916 remains one of the great creative convergences in American history. Already stocked with fishermen, families, and painters, the town was now bursting with thousands of tourists thanks to the ferry from Boston, the train from Fall River (where New Yorkers, including a small but growing number of writers, arrived by steamship), the increasingly popular car, and hundreds of drunken sailors, assigned to practice naval maneuvers in the harbor. At this point, the tourists were coming to see the artists, and the artists filled the benches in the playhouse. With creative, recreational, and sexual energy flowing, the summer would be remembered as a last hurrah before the United States entered the war the following spring. The players staged 16 one-act plays, an astonishing nine of them premieres and the others reprises of recent work.[32]

Yet after this burst of glory, nature roared right back, as though Provincetown's artists had flown too close to the sun. Under the name the Provincetown Players, the troupe moved to New York and enjoyed several years of success. Painters crept back onto

Lewis Wharf, and for two summers a group of art students ran a coffee shop and nightclub in the fish house. But in late 1921, the fish house burned down and the wharf was felled by ice floes, "leaving only Lucy L'Engle's studio tottering precariously on a few piles," wrote Vorse. By 1922, the wharf had disappeared, and the playhouse passed into legend in the annals of American theater.[33]

———————————

Lewis Wharf had been gone for almost two decades when the first generation of modern designers arrived on Cape Cod, yet it still stood as an early emblem of one type of work that defined them. Here, a group of avant-garde thinkers came into a historic building, almost comically intimate with nature, designed in a traditional style, and used for an age-old purpose. They adapted it at minimal cost, without compromising its core appeal, and employed it as a backdrop for hard, pioneering creative work.

Four years after the fall of Lewis Wharf, Le Corbusier, in Paris, published one of the key manifestos of architecture's modern movement. The first of his "Five Points

In a famous example of adaptive reuse, the troupe that became the Province-town Players staged its earliest public performances in this nineteenth-century fish house in 1915 and 1916. Despite its humble mien and lingering odors, the building seated at least 90 people and launched Eugene O'Neill as a playwright.[35]

of a New Architecture" was the elevation of buildings on *pilotis*, or pilings: now that technology had replaced stone foundations and walls with reinforced concrete and streamlined steel, Le Corbusier argued, all buildings should be raised off the ground on concrete posts to liberate the architect, client, and landscape alike. Good riddance to basements, which collect moisture and clutter, he wrote; humanity can now preserve the land it builds upon. When a building is lifted, "the rooms are thereby removed from the dampness of the soil; they have light and air; the building plot is left to the garden, which consequently passes under the house."[34] As we trace the rise of modern architecture on the Outer Cape, we will see that Marcel Breuer's long-house prototype, Serge Chermayeff's studio prototype, Paul

Weidlinger's house, Jack Hall's Hatch House, Paul Krueger's Mark House, and several others are all raised on pilings. Born of necessity on the waterfront — some of Wellfleet's oyster shacks were still standing into the 1960s — pilings would reappear on dry land for a host of practical and environmental reasons.

With the passing of the golden age of painting and theater in Provincetown, and the onset of the Great Depression, creative energy ebbed on the Outer Cape. The next generation of artists — namely, architects and writers — would find their way to a new neighborhood. Freed by circumstance to experiment with forms and materials, a group of self-taught designers began in the 1930s to build something that would grow much larger than themselves.

Notes

1. National Park Service, Cape Cod National Seashore, "The Archeology of Outer Cape Cod," (http://www.nps.gov/caco/historyculture/the-archaeology-of-outer-cape-cod.htm); Howard S. Russell, *Indian New England Before the Mayflower* (Lebanon, N.H.: University Press of New England, 1980), 51, 53–55; Kittredge, *Cape Cod*, 27.

2. Morrison, *Early American Architecture*, 9–12.

3. Doris Doane, *A Book of Cape Cod Houses* (Old Greenwich, Conn.: Chatham, 1970), 12.

4. Morgan, *The Cape Cod Cottage*, 9; Thoreau, *Cape Cod*, 104; Morrison, 37.

5. Cummings, 134, 137–40; Morrison, 30–32.

6. O'Connell, *Becoming Cape Cod*, 72–73; Josef Berger (Jeremiah Digges, pseud.), *Cape Cod Pilot* (Provincetown, Mass., Modern Pilgrim/New York: Viking, 1937, repr., Cambridge, Mass.: MIT Press, 1969), 147.

7. Katharine Smith and Edith Shay, *Down the Cape: The Complete Guide to Cape Cod* (New York: Dodge, 1936), 78–79.

8. Morrison, 95.

9. National Park Service, "National Register Bulletin: Historic Residential Suburbs," http://www.nps.gov/nr/publications/bulletins/suburbs/part3.htm; O'Connell, 73.

10. Robert Hayden, interviewed by Christine Cipriani, June 9, 2012; Lombardo, *Wellfleet: A Cape Cod Village*, 22.

11. Vorse, *Time and the Town*, 87, 89–90.

12. Berger, 98; National Park Service, Cape Cod National Seashore, "Shipwrecks," http://home.nps.gov/caco/historyculture/shipwrecks.htm; University of Massachusetts and National Park Service, *People and Places on the Outer Cape*, 104; Lombardo, 48; Thoreau, 109.

13. Berger, 98; Shay and Smith, 66; Kittredge, 154.

14. Thoreau, 48, 50, 211, 214 (a reference to Highland Light in Truro); Beston, *The Outermost House*, xxxiv.

15. Shay and Smith, 149; Thoreau, 147.

16. Freeman, *A Description of the Eastern Coast of the County of Barnstable*, 6–7.

17. Freeman, 14; Kittredge, 225–26.

18. Thoreau, 60.

19. Egan, *Provincetown As a Stage*, 146.

20. Egan, 104, 146, 244–45; Susan Glaspell, *The Road to the Temple: A Biography of George Cram Cook* (New York: Frederick A. Stokes, 1927, repr. Jefferson, N.C.: McFarland, 2005), 226; Wilson, *The Twenties*, 125.

21. Huntington, *The Salt House*, xi, 4; National Park Service/Cape Cod National Seashore, press release, Mar. 19, 2012, http://www.nps.gov/caco/parknews/national-park-service-formally-lists-the-dune-shacks-of-peaked-hill-bars-historic-district-on-the-national-register.htm.

22. David Dunlap, "Dune Shack 9: Kemp-Tasha," Building Provincetown, http://buildingprovincetown.wordpress.com/2010/01/10/cape-cod-national-seashore-great-beach-dune-shack-9/#more-10890.

23. Bill Burke e-mail interview with Christine Cipriani, June 1, 2012; Dunlap, "Dune Shack 9."

24. Robert Finch, *Common Ground: A Naturalist's Cape Cod* (Boston: Godine, 1981), 5.

25. Lombardo, *Wellfleet: Then and Now*, 39–40.

26. Doug Roberts, quoted in D. B. Wright, *The Famous Beds of Wellfleet: A Shellfishing History* (Wellfleet, Mass.: Wellfleet Historical Society, 2008), 71.

27. "The Camera's Coast," *Historic New England,* fall 2003; Lombardo, *Wellfleet: A Cape Cod Village,* 110.

28. O'Connell, 84; A. J. Philpott, "Biggest Art Colony in the World," *Boston Daily Globe,* Aug. 27, 1916.

29. Egan, 13–17.

30. Vorse, 118–19.

31. Egan, 11–12; Glaspell, 204.

32. O'Connell, 84–87; Egan, 157–58, 169.

33. Nyla Ahrens, *Provincetown: The Art Colony: A Brief History and Guide* (Provincetown Art Association and Museum, 2000), http://www.iamprovincetown.com/history/wharves-history.html; Vorse, 115.

34. Le Corbusier and Pierre Jeanneret, "Five Points of a New Architecture" (1926), in *Programs and Manifestoes on Twentieth-Century Architecture*, ed. Ulrich Conrads (Cambridge, Mass.: MIT Press, 1970), 99.

35. Robert Károly Sarlós, *Jig Cook and the Provincetown Players: Theatre in Ferment* (Amherst: University of Massachusetts Press, 1982), 17.

2

THE BRAHMIN BOHEMIANS
"A VERY NICE SHACK"

Why should they be different from the others . . . the ex-lawyer who ran a duck farm, the oysterman who had gone to Harvard, the French vicomte who had an antique shop in the summer and clerked in the liquor store in the winter, the plumber with his degree in fine arts, the illustrator who had once been married to a screen star, the former Washington hostess who now took paying guests?

— MARY MCCARTHY, *A CHARMED LIFE*

Art is not produced by one artist but by several. It is to a great degree a product of their exchange of ideas with one another.

— MAX ERNST

On Christmas Eve in 1922, a Boston dentist sat in his Wellfleet camp, drawing a lot plan. "Gull Hill Lot. Now on Atlantic Ocean back to Mile Lot Line," he wrote in his journal that night. "I have but one break in my Gull Hill Tract that is now over 3500 ft. on ocean. I am now down to Baker heirs on South." Normally, when he finished a plan, he carefully noted the book and page where the lot's deeds had been recorded at the Barnstable County registry — but the deeds for this parcel were still outstanding. "It is a bother having this matter stand for over 10 years," he wrote, "but then the Cape people are very odd and slow about deciding on land sales. They seem to hate to part with earth."[1]

William Herbert Rollins (1852–1929) was no ordinary tooth-puller. Decades after his death, a historian called this Renaissance man "the greatest genius the dental profession has ever known." The American Academy of Oral and Maxillofacial Radiology calls him "a remarkable man, born perhaps a century ahead of his time." Educated at Harvard's dental and medical schools, Rollins was a mechanical wizard who spent his evenings compulsively engineering better versions of nascent technologies. Sequestered in his Back Bay brownstone or one of his two vacation homes, he established the precise nature, optimal uses, and many of the benefits and dangers of the newly popular X-ray; made his own cameras, grinding the lenses by hand; hybridized plants in what he called his "experimental garden"; milled his own whole-wheat flour, finding the white stuff "poor food"; and stubbornly tried to build the perfect radio receiver. But with neither academic appointment nor taste for self-promotion, Rollins labored in obscurity — when others duplicated his findings in institutional settings, often decades later, they were lauded for their insights. "It seems to be my fate," he wrote in his journal in 1927, at the age of 75, "to have all my work forgotten and attributed to others later on."[2]

When, in the early twentieth century, he started buying land in Wellfleet and Truro, Rollins didn't just sign the papers. Swathed in calculated layers of wool, leather, and cotton, he personally tramped through mud, brush, and snow to survey his properties, mark them with traditional stone posts, and catalogue them in writing. Uninhabited land in the area had been used for generations as woodlots, divided by household to give each family access to firewood. But when kerosene

Jack Hall, Hatch House, Wellfleet (1962), west facade of guest room

Spanning Cape Cod at one of its narrowest points, from the Atlantic to Cape Cod Bay, this 1960 aerial view shows seven ponds: at left, from bottom of photo to top, Horseleech, Williams, Higgins, and Gull, and at right, Round, Slough, and Herring. Now protected by the Cape Cod National Seashore, some 800 acres of these wild lands were accumulated in the early twentieth century by Dr. William Rollins, who paid almost nothing for them.

replaced wood as a heating fuel, the lots were gradually abandoned as mosquito-infested wastelands, marked only by the odd hunting or fishing cabin. Rollins, seeing four seasons of exquisitely wild beauty, bought them, parcel by parcel, for a few dollars an acre until he owned some 800 acres.

Around 1910, Rollins ordered and assembled a 14-by-28-foot Hodgson portable cottage — one of the first prefabricated homes on the market — and he and his wife, Miriam, began to spend time on Wellfleet's Horseleech Pond. "Much trouble surveying with wind," reads a typical winter journal entry; "I can't hold myself rigid enough with gusts to read carefully. This work took me six hours as I had to try many times . . . . The tachymeter levels would not stay still." Even after Miriam died and he sank into depression, Rollins found comfort in documenting Cape Cod land. In 1927, on a brisk autumn day at his camp, he wrote,

> It is now noon and the temperature is up to sixty-four, the sun bright and the S. W. wind soft. I send old deeds to be registered. Worked on old deeds the whole morning. Picture puzzles never interested me but I can spend hours in trying to locate land described in old deeds, and be totally unconscious of time. The oak leaves come sailing in the door and over the roof like flying brown birds.[3]

Dr. Rollins was an extreme example, but his Yankee do-it-yourself determination and Thoreauvian love of the land would define the American architects who brought modern design to Cape Cod — starting with Miriam Rollins's great-nephew, John C. "Jack" Phillips. When Dr. Rollins died, in 1929, he left all of his Outer Cape property to Phillips, then a Harvard undergraduate. After a few years in France, Phillips moved to Wellfleet and quietly planted the flag of modern architecture, to be followed by three other American designers: Jack Hall, Hayden Walling, and Nathaniel Saltonstall. In most of that group, a collaborative design-build ethic took hold, a willingness to work as both architect and carpenter that harked back to the earliest coastal settlers. Incredibly, Rollins, Phillips, and Saltonstall were all descended from passengers on the same transatlantic crossing: the voyage of the *Arbella*, which carried prominent English Puritans — chartered as the Massachusetts Bay Company, governed by John Winthrop — to the New World in 1630.[4] All four designers were raised in cosmopolitan environments, all were expensively educated, two were Boston Brahmins, and not one had a degree in architecture.

JACK PHILLIPS

Jack Phillips belonged to a family that helped build the United States and hasn't sat idle since. Cambridge-educated minister George Phillips founded America's first Congregational church in Watertown, Massachusetts, in 1630. Twenty years later, his son became the family's first Harvard graduate. Another Phillips cofounded Phillips Academy, Andover, in 1778, and his uncle opened Phillips Exeter Academy in 1781. Boston's first mayor, elected in 1822, was John Phillips; his son, Wendell, became a well-known abolitionist who worked closely with William Lloyd Garrison. In the twentieth century, Jack Phillips's father, John C. Phillips, was a conservationist, ornithologist, and creature-loving hunter in the tradition of Theodore Roosevelt. His monumental series *A Natural History of the Ducks*, first published in 1922, remains the definitive work on the subject. Jack accompanied his father on many an expedition, including, at age 15, a safari in Kenya, where, he said, his father collected "fish, birds, small rodents and occasional heads and horns." He remained a lifelong woodsman in the New England mold, said his daughter, Hayden Herrera: "His spiritual center was Thoreau and Walden Pond. Nature was everything to him."[5]

Born in 1908 and raised in Boston's historic Back Bay and Beacon Hill, Jack Phillips was educated at private schools including the unorthodox Rivers Open Air School in Brookline, Massachusetts, the exclusive Le Rosey, in Switzerland, and Milton Academy, in Milton, Massachusetts. He majored in fine arts at Harvard and, after graduating in 1930, moved to France. Based in Fontainebleau and Paris — on the Left Bank near the Place Saint-Sulpice — Phillips studied painting with Fernand Léger and André Lhote and aquatint etching with the master printmaker, illustrator, and film animator Alexandre Alexeieff. He later shifted to intaglio monoprints and experimented with new printmaking processes, rounding out a body of artwork that was featured in solo shows at the Art Institute of Chicago in 1948 (facilitated by his Wellfleet friend Serge Chermayeff) and the Century Association, in New York, in 2001. His early subjects were people in urban settings, but later he made primarily Cape Cod

As a 20-year-old Harvard senior, Jack Phillips inherited 800 acres of land in Wellfleet and Truro, including his great-uncle's camp on Horseleech Pond.

landscapes, focusing on process rather than emotional effect, said Herrera, an art historian. "He was so different from any of the Abstract Expressionists," she said. "He was too modest to think that self-expression was the thing."[6]

Phillips had been to Cape Cod several times in the 1920s, touring with his father and camping on the beach with a friend from Harvard. At the time, the Outer Cape was an outback. Before the construction of the Mid-Cape Highway, now Route 6, in the 1950s, it took a full day to drive from Boston to Wellfleet (today, it takes two hours). Tourism on the Cape evolved gradually starting in the late nineteenth century, following

Jack Phillips, *Beach Picnic*, intaglio monoprint (1990)

Jack Phillips, *Horseleech Pond I*, intaglio monoprint (1972)

depressing air." Wellfleet and Eastham did not provide electricity until 1926, lagging behind the Upper Cape by more than a decade.[7]

Resorts such as the Chequessett Inn had catered to those arriving by train or boat. As the family car gained prevalence over the first half of the twentieth century, resorts gave way to casual campgrounds, boarding houses, and the cottage colonies that are now fixtures on the Outer Cape's automotive landscape. Restaurants and drive-ins sprang up to feed the new renters, and dance halls, theaters, and bars kept them out after dark. At the same time, the long decline of the fishing trades had decimated the local population; between the 1870s and 1920, the number of people living in Wellfleet alone plunged from 2,135 to 826. The exodus of year-rounders kept a damper on prices for Outer Cape real estate, making it possible for the occasional visionary to buy a piece.[8]

During the Great Depression, as the national malaise spread throughout the Cape, something else happened: Americans looked back in time. "Americans were seeking cultural antidotes to the social upheaval and uncertainty bred by rapid urbanization," O'Connell found.

changes in travel patterns from boat to train to car; not until after World War II did it reach its current level of frenzy. The Outer Cape was the last part of the peninsula to be discovered, because its coast had so long been thought hostile. "Nobody, even in the twenties, wanted to be on the Back Shore or the ponds," Phillips recalled in 1998. "They didn't swim there or lie on the beach. The only reason to go there was to collect seaweed for their gardens, or to go to the ponds for their woodlots. Even in the twenties, people thought of the ocean as having undertows, sharks — the beach was deserted." Out-of-towners absorbed this dim view, writes James O'Connell in his history of Cape tourism, *Becoming Cape Cod*: "Travelers perceived the Outer Cape as an entirely different place from the rest of Cape Cod. The Cape's outer arm and the forbidding sea beyond gave off an air of desolation. Because of the stormy ocean, no settlers had ever established villages on the Atlantic shore." Most of the towns they did establish "had a quiet and, in the off-season, even

A wish for a simpler and more natural era had arisen. Vacationers sought storybook historic architecture, colorful rural characters, and legends of bygone New England. . . .

An intensive interest in American history developed during the 1930s, as Americans sought to cope with the Depression and European totalitarianism by reaffirming their national identity. . . . The more traditional seafaring Cape Cod receded into the past, the more writers, artists, and tourists sought to recapture it. The modernizing decades between the two world wars witnessed the elaboration of the myth of "olde Cape Cod" that the region lives off to this day.

In architecture, the heritage boom pulled Cape Cod into the national Colonial Revival, which soared from roughly the 1920s to the postwar Levittown years. For most of the previous century, Victorian and Greek Revival styles had prevailed here as elsewhere, but now the Cape house came home. New Capes were built and old ones restored with fresh fervor.[9]

Jack Phillips's father advised him to refuse Rollins's acreage, saying the young man would be felled by property taxes if the mosquitoes didn't get him first. "Fortunately, Jack didn't pay attention!" said his widow, Florence Phillips. After a brief first marriage to a fellow art student in France, Phillips moved to New York and married Elizabeth Blair. In the late 1930s, their growing family and two servants moved into Dr. Rollins's old modular camp on Horseleech Pond, and gradually added rooms — "like a railroad train," Phillips said, with "end-to-end growth" — until the building was nick-named the Big House. The couple began making friends and hosting them for dinner, including Wellfleet's mete-orically short-lived literary couple, Edmund Wilson and Mary McCarthy, and the painter Edwin Dickinson and his wife, Pat. "The backwoods were very, very neigh-borly in the forties," Phillips explained, "and there were about fifty people in the three towns of Wellfleet, Truro, and Provincetown that one saw."

Pleasing views and a sense of having neighbors were as important to Phillips as they would be to the Cape's best-known modernists, Marcel Breuer and Serge Chermayeff. The Outer Cape looked different in the early twentieth century: starker, denuded, with fewer of what Phillips called "those damned pitch pines." Generations of deforestation and replanting had skewed the area's natural diversity of species, making way for a glut of Cape Cod's iconic tree and a constantly changing landscape. "Bound Brook Island [in Wellfleet] was a bare place, now it's a forest," Phil-lips complained in 1998. "You could see everywhere. You felt you could breathe better. . . . It was wild, but more like moors, open country: you could see people's houses much more than you can today." You could stand on Gull Pond, he remembered, and see homes on Higgins and Williams ponds.

Few buildings had better views than the ones Phillips created in those early, quiet years. Dogged by a yen to study architecture, he realized he first needed to build something, so around 1938 he designed and raised a spacious, roughly square-plan art studio facing the ocean north of Newcomb Hollow Beach, in

Days' Cottages, a bayside North Truro rental colony built in the 1930s, is marked by density and architectural uniformity.

Truro. He flipped traditional clapboard siding on its head, echoing the vertical sweep of the windowpanes on the glass wall; in turn, his shed roof echoed the gentle slope of the surrounding sand dunes. With the wind whistling through its unfinished interior walls, the building could scarcely have been more intimate with its environment, making it at once thrilling, perilous, and distracting. "It wasn't a very good place to work," Phillips admitted. "You saw anybody down on the beach and you got full of curiosity! And you got extremely tired of the southwest wind." But Herrera loved the effect:

> That place was so beautiful. It was the most beautiful space. If you're facing the ocean it was slightly turned to the left, but it must have gotten all the wind because the glass eventually became completely frosted. . . .
>
> The room itself was beautiful. I think it was the volume of the space in relationship to that huge window: it was dark in the back of the room, but then you moved toward the ocean and all this light, and so the back of the room felt protective, and the front, which was all this glass facing the ocean, was extremely exposed. I think it was a combination of being in a little bit of a hovel in the back and being completely out there in the front. It was a really nice piece of architecture.[10]

Self-taught designer Phillips built this studio on a choice piece of his waterfront land around 1938. With its soaring glass wall, vertical cedar siding, and roof with a dunelike pitch, the building engaged its environment without defacing it.

Top: Facing northeast for the best painterly light, the studio was spacious enough for working, dining, sleeping, and dancing. *Above left*: In the postwar years, the painter and sculptor Xavier González, who ran a summer art school in Wellfleet, rented Phillips's studio for his own work. *Above right*: Like Eugene O'Neill's former home, Henry Beston's Outermost House, and the Lewis Wharf theater in Provincetown, this artist's retreat (shown with later additions) was a victim of its glorious site.

Phillips clad this 1938 house in Homasote, an innovative wallboard made of pressed paper. Overlooking the Atlantic and a freshwater pond, it became known as the Paper Palace.

Phillips and his wife held dance parties here for several years, and after the war, the painter and sculptor Xavier González rented the studio for his own use. Later expanded into a house, it finally paid the ultimate price for its site, falling to the sea in the 1970s.

Phillips's next foray into what he called "improvised building," also around 1938, was another oceanside redoubt that became a social nexus. This one, however, combined the local tradition of recycling with cubist forms inspired by European high modernism. Nodding to Le Corbusier's residential work in stucco, Phillips massed a series of cubes on a roughly L-shaped plan, pulling some of them back to form Corbusian rooftop terraces, and painted the house bright white. (It is worth noting that Walter Gropius was building his own white cubist house in Lincoln, Massachusetts — with vertical wood siding — at virtually the same time, in 1938, although Phillips likely had not seen it.) Playing a bit with the lines, Phillips curved the corners of the terraces with Art Moderne nautical rails. The structure was built of reclaimed lumber and clad in Homasote, the first American construction product made of recycled material: a pressed board of pulped paper and newspaper. Set on an undulating dunescape off Ocean View Drive, between Newcomb Hollow and Cahoon Hollow beaches, the house peered down on a small freshwater pond and out to the Atlantic. Looking rather like a papier-mâché gun battery, it was nicknamed the Paper Palace.

During World War II, when Europe's intellectual refugees were looking for places to play, the Paper Palace became the unlikely home of a circle of avant-garde artists. Phillips had designed it as a rental property, so Surrealist painter Roberto Matta took the house and hosted Max Ernst, Peggy Guggenheim, Robert Motherwell, and their friends — "a pretty unconventional bunch," Phillips said, with some understatement. No Puritan he, Phillips was still taken aback by stories of the games played on his property, including a form of Truth or Consequences in which one consequence was to masturbate in front of the group. "They thought I was a very conservative type and teased me about being a stuffed shirt," he told *Provincetown Arts* in 1994.[11]

But with wartime mistrust in the air, especially on the Atlantic coast, the presence of foreigners in a foreign-looking building raised federal authorities' eyebrows. Ernst, considered an "enemy alien," was hauled off by the FBI in Provincetown during his brief stay in 1942 and questioned about whether Matta was using ladders to climb from roof to roof on Phillips's cubist creation. Phillips recalled, "The fact that [the house] was on the seacoast and had some shutters used to protect the glass from blowing sand — and that flat roof — led the FBI to wonder if Matta, as a Chilean, with German guests, might be sending signals to offshore subs via the shutters or on the flat roof." As farfetched as that sounds, the only attack on the U.S. mainland during World War I had come from German submarines off Nauset Beach.[12]

In her biting 1955 novel *A Charmed Life*, Mary McCarthy mocked the lives of intellectuals and also-rans in a fictionalized Wellfleet that she called New Leeds. McCarthy made a number of enemies with the book, as many of its characters were cruelly obvious caricatures of people in her social orbit. Modern architecture makes an appearance in the form of a house that sounds decidedly like the Paper Palace:

> The Coes lived in a modern house that had been designed for them by a cousin of Jane's. It stood on a bluff, overlooking the open ocean; the Coes now wished they had built in a hollow, the way the old settlers had, for the situation was very windswept, and nothing but dune grass and dusty miller and wild beach peas could get a footing in the whirling, shifting sand. In their early years, they had tried to keep a goat there; Jane had read that goat's milk was terribly good for you and they were going to write to the Trappists for their receipt for cheese.... Yet the windy, barren, desolate setting had, it turned out, one unexpected advantage. Beaten by the storms, the house had weathered, so that it now seemed to belong to the landscape. The squat rectangular building, with futuristic hardware, painted gray originally and topped by a roped-off sundeck, now looked like an old-fashioned wooden icebox that had been wintering for generations on a New Leeds back porch. The Coes liked this effect and assigned credit to themselves for not having fought Nature. Everything fitted in, the worn tarpaulin covering the sundeck, the goat's post — even the cylindrical bottled-gas tanks by the kitchen door, which looked so unsightly against a traditional house — harmonized with the main structure and with the sand heaped around it and the patches of reindeer moss and the gray sea birds circling above.[13]

Near the Coes' house, McCarthy tells us, is an art studio, its two-story north-facing window "obscured by three army blankets tacked up to keep out the cold." Here, modern architecture is impractical, unserious (designed by a family member), even ridiculous. Yet even this satire stresses the way in which the unpolished house melds with its environment, biodegrading aesthetically over time. Today, the Paper Palace survives but is no longer paper, having been expanded and shingled.

Phillips had no delusions about his deficiencies in structural principles. Hugh Stubbins, later the architect of New York's Citicorp Center and other institutional landmarks, was an early critic, Phillips said: "Hugh Stubbins came up when I built the Palace and said, with the wind blowing, 'Look here, do you realize you have no diagonal bracing to keep the structure rigid?'" In 1939, Phillips applied to Harvard's Graduate School of Design, where Walter Gropius and Marcel Breuer were two years into their pivotal reign as department chair and associate professor of architecture. Gropius had already traveled to Wellfleet with his family and seen Phillips's dune studio. Phillips met him in Cambridge:

Phillips joined two surplus wartime barracks and added a fireplace to form this house on Slough Pond, which was co-owned by Gustav and Vita Petersen and Arthur Schlesinger, Jr., and his first wife, Marian. At ease in the cottage in 1961, Schlesinger talks on the phone line he shared with Serge Chermayeff.

When I went to see Gropius, I took with me, among other things, some photographs of things that I'd built. He looked at the photographs of the Palace and asked, "Did you have any trouble with leaks?" Because he had seen my two second-floor balconies, each connected to a bedroom — and seen they weren't supported by any structure. Below them was a living room, and he could tell from the fenestration that there was no supporting beam to hold up the balconies — [they] were resting on the living room's structure. Well, I had had problems with leaks. I'd tried marine scraps of lead [as flashing at the threshold of the balcony] . . . I admitted the mistake. I didn't know a goddamn thing. . . . Gropius was very detached but also friendly.

Phillips did not earn a degree in architecture, sensing there was no money in the profession. Excused from first-year fundamentals, he simply dipped into Harvard's second-year graduate curriculum. "He never would have wanted to be a full-time, capital-*A* architect," said

Florence. He just "thought it was sort of a natural thing to try." When the United States entered the war, he and his family were living in New York, where, for a while, they rented a new apartment each fall, stuffing their furniture into a huge truck they called the Blunderbuss. Phillips went to work as a civilian camouflage designer at the Brooklyn Navy Yard, but when his superior tried to draft him into the Navy, he decamped to the Cape and threw himself into turkey breeding, which the Selective Service considered "essential farming." Working with Hayden Walling, a conscientious objector, Phillips ordered 3,000 chicks by mail and converted his modern dune studio and other holdings into turkey barns. For about three years, Phillips and Walling had their hands full building barns, fighting off predators, incubating chicks, and battling disease, which ultimately got the better of the birds.

Phillips's most conceptual (if unintentional) contribution to Outer Cape modernism, in the late 1940s, was the purest form of architectural salvage. At the end of the war, his brother-in-law noticed an ad for some abandoned prefab army barracks in Georgia, free for the taking. Inspired, Phillips ordered them in February and had them shipped to Wellfleet for $400 on open rail cars. After passing through rain and snow en route, the little bunkhouses froze together like shrimp. Phillips pried them apart with a pickax and backhoe, cleared the roads to five sites with a bulldozer, and had the units towed by tractor, one by one, to the woods and dunes of South Truro. He combined them to form five houses, connected them to the power grid (unlike most of his other constructions, which were powered by unreliable generators), and added plumbing, fireplaces, and concrete patios. Nestled in choice sites on Slough Pond and the Atlantic — accessible by Wellfleet roads in such a way that most owners identify with Wellfleet, not Truro — most of the barracks survive, some as nuclei of larger homes. They have been summer retreats for historian and Kennedy presidential adviser Arthur Schlesinger, Jr., and *New Yorker* writer and *Partisan Review* editor Dwight Macdonald and their families, who still use their pondside cottages; and for Charles Jencks, the architectural theorist and landscape architect, whose house is on the ocean. Schlesinger's first wife, Marian Cannon Schlesinger, remembers staying in their house in the 1950s:

Phillips in the 1960s, photographed by Tamas Breuer

> We acquired [a] delightful shack on Slough Pond, a five-minute walk from the beach on a sandy path skirted by beach plum bushes and low-growing wild cranberries and permeated in the early summer by the intoxicating fragrance of pink wild roses. Another sort of sunrise took place on our peaceful pond, the rays of the sun filtering through the branches of gnarled pines, so Japanese in feeling. The only sounds were the intermittent calls of the quail, which rustled through the underbrush, and the almost noiseless splash of the Chermayeffs, our neighbors, and their two German shepherd dogs, as they took their morning swim across the pond. Such peace!

The Schlesingers originally shared a phone line with the Chermayeffs — whose house and colorful new studio were next door — and "there was a certain

amount of complaint when Arthur served in the Kennedy Administration and tied up the line with talks to the White House," Marian recalled. The Schlesingers got a private line.[14]

Soon after Phillips finished the barracks project, his friend Breuer, now building in Wellfleet himself, told him he could have saved himself the trouble. "I could have made all of them very easily in my office — from one design," said Breuer, who was hatching his own prototype for a group of summer cottages. Taking the salvage scheme to its conclusion, Phillips started work on a house for his family, on Horseleech Pond, by turning a leftover 16-by-16-foot barracks unit (with only three walls, as a friend had used the fourth to build a fish trailer) into a living room, and adding a modular tool shed before designing new sections himself. Like all of Phillips's houses, it was, said longtime friend Gloria Watts, a "very nice shack." Peter Watts, who helped Phillips build the house, noted that "Everybody else was overbuilding and he was underbuilding. The two-by-four was the common structural element in

The painter Paul Resika, Phillips's son-in-law, at work near the Phillips family camp on Horseleech Pond

the house, and when everybody else was going from two-by-four to two-by-six, Jack was going from two-by-four to two-by-three. . . . He just liked the idea of not being overly built."[15]

With five wives in three decades, Jack Phillips was the most married in a much-married crowd. Breuer's son, Tamas, compared him to Cary Grant, and his plummy Brahmin accent won him a spot in the Tetley tea commercials shown at the New York World's Fair in 1964 ("Tetley uses only tiny little tea leaves," Phillips intoned. "The tinier the leaf, the tastier the tea!").[16] In 1948, Arshile Gorky, Agnes Magruder ("Mougouch") Gorky, and Matta were embroiled in drama that Phillips would, in a sense, resolve: Mougouch and Matta had an affair, she left her deeply depressed husband, and Gorky committed suicide at his home in Connecticut. Phillips fell for the young widow in New York while she was still seeing Matta; he met her at a dance hosted by Serge and Barbara Chermayeff at an apartment on New

York's East River owned by the Edgar J. Kaufmann family (patrons of Frank Lloyd Wright's Fallingwater). A month later, in Wellfleet, Phillips came home one day to find Mougouch and Matta dancing to the gramophone in his living room, and Phillips gradually won her over. The two were married in Paris in 1949 and spent the early 1950s in France.[17] At one point, Phillips worked for the U.S. Embassy, joining a group of architects to design exhibitions for the Marshall Plan's information service. After he and Mougouch separated, in the late 1950s, Phillips married Florence Hammond in 1965, and the couple divided their time between Wellfleet and Cos Cob, Connecticut, until his death, in 2003. His ashes are buried on the shores of Horseleech Pond.

As an accidental landowner committed to honoring and sharing the bounties of his property, Phillips contributed to Cape Cod modernism as both designer and facilitator. He was too easygoing to excel in business; he priced his plots too low, and more than once he sold

A modernist with a taste for history, Jack Hall painted in a style that owed something to American folk art. Here, in the late 1970s, speculative portraits of his ancestors line his Wellfleet studio.

land to friends who broke their promises not to flip or build on it. Yet his houses established the self-taught design-build tradition that would define so much of the Cape's new vernacular. Writer Phillip Lopate, who spent time in Wellfleet in the 1970s, said that Phillips was, even in his later years, a friendly presence at Dwight Macdonald's legendary softball games — an enduring tradition started by the writer in the forties, pulling in such athletes as Schlesinger, Norman Mailer, and *Dissent* editor Bernard Rosenberg. (Macdonald's son was once photographed reading the *New York Times* at third base.) Phillips "seemed to have some real stature in that world," said Lopate, "because he had put together some of the houses early on."[18] Although they echoed the high modernism he had seen in Europe, Phillips's buildings had an undeniably casual charm. They are remembered as much for their functions — waterfront studio, party space with no neighbors — as for their forward-looking designs.

JACK HALL

As he entered his sixties, self-taught architect, carpenter, and painter John Hughes "Jack" Hall began to research the lives of his ancestors. Based on his findings — including the fact that one of his mother's forebears had sailed on the *Mayflower* — he began to paint portraits of his ancestors as he imagined them, and then to make up stories about the paintings. Over the course of 20 years, Hall crafted dozens of these character sketches, and compiled the results in a makeshift book called "Visible Ghosts: Portraits of an American Family" (1992). In the introduction, Hall, a recovered alcoholic, explained that he had once "rejected everything connected with ancestors as a form of snobbery." Now, he hoped for some insight into "those people whose problems had helped create the problems that helped create my problems."[19]

Hall's tone in these tales mixes respect for his predecessors with flashes of mischievous humor — a

Jack Hall, *Family—1874*, oil on canvas (1974). Hall's caption: "Here is William Henry Hall with his motherless children the year that his wife died. Gus, at 17, is trying to look sophisticated; Henry J. S. II, at 14, is constrained and tense and obedient; Martha, 12, is trying to manipulate her father in some fashion; and Billy and Agnes are simply young, pretty, and uninhibited."

combination that imbues much of his work. John Lothrop, born in England in 1584, was "that rare bird, that contradiction in terms, a liberal Puritan minister. One suspects that theology bored him." John Hughes, a Catholic born in Northern Ireland in 1774, "liked to say that he left for religious freedom, but he soon married a Methodist, fathered twelve Protestant children, and himself became a Methodist and a Mason." As for Bennaiah Dunham, born in Plymouth, Massachusetts, in 1640, Hall mused, "I've always thought of Bennaiah as a Yankee womanizer."

Born in New York in 1913, Hall grew up in what he called "an ordinary middle-class family with a mixture of origins . . . almost, but not quite WASP. Its members weren't famous or notorious. My father's family were, for the most part, business people, and my mother's family, farmers, clergymen and physicians." In reality, raised mostly by a nanny in Manhattan apartments and a neoclassical summer mansion in Smithtown, Long

Island, he was led to believe he would never have to work for a living. After attending St. Paul's School in New Hampshire, he arrived at Princeton with his own polo pony and took a degree in English in 1935. But Hall's father, who worked for a pharmaceutical firm, did not manage his wealth wisely, and the Great Depression destroyed most of his remaining assets. Telling his own life story in "Visible Ghosts," Hall highlights the defining jolt he experienced when his inheritance failed to materialize:

> He was the only child of Helen Hughes and Henry J. S. Hall II. Despite his mother's assurance that it would never be necessary, he discovered after her death, when he was thirty-three, that he would have to earn a living. Up until that time he had done some writing and some painting, married several times, served briefly in the army, had a tiny farm on Cape Cod and three children, and had stopped drinking, but it had never occurred to him to make any money. He became a carpenter, then a designer-builder on Cape Cod, then a designer in New York, without benefit of special schooling, and much to his astonishment earned a modest living for the next forty-odd years. His fourth marriage was happy. In his sixties and seventies, having returned to Cape Cod, he spent more time painting, and painted, among other pictures, a series of imaginary portraits of his forbears [sic].[20]

Hall would never quite settle on a career, but he would find satisfaction in several and achieve a flash of greatness in one. Ironically, it was because of his aimlessness that Hall left a diverse body of work in both art and craft: architecture, painting, carpentry, and writing. His architecture library held equal numbers of books on modernism and early American building types.

In the late 1930s, Hall and his first wife, Camille L'Engle (daughter of the Provincetown painters William and Lucy L'Engle), moved from New York to Wellfleet. The marriage imploded within two years, but by then Hall had bought an eighteenth-century farmhouse on several acres on Bound Brook Island — birthplace of

In 1937, Hall bought this antique Cape from John and Katy Dos Passos. A picket fence created some intimacy for a house that was otherwise adrift on its coastal prairie, the moors of Bound Brook Island.

Hall used an old barn on his property as a painting studio and a makeshift garage for some old carriages. When the building burned down, in the early 1940s, Hall salvaged some lumber from another derelict barn and reconstructed the post-and-beam original.

the banana magnate Lorenzo Dow Baker, builder of the Chequessett Inn. Hall purchased the property in 1937 from John and Katharine (Katy) Smith Dos Passos, who were leading the southward trickle of artists from Provincetown to Truro and Wellfleet. In a letter to Edmund Wilson in 1936, Katy Dos Passos wrote, "Provincetown has collapsed intellectually and is now turning into a mild country honky tonk with all the Café Azuls and second hand tourist traps filled with fishermen A&P boys and girls and the last thin line of Bohemia drinking harmless whiskeys and ale in the evening up till ten. The movie house is done over in plush." Whatever her objections to Provincetown's decline, Katy also had a weakness for cheap real estate; but she and John, who already owned a house in South Truro, had no need for the Baker homestead and sold it at no profit within a year. Hall kept the property until 1949, modernizing only the kitchen while maintaining the wide pine floorboards, original fireplaces, and nineteenth-century paneled pocket shutters.[21] Hall's photos of his new home betray an obsession with historic houses and landscapes that would last the rest of his life. Soft, finely textured, and unmistakably moody, the images embody what we might call Cape Gothic, the sense of desolation and unfulfilled promise that haunted the lives of some of the Brahmin Bohemians and the entire cast of *A Charmed Life.*

Bound Brook Island, which borders Truro on the bay side, is Wellfleet's most pristine backcountry, a silent swath of rolling heathland once "bound" by a brook and the Herring River in addition to Cape Cod Bay. Then an actual island, it gradually became attached to the mainland by shifting sands, silt, and salt marsh, and is now one of the few bay areas in the Cape Cod National Seashore. As Jack Phillips lamented, pitch pines have broken the old sightlines across these moors, but out toward the shore, the pines and oaks taper off, the sand comes into view, and the heath presents a unique ecosystem hospitable to rare plants, animals, and, as it turns out, architecture. Sloping down to the dunes are acres of hardy, softly colored grasses, lichens, and blooming shrubs including beach and golden heathers, bayberry, and blueberry. Even today, the few roads are single narrow lanes of pure sand. In the event that you face an oncoming car, one of you backs slowly up to the nearest turnoff point and waits for the other to pass.

The small community of farmers who had originally populated the island moved into town over the course of the nineteenth century, sometimes taking their homes with them. By the time Hall arrived, there were only a handful of houses left. He soon found a distinctive way to drop out of the rat race he had never really entered: tooling around in one of his two Rolls-Royces, he was nicknamed the Squire of Bound Brook Island, and within a few years he was a fixture on Wellfleet's nascent party scene. Ati Gropius Johansen, who began visiting Wellfleet in the late 1930s with her parents, Walter and Ise, remembered Jack as a whirlwind: "He was legendary with his . . . wives, every one of them a beauty, and somehow cut a swath through those quiet woods." Hall's friend Gloria Watts said he was "a big, handsome, very assertive person. He could be very charming and he could also be very stubborn." When Hall decided to try his hand at commercial fishing, even Wilson was on the scene, writing to McCarthy in 1944: "We went over to Ptown Monday with the Geismars and found the town full of exhilarated friends who were celebrating the christening of a magnificent new fishing boat which Jack Hall has had built for himself and which he is going to operate with a Portuguese crew. Matsons, Bubs Hackett, Joan Colebrook, Harl Cook,

Left: Jack Hall and Warren Nardin, Hall House, Wellfleet (1950). *Right*: Hall, right, dabbled in commercial fishing in the mid-1940s, buying a boat and hiring a captain who, while Hall served briefly in the army in 1945, took up with his second wife, Dodie. Hall sold the boat to the famous Provincetown rumrunner and fishing captain Manny Zora, left.[23]

the Portuguese crew and many others were all on board drinking various kinds of liquor."[22]

Having found his way into architecture through renovation, Hall engaged a friend, New York designer Warren Nardin, as a mentor for his first design project in the late 1940s: a modern house on a piece of his extensive property. "My father always had wanted to be an architect," said Hall's daughter, Noa. "He was crazy about beautiful things and beautiful designs. [But] he wanted to do things his own way." While living in the Baker residence, Hall built his new house section by section by hand (with help), and in 1950, now remarried, he moved in with his blended family. The house introduced the butterfly roof to Wellfleet, albeit on such a secluded site that only Hall's friends ever saw it. Butterfly roofs have always been counterintuitive in snowy climates, but midcentury architects, especially Breuer, were starting to build and promote them in New England, arguing that, when properly constructed, they were just as practical as their trusty peaked counterparts. The Museum of Modern Art popularized the profile by inviting Breuer to build a model home in the museum's Manhattan courtyard in 1949. In the 1950s,

butterfly roofs spread their wings nationwide, most notably in Palm Springs, California, where architect William Krisel put them on thousands of cheerful, affordable tract homes.

Hall's first design typifies the Brahmin Bohemian blend of innovation and patrimony. Like its colonial forebears, the house sits in a hollow to avoid the worst winter winds — but this hollow is on the leeward side of the dunes overlooking Cape Cod Bay. Hall angled the house so that people in the living room can see a slice of the bay through a break in the dune. By turning the traditional roof pitch gently upside down, Hall made space for dramatic full-height windows and screens and some high ribbon windows that pulled in the landscape and light. Inside, the centrifugal plan shoots three wings out of a central kitchen: the living room, screened porch, and master bedroom; dorm-style children's or guests' sleeping quarters; and a garage with utility space. In both plan and detail — a large screen of vertical wood slats divides the living room and bedrooms — the house was more stylized than anything Hall built afterward, perhaps due to Nardin's involvement. Hall's furnishings included an Eero

When Hall bought the early-eighteenth-century Joel Atwood farmhouse in 1953, it had been abandoned for 40 years. Hall's renovations included plate-glass windows that opened a sight line from the kitchen through the dining room to the living room. In the background, left and center, are Hall's Saarinen Womb chair and Hardoy "butterfly" chair.

Saarinen Womb chair, a Hardoy "butterfly" chair, and six chairs by master woodworker George Nakashima, a personal favorite. "He was *crazy* about this man," said Noa Hall, "and now has only one remaining chair that's not in great shape because he didn't take care of things!" Hall spoke with fond exasperation of her father's unique treatment of fine *objets*: "If he had something . . . that he thought looked beautiful outside, he would just leave it out, all through the snow and winter, and then it would just deteriorate."[24]

In 1953, Hall bought the early-eighteenth-century Joel Atwood House, where he would spend much of his vacation time and, after 1970, the rest of his life. "It was just a shell, it had been abandoned for forty years," said Noa Hall, "and people had stolen paneling and things out of it, mantels, and so he had to go [and fix it up] for a year and a half after he bought it." Hall traveled to Wellfleet to work on the house whenever he could, drafting his children to help. After restoring it, he blew out the back wall and part of the ell for a glazed corner of plate-glass windows overlooking the patio, a gesture that captured his dual affinity for antique homes and modern features. Over the next few decades, he made similar interventions in many of his friends' and neighbors' historic homes. Gloria Watts, whose husband, Peter, paints in a Hall-designed studio attached to their eighteenth-century Cape, said, "He

had this principle that you could change the interior but you could never change the front facade. . . . The facade has to stay." The Joel Atwood House is a perfect example of a centuries-old Cape that has been repeatedly modified in back yet looks unchanged in front (see page 23).[25]

Because he lived on the Cape year-round for many years, Hall worked as a carpenter and property manager for friends including Phillips. Promoting himself as a designer-builder, he completed his first commercial project in Truro: in the mid-1950s he designed an airy summer restaurant, Peters Hill, on the bay side of Route 6, the site of today's police station. Marked by exposed cross-bracing outdoors and a network of exposed wood trusses indoors, the building was an unprepossessing shed-roofed box that used sliding shoji-style screens to control light and breezes. Screens on the back wall slid open to a patio, and diners indoors and out enjoyed the strains of a jazz harpist. During the few years of its life, Peters Hill was a popular gathering place for writers and artists. "It was a wonderful building, and it was a wonderful community" of all ages, remembers Noa Hall. "Everybody we knew would go there and have dinner, because it was very homey food . . . and it was a very nice atmosphere. Things like kale-and-linguiça soup and garlic bread . . . very simple."[26] The restaurant occupied a

Right: Peters Hill restaurant and nightclub, which Hall designed in the late 1950s, was a hot spot in the quiet hamlet of Truro. *Below*: Inside, exposed wood trusses, cane furniture, and sliding shoji-style screens speak to Hall's taste for natural, historic materials and weather-sensitive versatility.

This model of the so-called Jungle Gym at the 1959 American National Exhibition, designed by George Nelson Associates (and here tweaked by Dolores Engle and Albert Woods), gives a sense of its enormous footprint—and the skeletal cubes that would reappear in Hall's Hatch House.

short but beloved place in Outer Cape history, as it hosted the kind of no-frills gathering that now defined summer culture there.

In 1954, his third marriage over, Hall started drinking after years of shaky sobriety. The following spring he joined Alcoholics Anonymous, became a Quaker, and began a process of personal and professional redemption. At Nardin's invitation, he moved to New York and committed himself to learning the art and craft of design. Soon he was working not only for Nardin's design firm, Nardin, Radoczy and Mayen, but also for the famed George Nelson Associates. Nelson was in the middle of his twenty-five-year reign as design director at Herman Miller, and his firm had become an institution. "The office was straight out of *Mad Men*," mused *Metropolis* magazine decades later, "with men in crisp white shirts and ties, and the few women in black dresses — cigarette smoke everywhere, classical music in the background, and Nelson, ever the impresario, standing in the middle of the tumult with a

camera dangling from his shoulders."[27] Plunged into pressing work on exhibitions, furniture, lighting, and commercial and office interiors, Hall, now in his forties, could scarcely have been better placed to join the national design discussion.

In 1959, Hall spent four months in Moscow with Nelson, whom the United States Information Agency had asked to oversee the design of the mammoth American National Exhibition, which drew 2.7 million Soviets to see the trappings of U.S. culture. Among other tasks, Hall helped supervise construction of a geodesic dome designed by Buckminster Fuller to show Charles and Ray Eameses' spectacular, seven-screen film, *Glimpses of the U.S.A.* Most notably, he also helped build the Jungle Gym, designed by Nelson's Richard Barringer — a building-sized, two-level, open steel grid of 4-cubic-yard modules that could be arranged to display hundreds of consumer products of various sizes. Upon his return to New York — still unencumbered by formal training in architecture — Hall opened his own firm. His design and renovation projects in the 1960s included a light fixture for Charles and Ray Eames, Plexiglas retail fixtures for the linens giant Fieldcrest Mills, several schools, and more than 20 houses and artists' studios in New York and Wellfleet.[28]

Around 1960, Robert Hatch, a film critic (and later executive editor) at *The Nation*, and his wife, Ruth, a painter, approached Hall to design a summer cottage on Bound Brook Island. The Hatches had bought almost three acres overlooking Cape Cod Bay from the pianist and composer Gardner Jencks and his wife, Ruth, who lived just up the hill — out of sight, of course. They considered moving an antique Cape to their plot, but this proved impractical. Hall, steeped in modern design after several years in New York, fresh from a celebration of the best in the field in Moscow, and at last happily married, was poised to create the house that would become his one masterpiece. Elements of his work in the 1950s, from the screens at Peters Hill to the Moscow Jungle Gym, now flowed into a building that became, against all odds and intentions, the quintessential Cape Cod modern house.

Hall's 1956 marriage to the genial, cosmopolitan life-of-the-party Martha (Marty) Parker was the one

Friends gather in the 1960s at Jack Phillips's house on Horseleech Pond. From left: Anne Özbekhan (an architect who studied with Mies van der Rohe), Jack Hall, Mary Ellen Johansen (first wife of architect John Johansen), Natasha Gorky (daughter of Arshile Gorky, and Phillips's former step-daughter), Phillips (leaning on deck), Marty Hall (Jack's wife), Alfred Thornton "Bobby" Baker (standing), and Hasan Özbekhan (economist and cofounder of the Club of Rome)

that stuck, ending only with his death in 2003. Over that same period, his weekly attendance at Quaker meetings — at which congregants gather in silent meditation, speaking only when they feel moved to do so — was another source of peace. In 1999, he told Seth Rolbein of the *Cape Codder*, "I suppose I've been doing this for forty years, driving forty-five minutes to sit quietly for an hour, driving forty-five minutes back — and somehow it's never felt foolish."[29]

HATCH HOUSE (1962)

Of all the Cape Cod modern houses that have opened their doors to the public, Hall's Hatch House evokes the most visceral, astonished response, even from veteran architects. With soft fir cladding, a separate building for each of its three living spaces, and a spectacular sloping site overlooking Cape Cod Bay, the house is at once a sculpture on a pedestal and a piece of weathering driftwood, blending slowly into its landscape.

The building's unique plan had a unique inspiration: some old chicken coops in a Wellfleet artist's backyard. In the 1950s, Ruth Hatch studied painting with Edwin Dickinson at the Art Students League of New York. She and her husband, Robert, grew friendly with Dickinson

and his wife, Pat, and spent several summers in a guest cottage on the Dickinsons' property in Wellfleet. The Hatches' daughter, Gilly, remembers:

On the hill above the cottage, there were two ex–chicken houses. They were turned into sleeping houses. I had one and my brother had the other, while my parents slept in the main house. . . . My mother [said] that those separate units gave them the idea of the main house/sleeping houses for our place. It was a way to have some privacy in a small space.[30]

Marrying the camplike appeal of little barns to a plan of Miesian rigor, Hall designed the Hatch House as a rectangular grid of 35 nearly cubic modules, each 7-by-7-by-8 feet, on concrete pilings. Taking a cue from Nelson's Jungle Gym, Hall created a structure like an open space frame and attached panels to form roofs, walls, and decks. The frame is a fir exoskeleton of 2-by-4 columns and 2-by-6 beams, and the panels enclose three volumes devoted to different functions: living space (living room, kitchen, and bath, comprising 10 cubes), master suite (master bedroom, dressing

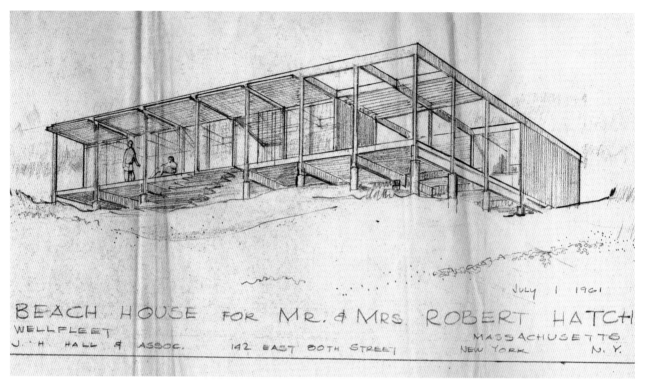

BEACH HOUSE FOR MR. & MRS. ROBERT HATCH
WELLFLEET   MASSACHUSETTS
J. H. HALL & ASSOC.   142 EAST 80TH STREET   NEW YORK   N.Y.
JULY 1 1961

Hall's rendering of the house, drawn while it was under construction in 1961. The bedroom modules on the far right migrated forward one bay in the built version.

area, and studio, three cubes), and children's or guest rooms (two bedrooms, one cube each). All three volumes open and close with the seasons thanks to full-height shutters, hinged at the top, that can be closed to block the weather or raised to form shaded verandas. Paul Rudolph had famously put such shutters on his Walker Guest House on Sanibel Island, Florida (1953), but the Hatch House is considerably more complex, with multiple indoor-outdoor zones. On walls facing the interior passageways, all rooms have screened clerestory openings with their own top-hinged shutters. The original enclosed floor space was 735 square feet; with the later addition of a guest-room cube, it is now 784.

Outside, the house holds an elaborate dialogue with the landscape: it is inexorably married to its wild site, yet often feels as though it could levitate away without leaving a trace. Between and around the interior volumes, instead of hallways, Hall laid an unbroken expanse of decking. He affixed fir deck boards vertically, leaving ¾-inch gaps between them to pull the

breeze onto bare feet and create a sense that the walking surface is dematerializing. With a foundation of narrow piers, a vanishing deck, and a total absence of guard rails, the house seems to hover weightlessly a few feet above the ground. Add the drama of a kettle hole, or glacial depression, on the slope just below the house, and the deck becomes a stage in a natural amphitheater. The rigor and simplicity of Hall's design form a strangely effective foil for the rolling heath and dramatic sweep of the bay. It is, says K. Michael Hays, professor of architectural theory at Harvard, "the perfect modern primitive hut."[31]

Hall was deeply invested in the idea of Bound Brook Island as a rural paradise. The neighborhood was electrified in the late 1940s, but Hall and two of his neighbors later paid the local utility to remove the poles and bury the cables. When he built the Hatch House, his clients were taken aback to learn that Hall did not want to install phone or electric connections. "He felt that they brought too much civilization to Bound Brook," said Gilly Hatch. The family made do for a while:

We used elegant, tall-chimneyed, mantled kerosene lamps and a hand pump that pumped, against pressure, into a tank. . . . I guess it was the pump that made my parents bring in electricity, as it was extremely hard work, not like a normal hand pump.

My grandmother asked my parents to put in the phone. They were always deeply concerned about the effect the house had on the environment (one reason it was on stilts), so had the line buried. The trench tore through the ground cover, so Pa and I spent a good deal of time, that summer, carefully replanting mock cranberry from our house to the telephone pole, several hundred yards to the northeast.[32]

The house could scarcely have had better stewards.

The largest interior space is the living room, where the sea-facing wall disappears in three layers: a fixed mosquito screen (hand-sewn, because no screen on the market was large enough), sliding Plexiglas doors, and, finally, the wooden shutters. A long, built-in banquette seats an audience for the bay view. The Hatches' decor was informal, with paintings by friends and family, found objects (the coffee table was an old ship's cable reel), miscellaneous chairs, and Design Research dining pieces including a Bruno Mathsson table and Alvar Aalto stools. "My mother had a knack for making a room feel right," said Hatch. "The lighting had to be good for reading; there had to be enough comfortable chairs for company; walls were for paintings; and there were always flowers, from her garden as well as wild, on the tables. She had no theory, didn't think about it, it was instinctive." For decades, the space was a casual meeting place for artists, scholars, and other friends, including Connie Breuer, Serge and Barbara Chermayeff, Noam Chomsky, Charles Jencks, Edmund Wilson, and Howard Zinn.[33]

Some people who visit the Hatch House, no matter how much they admire it, say they could not live in a place so tightly planned and so exposed to the elements. But friends of Ruth Hatch recall vividly that she used to stay in Wellfleet until November, even though the only source of heat in her windswept home was a wood stove in the living room. Eleanor Stefani remembered:

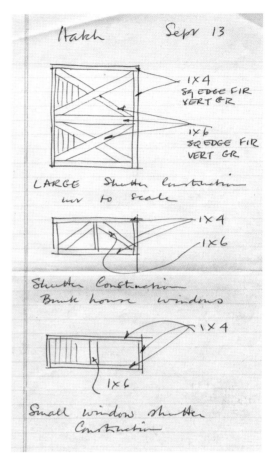

Hall's sketches for Hatch House shutters

She would stay till the last possible moment, especially after her husband died, for years . . . quite often we would walk down Bound Brook, park the car out in the road, and walk in, and there she would be, sitting in the freezing cold . . . you know, the sun was out but it was *freezing* cold — the wind was blowing, whitecaps on the bay, and she would be wearing mittens cut open at the tips . . . painting. Painting, sitting on a little chair with her watercolors, just working away, oblivious to everything.[34]

Artist Peter Watts, friend to both the Hatches and the Halls, was another frequent guest. "I used to love when we would go there," he said. "You could just be mesmerized sitting out on the porch. And the sun would go down and the colors would change, and I always thought it was like living in a Turner painting."[35]

The Hatch House, during and soon after construction, on what was then a treeless moor

Ruth Hatch enjoys her home's unique circulation, which moves a person outdoors — onto open-slat decking — for each trip between the living space, the bedrooms, and the bathroom. Above, shutters on the clerestory openings control wind and light inside.

Ruth Hatch spent as much time here as she could, often staying through the chill of November.

JACK HALL, HATCH HOUSE, WELLFLEET (1962, RESTORED IN 2013)

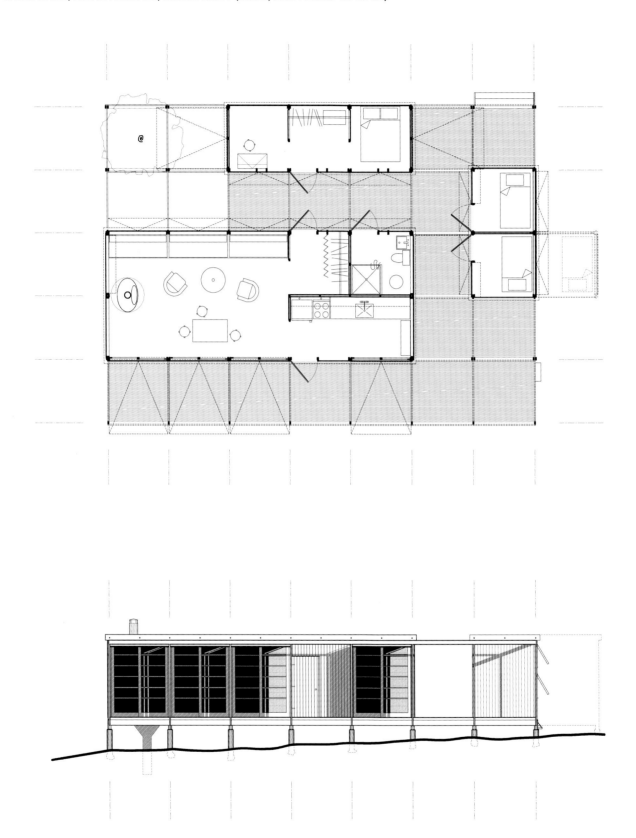

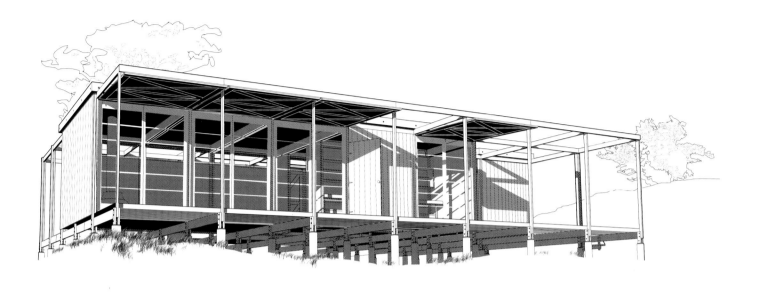

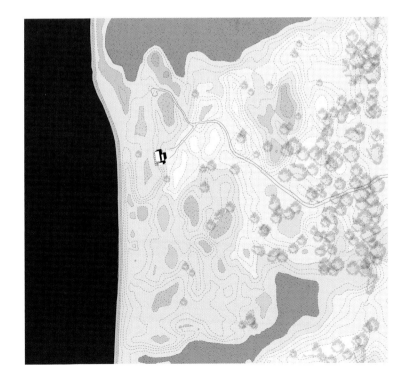

Opposite, top: Plan, with a later addition of one module (far right) expanding the guest room following all the rules of Hall's design. *Opposite, bottom*: West elevation with shutters open. *Above*: View from the northwest. *Right*: Site plan showing the glacial kettle holes of Bound Brook Island. Cape Cod Bay is to the west (to the left in site plan), the bed of old Bound Brook to the north, and a large vernal pool to the south.

Hatch House viewed from the kettle hole, or glacial depression, that separates it from the barrier dune

71

The presence of the kettle hole just below the house makes its hilltop site even more dramatic.
The sea-facing deck becomes a stage in a natural amphitheater.

The restored living room. All rooms in the house have apertures that can be adjusted to control ventilation, views, and light.
Opposite: Passageway between the living/dining area and master bedroom

The Hatches' pots, and fishing lures collected on the beach

Master bedroom

The Hatch House in the Bound Brook Island landscape. View to the south along Cape Cod Bay

HAYDEN WALLING

Hayden Walling was the fourth child of oppressively accomplished parents. Like Phillips and Hall, he defied his family's expectations in choosing to build houses — and a rural livelihood — out of old Cape Cod timbers.

Walling's mother, Russian-born Anna Strunsky, was a precocious political activist who, after attending the new, reform-minded Stanford University, became a darling of café society in San Francisco. William Randolph Hearst's *Examiner* called her the "Girl Socialist of San Francisco," and Rose Wilder Lane — daughter of Laura Ingalls Wilder — wrote in *Sunset* magazine, "No one who met Anna Strunsky ever forgets her, they say."[36] Strunsky formed an intense friendship with Jack London, and they coauthored the novel *The Kempton-Wace Letters.* Meanwhile, Walling's father, William English Walling, known as English, studied sociology and economics at the University of Chicago with Thorstein Veblen, author of *The Theory of the Leisure Class* and the term "conspicuous consumption." In 1905, after working as a factory inspector while living in a settlement house, Walling decamped to Europe to report on the Russian Revolution. Through activist networks, he began a correspondence with Strunsky and persuaded her, sight unseen, to join him in St. Petersburg. What followed was a heady period of impassioned journalism, covert assistance to revolutionaries, and all but inevitable love. When they married, in 1906, Anna Walling wrote loftily to London: "We mean never to have a home, never to belong to a clique, never to prevent life from playing upon us, never to shield each other."[37]

Back home, after the couple's deportation from Russia in 1907, English turned his attention to domestic affairs, publishing an impassioned essay on racial equality that led, ultimately, to the formation of the NAACP, and persuading W. E. B. Dubois to edit the new association's newspaper.[38] In 1916, the Wallings settled in Greenwich, Connecticut. But while Anna was a pacifist, English began to thirst for the blood of czars and aristocrats. His support for U.S. involvement in World War I — he was now informally advising the Woodrow Wilson administration — led to a complicated implo-

Hayden Walling in 1939 or '40. More than one female acquaintance remembered Walling as the handsomest man she had ever seen.

sion of his socialist beliefs, and his increasingly bellicose attitude destroyed his marriage, most of his friendships, and his professional reputation.

The youngest of the Wallings' four children, born in 1916 in Greenwich, was William Hayden English, known as Hayden. The family vacationed in Provincetown, where English and Anna's friends included members of the Provincetown Players. As a student at Greenwich's progressive Edgewood School, which was inspired by the teachings of Rudolf Steiner (founder of the Waldorf schools), Hayden was encouraged to learn through hands-on work, including carpentry, weaving, and maple-sugaring. From that time on, said his son, Christopher, Hayden Walling "could build anything." Alice Annand McMahon, an Edgewood student in the late 1930s, recalls, "The school was truly radical and

Walling in the Abruzzi, Italy, after World War II

diverse, as opposed to left-leaning schools today. The school nurse was a Nazi who stood up and shouted, 'Sieg Heil!' when Hitler's invasion of Poland was announced. The math teacher, an organizer for the Longshoremen's Union, would disappear during strikes."[39] Like other progressive schools of its day, Edgewood was informed by a cocktail of the Arts and Crafts movement, socialist and agrarian ideals, and old-fashioned Yankee self-sufficiency.

Ambivalent about his family's wealth, young Walling gave away much of his money, but what remained would fund his drive to build. In 1935, as a Bard freshman (he earned a drama degree in 1939), Walling showed up in Wellfleet wearing a white suit and carrying a clarinet. Phillips dubbed him a "jazz kid" and, despite Walling's tender age, sold him a plot between Slough and Round ponds, where Walling immediately started to build a house. Surrounding his site were the foundations of eighteenth-century houses that had long since been rolled to Wellfleet center; Walling gathered their left-over bricks and locust beams and added them to his materials. He built with only the most basic sketch or plan, preferring — as he would throughout his career — to see a building take shape organically, and blithely changing the size or shape of a room in progress to match the available beams.[40] He worked alone, or with just one assistant, as "he hated making money off another person's work," said Christopher Walling. Like Phillips and Hall, Walling designed mostly modern homes but lived in a hybrid: his new house was a meandering complex of mostly vernacular forms, opening to a modern expanse in the saltbox-shaped living room. When young Christopher found an old wooden water tower that was free for the taking, Walling took it apart, hauled it 2 miles down a dirt road, and rebuilt it as an annex to the house. Christopher Walling remembers the house as an architectural collage of old and new. "It was both — in delightful ways," he said, with oak floors and mahogany trim in the smaller, traditional rooms, flagstone floors and glass walls in the open, sunny modern living room, and a "great flow of traffic." Walling would work on this house for the next 30 years.[41]

Walling, like Hall, eventually became a Quaker. As a conscientious objector during World War II, he stayed in Wellfleet and helped Phillips with his trade in turkey husbandry. When the war ended, Walling and the second of his four wives, Elizabeth, traveled to Italy, where he helped the American Friends Service Committee

Walling and his eight-year-old son, Christopher, building a camp on Round Pond in Truro, 1956. The Wallings moved into the camp in summer to evade the many houseguests that their larger home could accommodate. The antique windows were salvaged from a wrecking company in Hyannis.

supervise the dangerous work of demining Nazi-mined hill towns in the Abruzzi. The Quakers also helped rebuild wood and stone houses using construction techniques traditional to the eastern Italian region, and Walling was in his element. "The mountain towns had rows of houses, each built on the roofs of the rows below," said Christopher Walling. "The Germans had blown up the bottom rows and the entire villages collapsed. [My father] brokered deals in which the hill-towners cut wood and delivered it to the valley-dwellers, enabling them to make bricks, which allowed everyone to rebuild." In 1946 the Wallings moved to Paris, where they raised an old barge from the bottom of the Seine and converted it to a houseboat, a project quirky enough to land them in the *New York Herald Tribune*. Their marriage ended soon after.[42]

In 1948, Walling met French journalist Odette Bonnat, who during the war had joined the French Resistance, carried out death-defying assignments for the British, and been imprisoned in a German concentration camp. The couple married in Rome and, with Hayden now working for the U.S. Relief and Rehabilitation Administration, traveled and worked in Albania, Beirut, and North Africa. In 1955, they returned to Cape Cod and settled year-around on Slough Pond, where they bought additional property to save it from threatened development.[43] Walling's life thus, in one sense, mirrored those of his parents: international adventure and idealism followed by New England domesticity.

Over the next 10 years, Walling built at least 14 houses on Outer Cape Cod. On some, he served as a contractor for established architects such as Olav Hammarström, who had worked for Alvar Aalto and Eero Saarinen: Walling built Hammarström's Saarinen House (1960) for Eero's first wife, sculptor Lily Swann Saarinen, and his Tisza House (1960). Hammarström was a demanding architect, and these commissions required a level of precision not found in the area's earlier, more ad hoc projects.

In addition to building others' designs, Walling was sometimes called upon to fix them. In 1954, Chermayeff designed a modern house for Charles Flato, a former U.S. civil servant who later was found to have been a wartime spy for the Soviets. Having suffered from polio as a child, Flato was very short, but Chermayeff's design did not account for his height. After Walling rebuilt the interior so that Flato could comfortably occupy it, Chermayeff never spoke to him again, although they were neighbors on Slough Pond for another 30 years. Around 1960, Walling renovated his friends Edmund and Elena Wilson's historic home.

Walling built at least five houses of his own design, some of which are still startling for the power they achieve despite his lack of training. His most fully realized work was a cottage and studio for the painter James Lechay and his family (1959). Using the most

The camp was, like Phillips's dune studio, a simple shed-roofed box. Walling, however, incorporated color into his modern design: having clad the house in Homasote, he broke the clerestory ribbon with panels in yellow and red.

prosaic materials — reclaimed barnboard, 2-by-12-inch rafters (doubled to increase the roof span), plate glass, painted plywood — and quite rudimentary carpentry, Walling fashioned an elegant shed-roofed house with a neighboring north-facing studio. In the living room, a glass wall looks west onto a large deck, which presides over an immediate steep drop and a distant bay view. Unfettered by railings, the deck gives a disarming sense of communion with the surrounding trees — one of several intimate yet dramatic experiences Walling created with the fewest possible moves. On the studio, using only materials from the local lumberyard, Walling created an unbroken wall of glazing by lapping narrow panes of plate glass like clapboards.

In the Halprin House (1965), on Horseleech Pond, Walling again makes a wall of vertical glass strips, this time incorporating casement windows. Inside, however, his mastery of woodwork is now apparent in handmade doors, pulls, and built-in storage. The Halprin House, more than any other in Wellfleet, evokes the Arts and Crafts, with its swaths of warm, stained wood, its built-in living-room couch, and the occasional through-tenon joint. In the living room, Walling used a shed roof to pull the glass wall upward, flooding the room with light, but he centered the sitting area on a brick-and-

slate fireplace flanked by stained pine. There are echoes of Frank Lloyd Wright's Usonian living rooms, and of Henry Varnum Poor's house, which Walling loved, in Rockland County, New York. But the L-shaped east elevation is Walling's alone. A second, steeper shed roof on the upper level extends part of the glass wall (and the chimney) upstairs into the wood-lined bedroom and work space, where 2-by-10 rafters flow uninterrupted across the skylights. Outdoors, a staircase leads from the ground-floor deck to a roof deck above the living room, where the sight line peers over the gently sloping shed roof toward what was once a clear ocean view.

The last two houses Walling designed, including his own second home on Horseleech Pond, still stand but were illegal constructions: he broke ground after the area had been protected as the Cape Cod National Seashore. Walling had bought the land from Phillips with a pledge not to build on it, and some never forgave his breach of promise. In both projects, Walling turns away from explicitly modern forms in favor of minimalist gable-roofed houses. At Deer Cove (1962), which Walling enjoyed off season and rented out in summer for income, exposed posts and beams, a cathedral ceiling, and a long, extruded plan recall a Japanese farmhouse, while modern elements include wide vertical siding, industrial light fixtures, and a wall of glass that bathes every room in soft northeastern light.

One acquaintance described Walling as "the handsomest man in the world," and more than one remembered him that way. He and Odette eventually divorced, and, in 1964, he moved to Manhattan and opened a cabinetmaking shop on Christopher Street. He married and divorced one last time, and in later years suffered from depression. Friends said he never felt he had achieved his professional potential, in contrast to his feverishly driven parents. In 1981, at the age of 64, Hayden Walling took his own life at Deer Cove. He is buried in Truro, his grave marked by a stone inscribed, "Master Builder."

Walling's own house, begun in the 1930s, marries traditional Cape Cod silhouettes to modern forms and interiors.

Walling framed his modern living room in the 400-year-old saltbox form (a gabled roof extended downward on the back side), creating an asymmetrical cathedral ceiling. Grounded by natural materials—cool slate, a brick fireplace surrounded by a wall of reclaimed stained-wood siding—the room draws in the outdoors with walls of glass.

A few steps down from Walling's Lechay House, Wellfleet (1959), artfully askew on the site, a north-facing studio provides a private space for painting, writing, or other work. Originally, the glass wall was made up of panes that were lapped, like clapboards; recently, full-height panes of thermal glass were installed for greater energy efficiency.

In the Lechay House, the living room fills with afternoon sun. Reclaimed barnboard frames the fireplace; on the right, the wide galley kitchen leads to a dining area with its own glass wall (shown opposite) and bedrooms on either side.

West-facing deck outside living room

Walling's Halprin House, Wellfleet (1965), has an unusual L-shaped east elevation thanks to an upstairs bedroom and work space with its own wall of glass and shed roof. Walling achieved a window wall using only 2-by-4's and strips of plate glass, giving the feeling of a standard stud wall dematerialized.

Living room

The floor in the upper bedroom steps up to follow the roof pitch.

NATHANIEL SALTONSTALL

Nathaniel Saltonstall was more Brahmin than Bohemian. Like the Phillips family, the Saltonstalls of Boston go all the way back to the *Arbella.* Sir Richard Saltonstall, a Yorkshire lord, was the only passenger with a title on that 1630 crossing; and when he founded what is now Watertown, Massachusetts, he named George Phillips — Jack Phillips's ancestor — minister of the town's first church. The Saltonstalls were active in American civic life, attending Harvard from its first graduating class and working mainly in law and government. The first Nathaniel Saltonstall made history as a judge at the Salem witch trials of 1692, when he resigned in disgust after the first conviction. Leverett Saltonstall served as governor of Massachusetts during World War II and a U.S. senator from 1948 to 1966, during which time he cosponsored the legislation, with junior Bay State senator John F. Kennedy, that ultimately created the Cape Cod National Seashore. By the time the seashore was established, in 1961, it held dozens of modern houses, including the exclusive Mayo Hill Colony Club vacation retreat, designed by Leverett's cousin Nathaniel.

Unlike Phillips, Hall, and Walling, however, Saltonstall embraced, rather than rejected, the visible privileges of his class. Far from the shacks of Wellfleet's Back Shore, he spent most of his time in sumptuous Back Bay brownstones, aiming not to subvert the social order but to gently expand its horizons and pursue his varied interests within it. An architect by profession, Saltonstall was equally active — and much better known — as a curator, tastemaker, administrator, impresario, and all-around bon vivant. His public persona, too, was multifaceted: while his courtly manner and even his modern architecture were rather conservative, he defied convention by living relatively openly as a gay man.

As a founder and the first president of what is now Boston's Institute of Contemporary Art (ICA), Saltonstall and his colleagues introduced modern art to their famously hidebound city, curating exhibitions, staging benefits, and gradually nudging Boston's other museums and galleries to show more contemporary work.

Nathaniel Saltonstall, shown in this undated photograph, straddled multiple worlds as an architect, art curator, impresario, and gay man in mid-twentieth-century Boston.

A fixture on the society page for almost 40 years, Nat, as he was known, seems never to have met a party he didn't like. Tall, graceful, and impeccably attired, he moved from debutante balls to black-tie Beaux-Arts blowouts to so-called bachelor parties with other well-heeled gay men. A trustee at Boston's Museum of Fine Arts and member of countless arts committees, he also assembled a personal collection focused on living artists. When first lady Jacqueline Kennedy decided in 1961 to restore her new home in Washington, she tapped Saltonstall for the Special Committee for White House Paintings. Upon Saltonstall's death, in 1968, the *Boston Globe*'s art critic wrote that "he was deservedly 'Mr. It' on the contemporary art scene."[44]

Born in 1903 in Milton, Massachusetts, Saltonstall was educated at Milton Academy, Harvard, and MIT,

For his own second home in Medfield, Massachusetts, outside Boston (ca. 1932), Saltonstall played with elements of the Machine Age—a curved stairwell, glass block—but grounded them in classic red brick. The window styles span three centuries.

though he never earned a degree at either Cambridge institution. A member of Harvard's class of 1928, he left in '27 and studied architecture at MIT until 1931, in the twilight of the Beaux-Arts era. In 1936, after touring Europe to study art and architecture, Saltonstall persuaded New York's six-year-old Museum of Modern Art to entrust him with a Boston satellite, and thus was born the Boston Museum of Modern Art. Following a fundraiser featuring music by Cab Calloway and the presence of Salvador and Gala Dalí dressed as sharks ("Modern Arts Ball Is Best Party of Year," said the *Globe*), Saltonstall and friends mounted Boston's first Gauguin exhibition. At the opening, Harvard undergraduate Leonard Bernstein — a Saltonstall discovery — played contemporary classical pieces on the piano. The museum, rechristened the Institute of Modern Art, was independent by 1939, and Saltonstall served as president for the next eight years. Bostonians, he insisted, were eager to stay abreast of "the changing panorama of modern sculpture, painting, architecture and industrial art," including "representative modern work from all parts of the world."[45] Architecture had a prominent place: between 1940 and 1950, the museum mounted the first U.S. retrospectives on Frank Lloyd Wright and Le Corbusier, and a major exhibition on the

importance of Walter Gropius. And in 1947, during the postwar housing crisis, Saltonstall and his colleagues organized a lecture series called Small House Designing, which offered "practical ideas for immediate use" from speakers Joseph Hudnut, Hugh Stubbins, Jr., William Wurster, and the suburban modernist and Techbuilt founder Carl Koch.[46]

Around 1952, Saltonstall redesigned the interior of an old Boston speakeasy to help create the Napoleon Club, a legendary gay lounge until it closed in 1998. The Napoleon was typical of his involvements, at once transgressive and upscale: police complained when it opened that the bar was filled with "girlie-boys," but it became a rather sedate gentlemen's club, with a jacket-and-tie dress code as late as the 1970s.[47] Because his architecture reflected this same genteel eclecticism, he was not an exclusive modernist: he designed suburban redoubts in Georgian, French chateau, and other traditional styles at his clients' request, and some banal modern motels. Yet his Mayo Hill Colony Club in Wellfleet, his modern residential work in the Boston suburbs and on the Outer Cape, and his solar-house innovations all speak to the influence of his formal sensibilities on his casual modern designs.

In 1931, after a spell at the Georgian Revival firm Little & Russell, Saltonstall joined another Boston firm, Putnam & Cox, founded by two École des Beaux-Arts alumni, and became a partner in 1939.[48] His main projects in the thirties were residential, including his own second home in Medfield, Massachusetts (ca. 1932), a characteristic example of early New England modernism in that it works historic elements — in this case, Boston red brick and divided-light windows — into modern forms. Here, Saltonstall mixes rectangular and rounded volumes of different heights and fenestration of every description: modified ribbon windows, Federal-style parlor windows with painted muntins, a curved wall of glass on the semicircular, south-facing sitting room at the back, and a three-story stairwell encased in a half-cylinder of Art Moderne glass blocks.

During World War II, after a stint in the Army Air Corps camouflage division, Saltonstall put his talents to work as chief of the Handicraft Branch in Special

Saltonstall and Morton designed this model in Natick, Massachusetts (1948), for a development of passive-solar homes meant for veterans. Horizontal louvers helped cool the rooms. At the time, large windows were seen as a threat to privacy; to ensure it, said the *Boston Globe* in its review, "Houses of this type require a large lot, and look their best when well landscaped."

Services, where he arranged the distribution of 400,000 craft kits to occupy idle soldiers with tasks including leatherwork, woodcarving, and clay modeling. After the war, in 1945, Saltonstall and his Putnam & Cox colleague Oliver Morton wasted no time in launching a new architecture firm. Together, they designed a prototype for a new, modern home for what was now called the ICA on the Charles River; a veterans' housing project in Boston; several motels including The Horizons, in North Truro; and several residential works in Wellfleet, including the Mayo Hill Colony Club (1949).[49] The club, a hillside grouping of tiny cottages and an art gallery, became Saltonstall's summer home, and he ran it from 1949 to 1963 as a retreat for patrons and practitioners of the arts.

In 1948, Saltonstall and Morton rode a national wave of passive-solar construction to design a prototype for a neighborhood of affordable passive-solar homes for veterans. Rising costs scuttled the developer's plan, but the sample house spawned one more, financed by Saltonstall's mother, and the homes were featured in the *Boston Globe* and *House Beautiful*.[50] Each house was sited to face the living room south, and the length of the roof overhang was calculated to welcome the sun in winter and block it in summer. Most windows were fixed, so the louvers below each window were backed with screens that could be exposed in warm weather.

THE COLONY (1949)

Saltonstall plunged into several progressive design initiatives after World War II, but no one could have mistaken him for an activist. At the Mayo Hill Colony Club, Saltonstall and Morton's best-known project, one had to furnish social and bank references just to rent a cottage. Far from the backwoods of Phillips, Hall, and Walling, The Colony was (and still is) next door to the Chequessett Yacht and Country Club, and it offered maid service and landscaped grounds with the aim of coaxing wealthy patrons down from Boston to see, and perhaps purchase, the work of unknown artists.

Saltonstall's masterwork — for the design was primarily his — is a series of 14 buildings spilling down a modest hill near the quiet end of Wellfleet Harbor. The original complex had 11 cottages (two have since been sold), six of them duplexes; a kitchen; an office and laundry building; and a storage shed, all anchored by a larger building housing an art gallery. From Chequessett Neck Road — which winds, heaves, and plunges across the Herring River toward the beaches of Cape Cod Bay — only the gallery building is readily seen. A privacy wall shields the complex but speaks to passersby: its concrete facade holds a sand-cast bas-relief by Xavier González, mixing geometric shapes with hardy plants, arthropods, and birds. Although The Colony's design was adventurous for its time and place, the roadside compound is insular and controlled;

R. D. Patterson's 1949 watercolor painting of The Colony shows how dramatically the landscape has changed in just a few decades with the proliferation of pitch pines. When The Colony was built, every cottage had a view of Cape Cod Bay.

nature here has been tamed. The club was clearly meant for consumers, not producers, of art.

Across the 10-acre site, the cottages are carefully positioned to capture the rays of the sun but not the gaze of neighbors. Cross-shaped in plan, each one is bisected by a wall of white-painted concrete block that extends beyond the house on both ends, creating privacy for duplex units; the roof and wall planes slide past each other. Owing something to the Dutch De Stijl movement, the rest of each exterior is plywood painted red, brown, or taupe. Plate-glass windows surround two opposing corners of each cottage, with an overhang to block the hottest rays. Inside, sisal rugs line painted concrete floors, and the furnishings include original pieces by Breuer, Harry Bertoia, Paul McCobb, and the Eameses.

As both architect and proprietor, Saltonstall used his social network to entice wealthy patrons of con-temporary art — and artists themselves, if they could pay — to little-known Wellfleet. Once ensconced in their cottage or duplex unit, guests enjoyed porter and maid service, a fire laid each morning, a snack in the fridge, and optional meals from the Continental Casse-role Kitchen (requiring only "brief reheating," the first brochure promised). They were also invited to gather bouquets from a "picking garden."[51] Still, these were spartan quarters by Brahmin standards: the units are 400 or 800 square feet, and in the duplex units the living room is the bedroom, with beds serving as couches by day. There were — and still are — no TVs, radios, or even clocks, only books, magazines, and journals. Saltonstall's brochure distilled the new ideal of the postwar vacation for an affluent audience, prom-ising "restful, comfortable and easy, leisure-time living" and "magnificent views of Cape Cod Bay and

Wellfleet Harbor, with long vistas of forest, dunes, marsh and moor. The surroundings are extremely quiet." Forestation has since blocked those views, but the lodgings are unchanged from those Saltonstall promised his first guests:

> The architecture is modern. Wide-vision windows
> look out over the views and vistas.
> Cross ventilation is provided by louvers.
> Furnishings and decorations harmonize with the
> architectural design. Varied color schemes,
> interior and exterior, pick up and blend with
> the natural hues of the site.
> The landscaping has been carefully planned to
> afford appropriate setting and finish,
> without artificiality. Crushed stone paths
> lead to the various Houses,
> and parking space is provided for each.[52]

The Colony was from the start an open-air art museum, from the Mayo Hill Galleries in the main building, which Saltonstall ran with his companion, Tom Gaglione, to the sculptures that still dot the property and the terrace fresco by Henry Varnum Poor, founder of the Skowhegan art school. Andrew Hyde, director of the ICA in the late 1960s and early '70s, wrote that Saltonstall occasionally surprised his Colony guests by giving them an original work of art, and "the presentation would be made with such characteristic grace that the recipient would be hard put to refuse it."[53] Around 1955, Saltonstall designed the Wellfleet Art Gallery on Route 6, and under Tom Gaglione's direction, it thrived for the next 30 years. The artists included Georgia O'Keefe, sculptor Sidney Simon, and painter Ethel Edwards; guests at gallery events included Jackie Kennedy and Supreme Court Justice Warren Berger.[54] Saltonstall next turned his attention to converting the Mayo Hill Galleries into a house and moved from his usual cottage (number 6) into the building.

In 1963, facing health problems, he sold the complex to a Boston artist and designer, Loris Stefani, and his wife, Eleanor, who shortened its name to The Colony and began renting the cottages to the public. Their one major

This postcard shows a hilltop Colony cottage around 1950, when the complex was the exclusive preserve of art patrons.

change to Saltonstall's plan was the addition of terraces and privacy screens with vertical slats, copied from a prototype Saltonstall had made for his own cottage.[55] The Stefanis retained Saltonstall's porter and maid service, kitchen service (until the Cape's new restaurant culture made it moot), gently resplendent garden, and studious discretion. The crowd, while still distinguished, became less pedigreed and more literary. The Colony has drawn a handful of Hollywood stars over the years: Saltonstall hosted Elizabeth Taylor, while Stefani has welcomed Paul Newman, Joanne Woodward, and Faye Dunaway. But the tone since the 1960s has been set by writers and intellectuals such as Lionel and Diana Trilling, Bernard Malamud, publisher Alfred A. Knopf, Jr., and child psychiatrist Robert Coles. After Lionel Trilling's death, Diana Trilling installed herself every summer in cottage 6 to write her memoirs; for a 1993 *New Yorker* profile, Richard Avedon photographed her through the plate-glass window to soften the lines of her 88 years.[56]

The Stefanis originally came to The Colony only in the summer. Eleanor settled in Wellfleet year-round in 1976, and has now run The Colony for more than half a century. Her devotion to the property has earned her a reputation as one of the area's most passionate preservationists. "We've just tried to use our common sense and pleasure," she says, "working with the basic original design and trying to be true, loyal to that design, and not offensive in any way."[57]

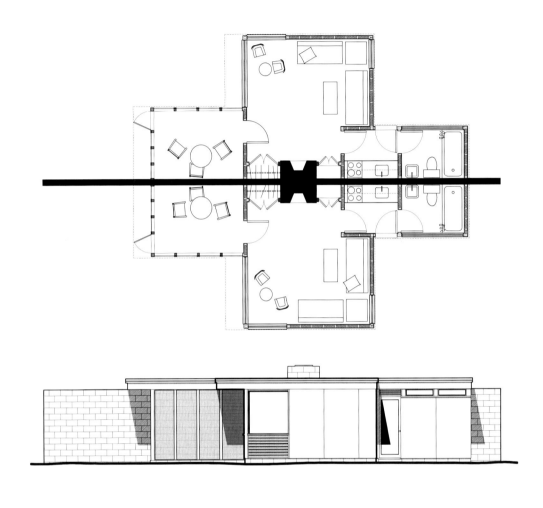

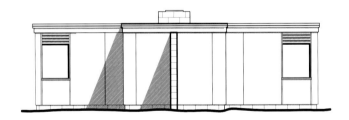

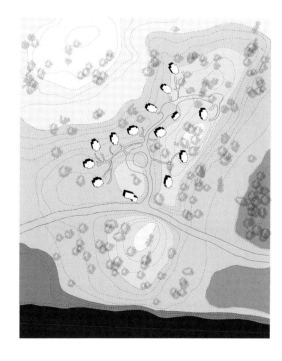

Opposite: Plan and elevations of a duplex cottage.
Above: Rendering of two cottages. *Right*: The site is
just north of Wellfleet Harbor.

The Colony's main building on Chequessett
Neck Road, with sand-cast bas-relief by Xavier
González. The cement relief panels on the left
shield a garden terrace.

A single cottage, left, and The Colony office, right. The projecting masonry planes serve as both privacy walls and surfaces for outdoor artwork such as this copper seahorse sculpture by Tom Brown and a fresco by Henry Varnum Poor at the office entry.

The Colony office

A duplex cottage. Original fixed glass and swing doors, on covered porches, were replaced with sliding doors in the 1960s.

Saltonstall and Morton's Harrod House, in Wellfleet (1950s), recalls the passive-solar house they designed in the Boston suburbs in 1948. Blocked by fixed windows, the breeze blows through a series of horizontal and vertical screened louvers, which double as a subtle colonial motif.

Saltonstall and Morton also designed four modern Wellfleet homes in the 1950s and '60s, all off Griffin Island Road near the bay. The Comfort, Harrod, and Yeston houses are rather sedate compared to other Cape Cod modern structures, in line with Saltonstall's reserve and traditional bent: they have flat roofs and large plate-glass windows with louvered vents below, but they attempt no reexaminations of what form a house could take. Still, Saltonstall's careful choices about materials, plans, and details add up to inventive, intriguingly personal, yet subtle designs, none of them derivative of any modern master; the houses are organized fairly traditionally, and nature is kept at arm's length.

The Comfort House (1951) is distinguished by discreet dentils above the ribbon window on the front facade, and a grasscloth wall covering in the bedroom hall. The Harrod House (1950s), which no longer stands, was a larger coastal version of Saltonstall and Morton's solar house, with fixed windows flanked by large ventilation louvers that resembled colonial shutters. For texture and variety on the facade, Saltonstall turned some of the louvers on their sides, creating full-height vertical slats, and lowered the roof height in the central connecting wing. The plan placed four small bedrooms

and two baths in one wing, a kitchen in the connecting space, and a living room and deck in the other wing, which was set askew from the first.

Saltonstall's debonair regional modernism reached its peak in the Kuhn House (1960), near Cape Cod Bay. Samuel and Minette Kuhn were progressive intellectuals from New York: Samuel was a Harvard- and MIT-trained engineer, Minette an editor who had studied at Vassar with Edna St. Vincent Millay. One of their sons, Thomas, was a physicist and science historian who established the concept of the paradigm shift in his book *The Structure of Scientific Revolutions* (1962). In 1956, the Kuhns hired Edward Larrabee Barnes to design a home for their retirement in Wellfleet, but the following year — apparently after a stay at The Colony — they changed their minds and hired Saltonstall before Barnes had finished his plans. The house was eventually used by Thomas, whose second wife, Jehane Barton Kuhn, had worked for a decade in the office of Charles and Ray Eames.[58]

The approach to the house features a gently winding staircase of three small decks leading to a roofed, deeply recessed entry centered on a simple yellow door with 2-foot-wide sidelights. Inside, the east-west entrance hall opens to the living room at the back of the house, forming an axis that captures the sunrise at one end, the sunset at the other. Light traversing the house streams through bubble skylights into the hall, kitchen, and guest bath. Skylights are framed in raw 2-by-10 timber, which crosses the exposed roof beams to create striking coffers. Birch paneling covers the walls in public spaces, and a full wall of birch cabinets and drawers, sporting Shaker knobs and modern drawer pulls, flanks a sleek slate fireplace in the living room. Wide plank flooring also recalls colonial homes, giving way to terrazzo in the kitchen.

The Kuhn House is organized as a classical 3-by-3 grid, with each bedroom and the kitchen occupying a square, but Saltonstall subverts this symmetry. He nudges the screened-in porch a few feet off the southwest corner of the house while maintaining access to the living room and west bedroom. On the facade, he varies the overhang of the eaves; the depth of recessed doors and windows; and the patterns of windows. Each

The Kuhn House in Wellfleet (1960) stands out for its elegant color scheme: bright-white trim on a dark stain.

element stands out because of Saltonstall's colors: the house is wrapped in diagonal tongue-and-groove siding stained wine-dark, which contrasts sharply with the bright white trim. Saltonstall also varied the direction of the diagonal on each plane to create visual tension between surfaces; where the siding on two adjacent planes or panels meets to form a V shape, the house looks as if it is about to take flight. The nearby garage wears the same finish. Today, the house is abandoned and derelict.

Saltonstall never stopped promoting new art and architecture. A week before he died, in 1968, he was working on an exhibition of young local artists to celebrate the opening of Boston's new City Hall. The *Boston Globe*'s art critic marveled, at an ICA display of

Saltonstall's art collection after his death, that "this lank, lean Yank with dark brown eyes, soft-spoken voice and a basically shy approach to people and situations, started shaking up the Boston art world some 35 years ago . . . [bridging the gap] between the ancestral portraits on family walls . . . and the public art of today. He did a tremendous job." The paper's society writer mused about the same event — with exhibition decor by Design Research — "The ambience was so much the feeling of his marvelous parties that it was impossible not to keep looking for that thin smiling face so familiar for so long to so many people — and there were a lot of them at 33 Beacon St., as the rainy dusk settled over the city."[59]

Now derelict, the house had a relatively formal entryway. Diagonal siding runs up, then down, creating a quiet visual dynamism.

The screened porch breaks away from the house for light and ventilation. A large barn door rolls back, making the porch an extension of the living room.

In the Kuhn House, Saltonstall created a casually sophisticated cottage by mixing rough and refined finishes, such as the raw ceiling beams, birch-paneled walls, and wide-plank floors in the living room. The modern lines are never broken, yet the hall's coffered ceiling and the cabinets' Shaker-style knobs hint at earlier periods.

Shaped by liberal education and international travel, each of the Brahmin Bohemians found his own way to modernism, and then to the practice of architecture. Phillips, Hall, and Walling were close friends and co-carpenters — members of a sort of back-to-the-land generation sandwiched between the Lost Generation of the 1920s and the Beats of the 1950s. All three had grown up with servants, but wanted lives different from their parents'.[60] All managed to avoid combat in World War II and, despite their prestigious degrees, all tried their hands at farming. With 13 wives among them, they had no claims on model domesticity — and yet they kept trying. As mostly self-taught designers, they left to the Outer Cape a series of small, almost threadbare modern forms built with local, often salvaged materials on quiet, sequestered sites. Saltonstall had more formal training and a sleeker, more refined use of materials, but he, too, worked with small footprints, affordable construction, and environmental sensitivity.

Each of these four designers used Cape Cod's building traditions to realize modern ideas in different ways. Yet even as the design-build ethos of the late 1930s looked back to colonial New England, its marriage of art and craft embodied the principles of the Bauhaus, which would soon come to Wellfleet in the person of Marcel Breuer. All four Brahmin Bohemians lived most of their lives in historic or hybrid homes, such as Hall's antique Cape and Saltonstall's brownstones. The same would not be true for the next wave of Cape Cod modernists, who began building on the Outer Cape within a decade of their emigration from Europe.

Notes

1. William Rollins, *Journal of Last Years: 1918–1929* (Topsfield, Mass.: Perkins, 1933), 56, 55.

2. A. Porter S. Sweet, D.D.S., *Dental Radiography and Photography,* 33 (1960); "William H. Rollins Award for Research in OMR," American Academy of Oral and Maxillofacial Radiology, http://www.aaomr.org/?page=RollinsAward; Rollins, 60, 78.

3. Rollins, 14, 89.

4. Charles Edward Banks, *The Winthrop Fleet of 1630: An Account of the Vessels, the Voyage, the Passengers, and Their English Homes from Original Authorities* (Boston: Houghton Mifflin, 1930), 86, 90, 92.

5. Unless otherwise noted, all quotations of Jack Phillips are from an unpublished interview with Michael Macdonald, July 2, 1998; Hayden Herrera telephone interview with Christine Cipriani, June 10, 2013.

6. Herrera interview with Cipriani.

7. O'Connell, 41, 44, 49.

8. Ibid., pp. 55–59; William P. Burke, "Atwood-Higgins House," *Park News,* Cape Cod National Seashore annual newsletter, 2009; O'Connell, 44, 62.

9. O'Connell, 63–64, 72–73.

10. Herrera interview with Cipriani.

11. Herrera interview with Cipriani; Phillips interview with Macdonald; Joan Marks, "The Seacoast of Bohemia," 41.

12. Anton Gill, *Art Lover: A Biography of Peggy Guggenheim* (New York: HarperCollins, 2002), 299; Marks, 41; Berle Clemenson, *Historic Research Study: Cape Cod National Seashore* (Denver: National Park Service, undated), 59–60, http://www.nps.gov/caco/historyculture/upload/Historic_Resource_Study.pdf; Mass Moments, "German U-boat Attacks Cape Cod," Massachusetts Foundation for the Humanities, http://www.massmoments.org/moment.cfm?mid=212.

13. McCarthy, *A Charmed Life*, 48.

14. Schlesinger, *I Remember*, 118–19.

15. Gloria and Peter Watts interview with Christine Cipriani, Wellfleet, Mass., Oct. 8, 2012.

16. Tamas Breuer interview with Peter McMahon, Wellfleet, Mass., Aug. 24, 2012; Marks, 40; Florence Phillips, telephone interview with Christine Cipriani, Apr. 14, 2013.

17. Hayden Herrera, *Arshile Gorky: His Life and Work* (New York: Farrar, Straus and Giroux, 2003), 622; Hayden Herrera, "Arshile and Agnes Gorky: Master and Muse," *Vogue,* Dec. 2009.

18. Suzanne McConnell, "Michael Macdonald" (obituary), *Provincetown Arts,* 2009, 101–2; Phillip Lopate telephone interview with Christine Cipriani, Nov. 16, 2012.

19. J. H. Hall, "Visible Ghosts: Portraits of an American Family" (unpublished, 1992), courtesy of Noa Hall.

20. Ibid.; Noa Hall interview with Christine Cipriani, Wellfleet, Mass., July 25, 2012.

21. Katy Dos Passos to Edmund Wilson, July 23, 1936, quoted in Reuel Wilson, *To the Life of the Silver Harbor,* 46; Virginia Spencer Carr, *Dos Passos: A Life* (Chicago: Northwestern University Press, 2004), 354–55; Jaci Conry, "A Storied History: A Family Parts with a Wellfleet Home That Once Hosted Great Literary Figures," *Boston Globe,* Oct. 9, 2008.

22. Ati Gropius Johansen telephone interview with Christine Cipriani, Aug. 13, 2009; Gloria Watts interview with Cipriani; Edmund Wilson to Mary McCarthy, July 13, 1944, quoted in David Castronovo and Janet Groth, eds., *Edmund Wilson, The Man in Letters* (Athens: Ohio University Press, 2002), 125.

23. Hall interview with Cipriani; Noa Hall telephone interview with Christine Cipriani, Oct. 15, 2012.

24. Hall interview with Cipriani.

25. Ibid.; Gloria Watts interview with Cipriani.

26. Hall interview with Cipriani.

27. Paul Makovsky and Belinda Lanks, "Nelson & Company: Iconic Workplace, 1947–86," *Metropolis,* June 2009, 90.

28. Jack Masey and Conway Lloyd Morgan, *Cold War Confrontations: US Exhibitions and Their Role in the Cold War* (Zurich: Lars Müller, 2008), 162, 179; Oklahoma City Museum of Art, *George Nelson: Architect, Writer, Designer, Teacher*, resource guide for traveling Vitra Design Museum exhibition, http://www.okcmoa.com/wp-content/uploads/George-Nelson-resource-guide.pdf, 2011; Jack Hall, curriculum vita, unpublished, courtesy of Noa Hall.

29. Seth Rolbein, "Driving to Quaker meeting recently with my friend John Hall," *Cape Codder,* Dec. 3, 1999.

30. Gilly Hatch e-mail interview with Christine Cipriani, June 2, 2012.

31. Christine Cipriani, "Bauhaus in the Breeze: Modernist Architecture on Outer Cape Cod," *Modernism*, winter 2009–10, 58.

32. Gilly Hatch e-mail interview with Christine Cipriani, Oct. 18, 2012.

33. Ibid.; Michael Gotkin, *Artists' Handmade Houses* (New York: Abrams, 2011), 206.

34. Eleanor Stefani interview with Christine Cipriani, July 22, 2009, Wellfleet, Mass.; Peter and Gloria Watts interview with Cipriani.

35. Peter Watts interview with Cipriani.

36. John Hamilton Gilmour, "Girl Socialist of San Francisco," *San Francisco Examiner,* Oct. 3, 1897, quoted in James Boylan, *Revolutionary Lives: Anny Strunsky and William English Walling* (Amherst: University of Massachusetts Press, 1998), 5; Rose Wilder Lane, "Life and Jack London," *Sunset,* Nov. 1917, 27–30, quoted in Boylan, 5.

37. Boylan, 95, 107.

38. Ibid., 171–72.

39. Alice Annand McMahon interview with Peter McMahon, Newton, Mass., Dec. 2012.

40. Peter Matson interview with Peter McMahon, May 15, 2012.

41. Christopher Walling e-mail interviews with Peter McMahon and Christine Cipriani, Jan. 12, 2013, and Nov. 6, 2012.

42. Christopher Walling e-mail interview with Peter McMahon, Aug. 10, 2012; David Perlman, "Americans Cement Paris Ties When Houseboat Springs Leak," *New York Herald Tribune,* June 21, 1947.

43. "Odette Walling, Truro" (obituary), *Provincetown Banner,* Jan. 22, 2010.

44. Edgar Driscoll, Jr., "A Memorial to 'Nat'," *Daily Boston Globe,* Nov. 16, 1969.

45. Oral history interview with Elizabeth Saltonstall, Nov. 18, 1981, Archives of American Art, Smithsonian Institution; Sebastian Smee, "A Beacon Among Its Contemporaries," *Boston Globe,* Sept. 11, 2011; "Modern Arts Ball Is Best Party of Year," *Daily Boston Globe,* Apr. 19, 1936; "The Institute of Contemporary Art," Metropolitan Boston Arts Center program, first season, 1959, 25–28; Harold Shapero and Sid Ramin interview with Ryan Raul Bañagale, Emily Abrams, and Corinna Campbell at Harvard University, Feb. 21, 2006, unpublished transcript, 7–8; Nathaniel Saltonstall, "The Boston Museum of Modern Art," *The Bulletin of the Museum of Modern Art* 5:3 (Mar. 1938), 3–4.

46. *ICA75: 1936–2011* (Boston: Institute of Contemporary Art, 2011); "Four Noted Architects to Lecture Here on Small House Designing," *Boston Daily Globe,* Jan. 23, 1947.

47. Keith Orr, "Napoleon's Closes," *Boston Phoenix*, July 1998, http://www.bostonphoenix.com/archive/1in10/98/07/CLUBLAND.html; John Robinson, "Napoleon Club: Still Fabulous after 41 Years," *Boston Globe,* Oct. 12, 1993.

48. *American Architects Directory*, 2nd ed. (New York: R.R. Bowker, 1962), 609–10; Kim Markert, "Nathaniel Saltonstall and America's First Solar Movement," Second Forbes Lecture, Back Bay Historical, Boston, Mass., May 6, 2009.

49. Major Nathaniel Saltonstall, "Why Crafts in the Army," *Craft Horizons*, Nov. 1945, 8–9; Preservation Revolving Fund Casebook, "Christian Herter Center," Historic Boston, 1999, http://www.historicboston.org/casebook/99cb/christianherter.htm.

50. "Harnessing the Sun," *Boston Sunday Globe*, Feb. 9, 1947; Jedd S. Reisner, "You Can So Have a Solar House in a Cold Climate," *House Beautiful,* June 1948, 84–91.

51. Jessica Lustig, "The Wellfleet Ten," *New York Times T Magazine,* May 13, 2011.

52. Sarah Korjeff, "The Colony," Inventory of Historic Assets, Massachusetts Historic Commission, July 2002.

53. Andrew C. Hyde, foreword, *A Memorial Exhibition: Selections from the Nathaniel Saltonstall Collection* (Boston: Institute of Contemporary Art, 1969), unpag.

54. Carol Baldwin, "Art Critic's View of Wellfleet Art Gallery," and "Era Ends As Wellfleet Art Gallery Closes," *Nauset Weekly Calendar,* undated.

55. Stefani interview with Cipriani.

56. Lustig; "Avedon," *Newsweek*, Sept. 12, 1993.

57. Eleanor Stefani interviews with Christine Cipriani, July 22, 2009, and spring 2013.

58. Jenny Fields Scofield and Virginia H. Adams, National Register of Historic Places Nomination Form for Kuhn House, unpublished, courtesy National Park Service, U.S. Department of the Interior; abstract for J. Kuhn, "A Consistent Man," *Constructivist Foundations,* vol. 6, no. 2 (2011), p. 138, http://philpapers.org/rec/KUHACM.

59. Edgar Driscoll, Jr., "A Memorial to 'Nat'," *Boston Globe,* Nov. 16, 1969; Marjorie Sherman, "Nat Would Have Felt At Home . . . ," *Boston Globe,* Nov. 12, 1969.

60. Helen Miranda Wilson interview with Peter McMahon, Aug. 8, 2012.

3

COMMUNITY AND PRIVACY
THE EUROPEANS

The modern architect is no vandal but the lover of all that is best in all periods, who is anxious ... to preserve beauty and recapture for us today and for the future some of the preindustrial orderliness and quality which we are rapidly losing.

— SERGE CHERMAYEFF, "REBUILDING ENGLAND"

One woke early to see the gorgeous, uncluttered rise of the sun and then slide down the dunes and take a first dip in the sea, the beach empty as far as the eye could see. Housekeeping was nil, merely a swish of the broom to sweep the sand out the door.

— MARIAN CANNON SCHLESINGER, *I REMEMBER*

Like many of the American arts and sciences, Cape Cod modernism owes its postwar richness to talented Europeans fleeing one or more perils of the 1930s, from Nazi oppression to economic insecurity. Once here, émigré architects fanned out to positions at East Coast and Midwestern universities and design firms, and came to Cape Cod in the 1940s in a swiftly issued chain of invitations. Serge Chermayeff was coaxed out to Wellfleet by a friend who had rented Jack Phillips's Paper Palace; Chermayeff urged Marcel Breuer to see the Outer Cape for himself; and Breuer lured Walter Gropius and Paul Weidlinger. Olav Hammarström came with a fellow Finn who had visited the Cape with the Saarinen family. When Chermayeff bought land from Phillips, the European and Brahmin Bohemian contingents were joined as a community, albeit a loose one. All of them, with the possible exception of Nat Saltonstall, lived or summered on the Cape for the rest of their lives.

What the Europeans found — and what appealed to some of them as foreign to their experience — was a frontier. The Brahmin Bohemians had only just established their toehold; there were still no tourists, no restaurants, no nightlife. Eleanor Stefani compared the designers' outpost to that of the first Pilgrims because, socially and architecturally, "they were able to do pretty much what they wished at that time. There weren't any zoning laws, and life had a great deal more freedom." Since they had not only the woods but also the beaches to themselves, their parties, picnics, and love lives were "a three-ring circus," said Ati Gropius Johansen:

The only people on the beach at Newcomb were the people who lived in the woods — there was no "public." So every Saturday night, different families like the Chermayeffs would have a big bonfire, and ... there was singing and roasting and several fires going on down the beach, and it was very, very nice .... Jack Hall would be there with children from one marriage or another, and with one wife or another.... That's where, I think, all the great love affairs sprang from ... people went off on starlit nights.

It was juicy living ... rampant love, is all I can tell you.

Many in the community expressed their sensuality by swimming, sunbathing, and walking the Atlantic shore in the nude. And why not? "There was nobody around!" exclaimed one architect's relative. "You could walk all the way to Provincetown and not see anybody in those days." Hayden Herrera, Phillips's daughter, said that in her childhood circle, "it was almost considered

Serge Chermayeff and Marcel Breuer at Breuer's house on Williams Pond, ca. 1975, more than 30 years after Chermayeff convinced Breuer to visit the Cape and buy property near his own.

reactionary if you wore a bathing suit. We were all naked until puberty." Breuer's brother-in-law, the painter Robert Jay Wolff, split the difference: he liked to walk into a pond waist-deep, stick a branch into the mud, take off his suit, and hang it on the branch for safekeeping. More than one of the children of these trailblazers has since decried their exposure to the bodies of adults they knew and loved; indeed, the quality of parenting among the architects was uneven. "The children in this particular backwoods world were completely left on their own," said Herrera. Many grew up to be extremely high achievers, usually in the arts; theirs was a cultured neglect.[1]

By the mid-1950s, however, postwar tourism had changed the face of Wellfleet. The beaches still drew an intellectual set, but now the artists and architects were joined by psychiatrists, scientists, political writers (Irving Howe), academics (Richard Hofstadter), civil servants (Arthur Schlesinger, Jr.), and a new generation of novelists (Saul Bellow, Philip Roth). Edmund Wilson was still there in his Panama hat, but now he complained about the crowds, famously calling the new scene "the fucking Riviera." The technocrats, he wrote in 1962, make "a striking contrast with the old Jig Cook Provincetown. . . . They were all writers and painters who were working and freely exchanging ideas; but these people are mostly attached to the government or some university. . . . They are accountable to some

institution." Literary critic Alfred Kazin, who vacationed in Wellfleet from around 1950, straddled the bohemian and professional eras, and hinted at the shifting vibe:

> Our happiest times were here, at the edge of the land, the ocean, the dunes. The beach was a great body, and on this beach we were bodies again. Beyond "Joan's beach," where a wartime army hut had been moved [by Phillips] as a summer cottage for a lady from New York and her painter boyfriend, still stretched the outermost Cape, forever beating in your ears from the ocean, the emptiness of that long wild ocean beach where you could still contentedly walk, make love, and skinny-dip.
>
> . . . The great beach was replaced every afternoon by the great society. Each year Joan's weathered old beach hut sank more abjectly into the sand while around it rose the mercilessly stylized avant-garde house [Phillips' dune studio, now expanded] of a wealthy Leninist from Philadelphia.[2]

Some of the architects mixed with the writers at casual dinners and softball games, but they were, on the whole, a more secluded bunch. They, along with their Provincetown forebears in theater and painting, had set the tone for an otherworldly idyll, and they quietly kept on building as the world moved in.

SERGE CHERMAYEFF

It seems apt that Chermayeff's neighbor Marian Schlesinger described the splash of his morning swim in Slough Pond as "almost noiseless": Chermayeff the architect was obsessed with noiselessness, centering much of his design philosophy and his best-known book on privacy within and around dwellings. His summer home, which began life as a rental cabin built by Phillips, was the ultimate refuge from a world of increasing noise, technology, and mobility. But Chermayeff himself was a walking volcano, often demanding peace for himself while shattering it for others. A 6-foot-2-inch intellectual omnivore, whose career spanned ballroom dance and Harvard and Yale professorships, he brought conceptual rigor and a deeply cosmopolitan flair to the woods of the Back Shore.

Sergei Ivanovitch Issakovitch was born in 1900 to a Sephardic Jewish family near Grozny, Russia, in what is now the republic of Chechnya. His grandfather was a gentleman livestock farmer who helped inspire a character in Aleksandr Solzhenitsyn's novel *August 1914*. In 1893, a British engineer struck oil in the area, and the Issakovitches and their neighbors found themselves rich. Serge's father, a banker, and mother took an apartment in Moscow and entrusted the children to German, French, and English governesses. Serge left Russia for an English boarding school at age 10, but his rural childhood was "undoubtedly influential," wrote his biographer, Alan Powers, in shaping his ideal of an architecture that preserved and interacted with the natural environment. "Among a generation which carried forward the experience of the more spacious and hopeful world before the Great War," Powers wrote, "he had seen places where modern life had hardly begun to have an impact."[3]

In London, Serge attended Peterborough Lodge and the prestigious Harrow School. Encouraged in his talents for painting and drawing, he won prizes from Harrow and the Royal Drawing Society and sold some of his work. His paintings, he said, were a mix of "imaginary submarine scenes, great lobsters and wonderful things floating around," while his drawings centered on "rude pictures . . . of naked girls wearing silk stockings or very rude caricatures of people that everybody hated." He was accepted at Trinity College, Cambridge, but was forced to decline when his family suddenly lost its oil fields and savings in the Bolshevik Revolution. His formal education aborted in 1918, he was briefly an illustrator before turning to professional ballroom dance.[4]

From 1919 to 1921, as American jazz penetrated London, Serge worked as a competition dancer — "What," he asked, "is a young man with expensive taste to do after dinner, so to speak?" — and as a teacher of the waltz, foxtrot, and tango. After a few subsequent years of work and study abroad, including a stint at an Argentine ranch and some desultory design studies in Europe, he returned to London in 1924 and changed his name. At the suggestion of relatives concerned about anti-Semitism, Serge took the surname of Tapa Chermoev — his "milk-uncle," with whom his father had shared a wet nurse — upon the older man's death; he tweaked the spelling to avoid liability for Tapa's debts. Through a Harrow School friend he got a job at an interior-design firm, where he worked on hotel decor and stage sets. In 1928, he married Barbara May, an Englishwoman whose father was a director at an upmarket building firm; and thanks to his father-in-law's connections, Chermayeff soon found himself director of the new Modern Art Studio and Department at the interior-design firm Waring and Gillow, which styled posh homes, hotels, and ocean liners.[5]

To engage a wary but curious public, Waring and Gillow promoted its new department by mounting a blockbuster modern-design show of 68 rooms. With 12 assistants, Chermayeff was now designing and producing furnishings — rugs, fabrics, and furniture, including some of Britain's first tubular-steel pieces — and curating every piece of each room down to the tableware. His emphasis on color, especially pale yellow and pale blue, took flight there and would reappear in his buildings and paintings throughout his life. Compelled by the show to ponder larger questions of functionality, comfort, and national taste, Chermayeff found his métier as both designer and thinker. Within two years, he had a citywide reputation, and in 1930 he left to start his own practice as an "interior architect." He began to give lectures, publish in design magazines, and appear in the popular press.[6]

Jealous, thanks to his travels, of the robustness of modern design on the Continent, Chermayeff found promoting modernism in Britain a thankless process. History-loving England must be careful, he wrote in 1930, not to fall into a "retrospective stupor." He forged ahead, renovating and reconfiguring older homes and offices, and the interior of London's new Cambridge Theatre (still largely intact). His renovation of his own rented house on Abbey Road — where he ripped out moldings, made generous use of wood veneer in gentle geometrics, and lured dubious guests into cantilevered Mies van der Rohe dining chairs — was widely published.[7] Chermayeff was adamant that such work be thoughtful. Railing, with what became his signature acidity, against slapdash updates of historic designs in the 1920s, he told the BBC in 1932:

> So-called modern things began to be created by conceited and under-taught amateurs and were collected by their idiotic friends. Chairs designed for wood construction were made in metal.... The first wood chair made as a support for the human body developed by gradual processes to a very comfortable and beautiful thing within the limits of materials and construction and reached its most finished form in the eighteenth century. To take such a finished product and begin to eliminate, for example, some carving or inlay, is merely walking backwards on the road of its evolution. It cannot produce a better article and robs the original of whatever merit it possesses . . .
>
> By buying intelligently we can all help in the fight against snobbery, sentiment and stupidity, and range ourselves on the side of simplicity, directness and usefulness.[8]

In 1932, the BBC invited Chermayeff to work with Wells Coates and Raymond McGrath on the interiors for its new Broadcasting House (1932), where Chermayeff's rooms laid the cool sheen of tubular-steel furniture over the warmth of sunset-colored textiles. In response, artist Paul Nash wrote that "Serge Chermayeff working

in partnership with Raymond McGrath, has probably done more to bring about a change of taste than any other designer in England to-day." Chermayeff was then hired to design his first residence, the Shann House, in Rugby (1934) — one of the first modern designs in the English Midlands. A 20-by-30-foot rectangle of white concrete with a rounded, concrete-rimmed terrace off one corner, the house featured built-in furniture and cabinetry made by expert joiners.[9]

In the mid-1930s, the rise of Nazism drove many ambitious German designers to London. Chermayeff got to know Bauhaus refugees Gropius, Breuer, and László Moholy-Nagy — unaware that they would all be in the United States within a decade — and, in 1934, he used Breuer's cane-seated B64 armchair in a showroom design, possibly its first appearance in England. Another German architect, the eminent Erich Mendelsohn, invited Chermayeff to go into business with him, and although their collaboration was brief, it produced one of Britain's most celebrated early modern buildings. Chermayeff called his work with the older architect an "invaluable" experience. He did not yet draw, however, entrusting others to set his schemes to paper. Said one assistant, "Serge had NO drawing board — and I never saw him sketch — he just came round each day — making notes or scribbles on others' drawings — but he was THE BOSS and we worshipped him."[10] Within months, Mendelsohn and Chermayeff had entered a competition for a public waterfront pavilion, a social and cultural center at Bexhill-on-Sea, East Sussex.

Bearing the clear signatures of both of its authors, the De La Warr Pavilion (1935) is Chermayeff's most monumental work. Commissioned by the competition to transcend what the *Architects' Journal* called the "monstrous blight of gloomy ornament" in Victorian resort towns like Bexhill, the pavilion spreads out on the English Channel in two long, three-story concrete rectangles, their junction marked by a spectacular half-cylindrical stairwell. Lined with glass walls, colonnaded balconies, and gleaming nautical rails, the bullnose and eastern half of the building face the water like a buoyant ocean liner. Chermayeff's interiors featured rich, bold colors, materials, and gestures; the ceiling in his theater echoed the seats below with rows of small recessed domes. The pavilion was popular with visitors and critics, one of whom praised its airy chambers and "exquisite finish," and Mendelsohn was thrilled: "The situation is first-class: seen from the sea, the building looks like a horizontal skyscraper which starts its development from the auditorium. Seen from the street, it is a festive invitation. The interior is truly music." George Bernard Shaw, chiming in via the *Evening Standard*, was "delighted to hear that Bexhill has emerged from barbarism." Chermayeff and Mendelsohn parted soon after the opening, and over the next several decades the De La Warr Pavilion deteriorated. After restoration, it reopened in 2005 as a center for contemporary art.[11]

As early as 1933, Chermayeff started arguing publicly that design should serve the public good. The ideals of an architect, an urban planner, and a socialist came together in his proposals for healthy, comfortable, affordable modern living at the community level. Invited to speak to the Royal Institute of British Architects (RIBA) on new methods and materials, he proclaimed that these things only mattered if they had "direct social significance," because architects should now be focused on "the practical and economic problems of housing, industry and transport; the problems of regional and town planning, slum clearance and the erection of new buildings in a manner and with materials which will not saddle the obsoleteness of a bygone age on ourselves or on those who will come after." For Chermayeff, as for other modernists, the "obsoleteness of a bygone age" did not mean historic architecture; it meant the continued production of historical styles and modes of living not suited for the present day. In 1935, he won an honorable mention in a private-sector competition for a complex of "working men's flats."[12] Though mostly unrealized, Chermayeff's many designs for communal living centered on comfort, respect for the surrounding environment, and, above all, privacy for people of every background.

By all accounts, not least his own, young Chermayeff was devastatingly debonair. "I was a dandy," he admitted of his dancing days. "The Savile Row tailors used to give me suits, tail coats, and evening stuff simply because I was such a classy dancer. I won

Overlooking the English Channel from Bexhill-on-Sea, East Sussex, the De La Warr Pavilion (1935), designed with Erich Mendelsohn, was Chermayeff's most monumental work. Henry-Russell Hitchcock, curator of a 1937 exhibition on English modernism at the Museum of Modern Art, called it "about the most conspicuous and successful modern building in England . . . amazingly finished in execution and full of minor elegances of detail."[14]

enough international competitions so that I was quite in demand as a showman." He was also, said Powers, in demand after hours, and "in the liberated climate of post-Armistice London, girls would often invite him home." Later, when Chermayeff was advancing as an architect, Peter Blake observed that he "kept the figure of a tall and (one assumed) irresistible gigolo. His English — enunciated with the perfection and precision of which only aristocratic Russians were capable — was Harrovian. . . . His suits were clearly made in Savile Row, and his manner was imperial (and imperious)." Although Chermayeff would soon prove an incomparable teacher of design, Blake said, he seemed at first "an improbable fraud."[13]

By the mid-1930s, Chermayeff was prosperous enough to buy 84 acres in Halland, Sussex, where he built his family a house that many consider his greatest work. In many ways, Bentley Wood (1938) anticipates the houses he would build on Cape Cod a decade later, and the arguments he would begin to make about privacy. Striking out into wood construction, Chermayeff commissioned a prefab eucalyptus frame on a

Bentley Wood (1938), Chermayeff's home in the English countryside, established him as a master at blending the rural and the urbane. He was already thinking about privacy here; one of his floor plans maps zones of noise, neutrality, privacy, and, for his study (bottom left), "silence."[17]

The view from the upstairs deck shows how Chermayeff used a network of solid walls and open grids to control the boundaries between public and private spaces.

rectangular 3-by-6 grid of 11-foot-square modules. He exposed the structure in bold columns on the garden side, painted them white for emphasis, and clad the other three sides of the building in natural cedar clapboards. On the garden facade, Chermayeff created two stories of glass walls. On the ground floor, behind the columns, full-height sliding glass doors open the living room, dining room, and study to the garden; the terrace pavers run under the glass, giving way to hardwood a few feet inside.[15] Upstairs, large casement bedroom windows and glazed doors line a full-length balcony with wood decking. Above the balcony, the ceiling joists float out to the flying girder, creating a full-length pergola. All of this indoor-outdoor flow would soon be widespread in California, but it was pretty well foreign in the English countryside. Within a decade, Chermayeff would rework elements of Bentley Wood in Wellfleet: the simple, expandable grid plan of structural bays, the polished forms and furnishings in a country setting, and the use of outdoor art — in this case, Henry Moore's *Recumbent Figure* (1938) — to blur the boundaries between nature and civilization, public and private. Made for Chermayeff of local stone, *Recumbent Figure* is now in the Tate Britain collection.

Complemented by the pared-down landscape design of Christopher Tunnard, who would soon move

to the United States to teach at Harvard with Gropius, Bentley Wood was widely praised and published. One critic called it "a regular Rolls-Royce of a house," while another marveled that it is "packed with ideas and works out so many experiments that I venture to think that it will continue for some time to be a source of stimulus." Frank Lloyd Wright, visiting Great Britain in 1939 for a famously contentious series of lectures at the RIBA, was driven to Bentley Wood by a group of architecture students. Wright carped that the bedroom ceilings were 7 inches too high — Chermayeff agreed — but was generally content with the place, and took tea on the terrace.[16]

The Chermayeffs lived at Bentley Wood for barely a year. In 1939, with his coffers empty and new projects choked by the prospect of war, Chermayeff declared bankruptcy and sold the house. Foiled in their quest for U.S. visas, the Chermayeffs sailed to Canada in January 1940. By March, they had documents, and off they went to Lincoln, Massachusetts, where they stayed with the Gropius family. Within weeks, the publisher of *Architectural Forum* threw the Chermayeffs a party on the roof of Rockefeller Center, and Chermayeff began lecturing about modern architecture on national TV and at universities including Harvard, Yale, and Michigan. With no money for lodgings, he and Barbara bought a station

Chermayeff bought this cabin from Jack Phillips in 1944. As resources allowed, he gradually added clapboard, colors, windows, and rooms until the building was unrecognizable. One of his first additions was this sprawling, sturdy deck made of 2-by-4's.

wagon and drove cross-country, touring Native American communities and New Deal building projects and visiting Wright at Taliesin West. In San Francisco, Chermayeff found fellowship in the idealistic Telesis design group, codesigned two houses, and began to turn his attention to architectural education. "I have lost all desire to build," he wrote to friends in 1940, "to practise here in making more houses for the well-to-do or to repeat anything approaching a successful career or Bentley for oneself. It is quite a relief to have got all that out of one's system."[18] In 1942, he was named chair of the Brooklyn College art department and began a new life on the East Coast. In preparation, he spent the summer at Chicago's Institute of Design (formerly the New Bauhaus), taking the rigorous foundation course with Bauhaus visionary Moholy-Nagy.

Around that time, in the early 1940s, Peter Harnden, a self-taught architect friend of Phillips, rented Phillips's Paper Palace, caught the Cape Cod bug, and coaxed Chermayeff to visit. Within a summer or two, Chermayeff and his family had rented a cabin built by Phillips on a steep Slough Pond bank on the Wellfleet-Truro border, accessible only by a rough dirt road. A far cry from plush Bentley Wood, this house had a hand pump, an outhouse, and a kerosene stove, but it also had a royal view of the sunset. The Chermayeffs bought the place in 1944, and, despite the lack of amenities, it immediately became an informal architects' hostel, hosting Walter and Ise Gropius and, on occasion, Eero and Lily Saarinen. At one point, Eero, consumed by geological curiosity, decided to map the floor of Slough Pond and set off in a rowboat with

Serge, Barbara, Ivan, and Peter Chermayeff at their new home on Slough Pond, ca. 1944. The curtain is a makeshift privacy screen to shield the house from the road. The Chermayeffs' sons have achieved their own renown in the design world, Ivan as a graphic designer and Peter as an architect.

Living and dining areas

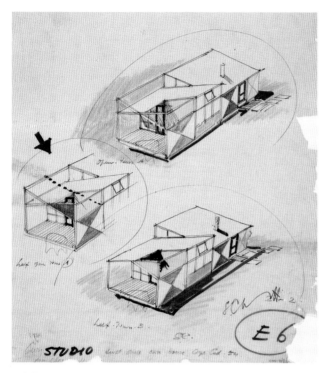

In ink and crayon, Chermayeff looks at various ways to resolve the end of his studio porch: an open truss, half-open, or a half-truss. In this early version, the studio faced in both directions.

Chermayeff and/or his sons, Ivan and Peter, taking soundings with a knotted rope weighted by a rock. (On another outing, Saarinen tried his hand at fishing and was pulled overboard by a giant snapping turtle.)

Over the next few decades, Chermayeff's Cape property became a laboratory for design experiments. Phillips's original house was a small, gable-roofed cabin with an exterior brick chimney and Homasote siding. Chermayeff, whose taste outran his salary for some years, made changes incrementally. The tiny living room is centered on the fireplace, but a cathedral ceiling makes it feel spacious, and Chermayeff gradually punched windows through the walls until the room felt distinctly modern. From here, a ship's ladder — handmade by Chermayeff and Breuer — leads to a loft bedroom, which Chermayeff expanded by creating a large dormer with its own gable roof and wall of glass overlooking the pond. The kitchen had a pass-through to the dining room, where, overlooking the water through a wall of windows, the family gathered on Thonet bentwood cane-backed chairs they had shipped from Bentley

Wood.[19] In 1950, extending the roofline north along the shore, Chermayeff added two bedrooms, at once darkened by interior walls of stained clapboard siding and brightened by full-height water views. In 1952, he built a freestanding, shed-roofed studio off to the side of the house, and, in 1957, for guest space, he created a mirror image of the studio about 8 feet away, connected by a shared entry deck. Finally, in 1971, Chermayeff added to the main house, down a small flight of stairs, a 28-foot-square, shed-roofed, skylit studio–living room, with paintings and built-in bookshelves reaching up toward the ceiling. At the very end of the house, where he once kept a freestanding summer workshop, he added a small apartment for Barbara's mother.

On Cape Cod, what any visitor to a Chermayeff house sees first is flashes of bright color. In a landscape where most buildings are clad in weathered cedar or classic white, Chermayeff's chromatics are statements. The architect never stopped painting, from his school years to his senescence, but only on Cape Cod did he build painterly houses, using color to celebrate, rather than imitate, the coastal surroundings. He had already established guidelines in a 1935 booklet on the use of color in modern buildings: eye-catching brights outside, then calming colors inside, where people spend most of their time. "First, the private, the domestic," he wrote, "requiring discretion, a background for personal preferences of colour, restfulness. Colours seen during prolonged periods of contemplation. Secondly, the public, the effective, stimulating, gay, startling, propagandist, permissible exaggerations for transitory contemplation." He saw bright colors as organic, not artificial; he warned only against deviating from "natural colours — of earth and of the primaries."[20] Photographer Norman McGrath, a family friend, found Chermayeff's cheerful compound fully at home in its landscape, indeed sometimes using nature as architecture.

It was such an unexpected experience to find a design like that in a place like Cape Cod . . . and yet it seemed very natural. It didn't seem out of place at all, and that was really one of the great charms of the thing. And, of course, the aspect of it that

Top: Serge Chermayeff, Chermayeff Studio, Wellfleet (1952), north facade as originally built, with four bays and semi-open porch. *Bottom*: A room in the guest studio, added in 1957

Chermayeff's modular concept was designed to allow growth by extrusion or mirroring. *Top*: Studio, south facade, after the porch was enclosed and another bay added (far left) to house a kitchen. *Bottom*: North side, showing expanded studio and guest cottage connected by entry deck

Serge was very proud of was the fact that he incorporated in that house parts of the garden. . . . He would even hang his paintings on the [exterior] walls of the house. There was one outdoor room, as he described it, where you would sit and . . . he had sculpture and things like that. It was really a room with the skies for a ceiling.[21]

Chermayeff's lightweight, panelized studio (1952), his first new construction on the Cape, became the prototype for most of his Cape Cod designs. Inspired by Phillips's use of Homasote on his cabin, Chermayeff used Homasote panels on the exterior and interior walls of the studio. He braced the exterior panels

diagonally, painted them in primary colors, and held them erect with overhead X braces that were exposed on the porch, creating exuberant geometric effects. With their bold white battens, the Homasote panels stretch out like painted canvases on a rack, blurring the distinction between a building and a painting. Over the next few years, Chermayeff built several iterations within a mile or so of his studio, and one commercial variation for the *Cape Codder* newspaper printing plant in Orleans. Two followed an original rectangular plan, at different lengths (the Wilkinson House and the *Cape Codder* plant), and two had additional wings, in an L- or T-shaped plan with a partial butterfly roof (the Sigerson and Flato houses).

Chermayeff clearly did not intend these wooded retreats to blend into the landscape. At first glance, they look like playing cards leaned up against one another, an assemblage of colorful planes with no depth; the effect is heightened when looking at the taller facade, where the shed pitch makes the roof disappear. And yet, because the bays are vertical rectangles rather than squares, the eye moves up and down rather than across the structure. Thus divided, said *House & Home* magazine in 1954, the studio and its counterparts "never seem to add up to a hunk of man-made stuff . . . plonked down rudely among the trees."[22]

Top: The Sigerson House (1953) looks down on Williams Pond from two glazed bays and a porch. (In this archival photograph, the yellow has shifted to orange.) *Above:* Chermayeff hated the visual effects of window screens, but, unlike the Wilkinson House, which is on a high site swept by ocean winds, the Sigerson House is in a wooded setting and needed protection from mosquitos. The two porches feel very different from one another.

The basic scheme is a standard 8-foot gridded platform, raised slightly off the ground, 16 feet wide, with 2-by-8 posts and a shallow, overhead X brace of doubled 2-by-10 beams. Chermayeff could make the shed roof face either direction, or alternate between the two directions on the same building, by excluding an upper leg of the X. By laying a roof or pergola on one of the porch trusses, then cocking the shed roof of the main house in the opposite direction, Chermayeff created a dynamic composition of complementary scissoring roof planes. Indoors, for additional bracing, cross walls are skinned with exposed tongue-and-groove planks on the diagonal; the same planks form the roof sheathing, which has additional flat diagonal bracing in each bay. Aside from creating a bold graphic effect, the continual use of X bracing makes for a very stiff enclosure using minimal materials.

This prototype delivers on the modernist ideal of modular flexibility. The interior is open, like a factory loft, free to be divided as needed. If the owners wanted more space, they could enclose the porch or add a new bay. Chermayeff's studio was originally four bays long, but, over the years, he enclosed the porch to make a bathroom and added a bay at each end to form a kitchen and bedroom, for a total of seven bays with no change to the basic modular system.

Chermayeff Studio, kitchen exterior (opposite) and interior. As the buildings based on this studio prototype were expanded and altered, the window panels were in some instances shifted to neighboring bays and replaced with solid panels.

Chermayeff's 28-foot-square studio–living room, built in 1971 for his retirement, was filled with books, artwork, textiles, and treasured objects from his travels, all bathed in natural light from above. The ceiling rises from 12 to 15 feet.

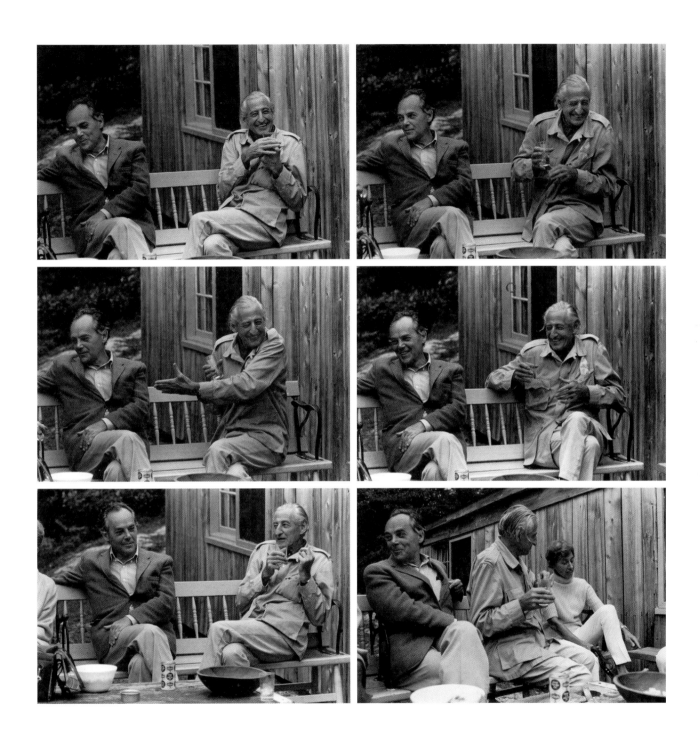

Famous for his ability to amuse and incite, Chermayeff tells a story in the company of friends György Kepes and Charlotte Borsody at the Petersen/Schlesinger House on Slough Pond in the early 1970s.

Chermayeff, in shirtsleeves and bare feet, enjoys a drink with Barbara (behind him), client Carolyn Wilkinson (center, in white), and Carolyn's sister- and brother-in-law, Helen and Charles Wilkinson, in the 1950s. Chermayeff called this social space an "outdoor room."

The Chermayeff deck today, overlooking Slough Pond

WILKINSON HOUSE (1954)

Chermayeff's Wilkinson House was built for a builder: Carolyn "Caps" Wilkinson, one of the first female contractors in the country, and her husband, Kirk. When Carolyn's father died relatively young, she joined her brother in taking over the family's homebuilding business. In the late 1930s, she went to work for *Woman's Day* magazine and helped pioneer the how-to article, illustrated with step-by-step photos. With her rare mix of editorial and carpentry skills, she became a mainstay of the *Woman's Day* Workshop, a program that took on real-life building jobs to use as feature material.

"My mother was in a sense the original Martha Stewart," said Stephan Wilkinson, Carolyn's oldest son,

Carolyn Wilkinson and Chermayeff discuss plans for the Wilkinsons' summer house in Wellfleet.

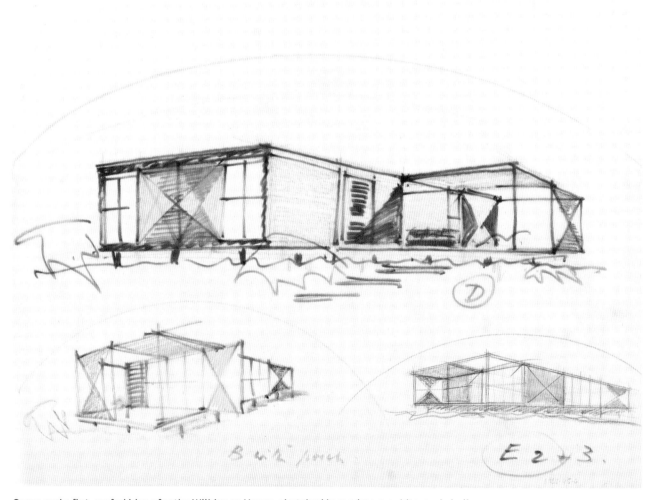

Some early, flat-roofed ideas for the Wilkinson House, sketched in marker, graphite, and chalk

Chermayeff's bowtie truss creates a frame for the Wilkinsons' ocean view.

who appeared as a young model in do-it-yourself demonstration photos. "She was a very hands-on sort of person." For the magazine, Carolyn dreamed up projects such as planting a spice garden in the "slices" of an old wagon wheel, and building an affordable postwar house starting with only a roof on a basement, to be expanded upward as a G.I.'s income allowed. After her first marriage ended, she married *Woman's Day* art director Kirk Wilkinson in 1946, and their

blended family eventually comprised four sons. In the early 1950s, they bought a high site east of Wellfleet's Gull Pond, overlooking the Atlantic, and hired Chermayeff to design a summer home based on his studio prototype.

The family pitched in with construction, driving up from their home in Westchester, New York, on off-season weekends. "My father was a very competent builder himself, an extreme handyman type," said

The bowtie trusses supported various kinds of enclosure. Chermayeff experimented with roofing on the Wilkinsons' deck, designing a thin-slat pergola that covers the space with delicate shadows.

The structural elements in Chermayeff's prototypes play visible roles. The X and Y roof trusses allow for a clear span with no bearing walls and a flexible layout; the windows and colorful infill panels hold up only themselves; and the shear walls (top photo, at rear of space), with diagonal 2-by-6 skins, help provide wind bracing and stiffen the structure. Though very lightly built, these buildings have survived hurricanes without a failure.

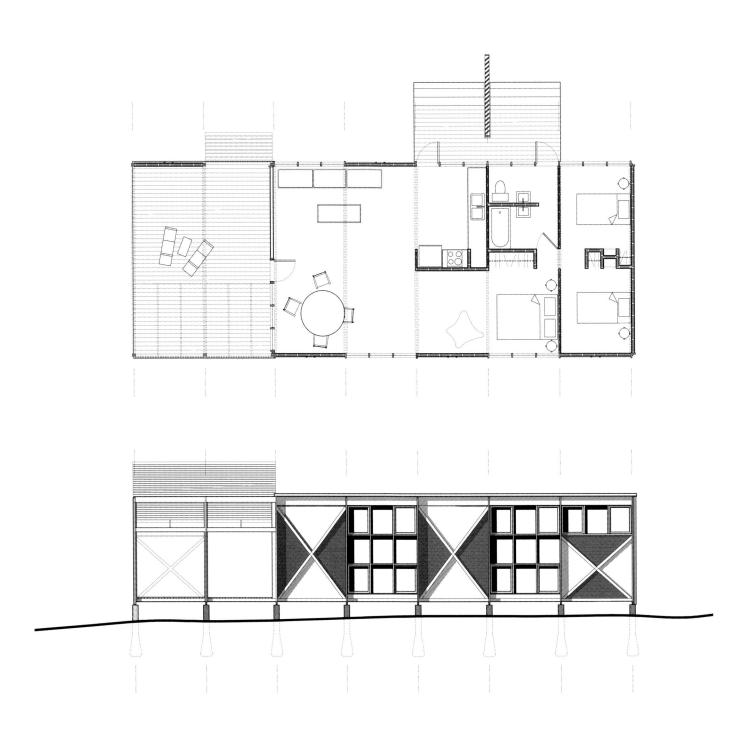

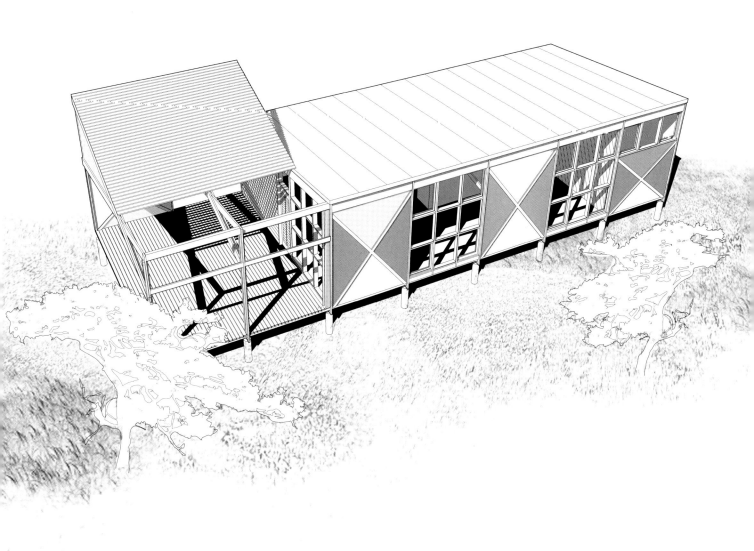

Opposite: Plan and north elevation. *Above*: View from the north. *Right*: Gull Pond is to the west, the Atlantic to the east.

Stephan. "He was very inventive and very skilled with tools. So between the two of them, they were about as involved a couple as you can imagine for someone like Chermayeff, for better or worse, to get involved with."

Chermayeff's studio prototype reached its apogee in the Wilkinson House. In this railroad assemblage of seven 8-foot bays, five were enclosed as living space and the last two left open as a porch. On the facade, Chermayeff used each bay differently, alternating solidity with transparency based on the interior plan: wall panels are solid, glazed, or half and half depending on how much privacy is needed behind them. On solid bays, he painted the triangles between the braces in patterns of red, white, black, light blue, and yellow. "He sometimes called them his flags," said Chermayeff's son Peter. "He enjoyed that kind of nautical image, those shapes in the landscape." Glazed bays were tic-tac-toe grids of nine vertical rectangular windows, a few hinged at the top for air.

Like the Brahmin Bohemians, Chermayeff built his Outer Cape designs with prosaic, locally available materials — nothing flashy, despite their appearance. Peter Chermayeff said that, while his father was obviously "playfully departing" from vernacular forms, he was happy to use classic 2-by-4 framing and a "light wood structure that would be lifted off the ground on . . . simple footings. He enjoyed doing those things in a way that he felt related to the traditions of the Cape." In an article titled "How to Have Fun: Pennants, Bow Ties, and a Keg of Nails," *House & Home* exulted:

No houses could look less like the traditional Cape Cod salt box — yet Chermayeff feels that these little cottages have much in common with that unpretentious product of Massachusetts. Like the salt box, Chermayeff's cottages are braced into the wind, the way a ship's carpenter might brace them; like the salt box, they are built of simple, thoroughly familiar materials: stock framing lumber, stock siding, stock fiberboards, stock windows, all put together with nails and bolts, and without preciousness.

Ivan Chermayeff added that being a polyglot and a professor helped his father stay on good terms with his craftsmen. "He always had a good relationship with carpenters and builders and the tradespeople that he worked with," said Ivan, "and could talk to them in their languages and was involved in the process." Construction costs for the Wilkinson House: $8,500.[23]

As Chermayeff experimented with the prototype, he changed the deck on each house. The Chermayeff Studio deck has one-half of a roof panel, the Sigerson deck has a fully enclosed roof, and the Wilkinson deck has a pergola of thin slats that cast delicate "corduroy" shadows on the space. In 1970, the Wilkinsons bought Wellfleet's Kendall Gallery, moved to the Cape year-round, and successfully reinvented themselves as art dealers. Like Chermayeff himself, they both lived to be almost 100 years old.[24]

——————

For the rest of his life in the United States, Chermayeff was better known as a professor than as an architect. (He received an architect's license in 1943, but renounced it in 1954.) Impatient with mediocrity, he gravitated toward the best design schools, and students raved about the interdisciplinary breadth of his learning and teaching. In his brief time at Brooklyn College, he refashioned the art department to focus on design, transforming the curriculum to include a Bauhaus-type foundation course and architecture projects that aimed to solve problems in the local community. Like Saltonstall, he engaged with the issue of affordable, prefabricated, passive-solar postwar housing, submitting a model housing complex to the 1945 Museum of Modern Art exhibition *Tomorrow's Small House.* At Chicago's Institute of Design in 1947, Chermayeff spent a few years building out Moholy-Nagy's foundation courses and offering teaching posts to the likes of Buckminster Fuller, Gerhard Kallmann (later best known as co-architect of Boston's City Hall), and Konrad Wachsmann (the German pioneer in prefab housing and space-frame structures). For fun, he went to hear Ella Fitzgerald at the Blue Note with Fuller and a few lucky students, and enjoyed regular late-night drinks with Mies van der Rohe, then at the Illinois Institute of Technology.

In 1951, Chermayeff left Chicago for a year at MIT, a move his family applauded because it placed them closer to their Cape Cod retreat. In 1953, he joined the faculty at Harvard's Graduate School of Design, where he created a first-year course called Environmental Design to immerse students of architecture, landscape design, and urban planning in the problems of all three disciplines. Finally, in 1962 he moved to Yale, where, under dean Paul Rudolph, he taught Norman Foster, Richard Rogers, and Robert A. M. Stern. Chermayeff "could have persuaded us to do anything," said Rogers. "He was a dominating figure, hugely intellectual in the best European mould and just as much of an influence on me as Rudolph." A faithful correspondent, Chermayeff maintained relationships with his best students throughout his life, to the point of staying with them when he traveled. When he and Barbara went on a world tour in the 1980s, said his son, Ivan, they "never had to pay a hotel bill, because he kept in touch with his students, who became famous architects all over the place."[25]

In New Haven, Chermayeff built himself a house that embodied his ideal of a single-family home in a dense neighborhood. The E-shaped plan preserved mature maples throughout the small urban site, especially in the two courtyards. The walls are unfinished concrete block, inside and out, yet it is hard to imagine anyone making a concrete-walled living room warmer or more inviting than Chermayeff did, with sun flowing in from two courtyards, paintings covering the walls, beloved objects on the periphery, and a ceiling of honey-colored pine.

It was not until 1963 that Chermayeff published his best-known book, *Community and Privacy: Toward a New Architecture of Humanism*, setting out the design principles he had been living by and teaching for decades, and crystallizing his obsessions with privacy, noise pollution, and the postwar car craze. His coauthor was Christopher Alexander, the architect-mathematician later known for the design classic *A Pattern Language*. An eloquent tract of twentieth-century urbanism, *Community and Privacy* rails against the design of communities, especially suburbs, around the automobile. The authors' utopia — a project Chermayeff assigned,

Chermayeff working on housing concepts at Yale, 1966. His students made the cartoon that hangs on the wall.

in different forms, to students for almost 30 years — was a dense, low-rise neighborhood where people lived in close proximity to one another but, even if they owned a car, had a quiet, private home and access to nature. Pleading for wider understanding that "the spaces between buildings are as important to the life of urban man as the buildings themselves," Chermayeff and Alexander go into breathtaking detail on the ideal transition from public to private space, down to the fact that trash should not be collected in front of each house because garbage trucks disturb the peace and pollute the air and overstuffed cans are unsightly.[26]

Although *Community and Privacy* is clinically precise about how to achieve its proposals, complete with computer-generated schematics, Chermayeff's vision

Above: The living room of Chermayeff's house in New Haven (1963) is an object lesson in making an inviting home out of industrial materials. Sunlight flows in from two courtyards. *Left*: The house's courtyards function as outdoor rooms that bridge nature and culture with original open-air artwork, much like Chermayeff's deck in Wellfleet.

was fundamentally romantic. "Why do you go to Rome? Why do you go to Paris?" he asked an interviewer in 1986. "To sit outside in the cafes and see people, the passersby, to see people, to see people, to see people." He developed a love-hate relationship with the city: he loved the ideal, and devoted much of his life to designing modern versions of it, but he hated what the car had done to the reality. "The street itself is no longer a promenade for friends and neighbors among whom pleasant exchanges can take place," he complained in *Community and Privacy*, "but a service artery carrying dangerous trucks and other high-smelling vehicles filled with strangers. It is no longer a place for a community of children at play, or strolling lovers. Nor is it fit for a dog. The unresolved conflict between pedestrians and vehicles has made it obsolete." Add to this the racket of the ubiquitous TV and stereo — Chermayeff's other bugbears — and you have an endless whir of "often useless mobility, the ceaseless sounds and noises of communication and machinery, and the dissolution of the tranquillity and independence known to earlier cultures."[27]

Chermayeff found that tranquility on Cape Cod. As a nature lover, he especially railed against the expansion of motorized suburbia into the wilderness, draining vitality from the city and serenity from the country, with commuters now "shuttling between them in a desperate search for satisfaction which neither can provide." Every dwelling, he argued in *Community and Privacy*, and especially family homes, must interact thoughtfully with nature regardless of location: "Just as there must be a hierarchy of man-made domains in the city, so, too, the enjoyment of nature demands its own hierarchy of scale and subdivision, ranging from the great natural landscape to the tiny cultivated outdoor room of one's own." At his home in Wellfleet, he managed the transition from public (such as it is, in its remote locale) to private with a series of small clapboard barriers between the driveway and the house. The barriers protect those inside from the gaze of visitors, and force a transition for those arriving: from public (driveway) to semi-private (approaching house) to private (indoors). Inside, the railroad plan of the house maintains privacy between each section.

Chermayeff and Alexander criticized the open plan favored by other modernists; while allowing that Victorian houses had been too severely carved up, they felt that people who didn't want to hear the TV all evening shouldn't be stuck in the entertainment room. And the stereo must not drown out the songbird: "Every dwelling must contain an acoustic hierarchy, closely linked to the enjoyment of sun, air, and light, so that even in the outdoor room of one's own, the smallest desired sound can be heard and enjoyed."[28]

When the Cape Cod National Seashore was proposed in the late 1950s, debate was furious, with many residents decrying the plan as a federal "land grab." (Less publicly, some bohemians worried that vigilant rangers would scotch their nude swims.) Chermayeff, whose house would fall within seashore boundaries, was one of the plan's most illustrious proponents, attending local hearings and firing off letters to newspapers. He was especially concerned with the motels and cottages sprouting up on the southern end of Provincetown; in a letter to the *Boston Globe* — to which he attached a photo of his studio for publication — he blamed "greedy developers" and "callous" residents and tourists for allowing Cape Cod to be slowly destroyed by new construction. "We are quite sure that the only way to stop the rot and to restore the area to its natural charm and beauty is through a program of strict conservation and enforcement as quickly as possible," he insisted. "It will otherwise vanish in all too short a time forever."[29]

Chermayeff's handicap was his explosive temper. Blake, who had been his apprentice in London, goes so far as to say that Chermayeff would have built more in Britain had he not antagonized so many clients. Everyone who knew Chermayeff has a story about his irascibility, yet Chermayeff was such a talented thinker that he was hard to quit. Blake wrote:

Unhappily for Serge and all those close to him, he had a monstrous temper and delighted in reducing everyone — his wife, his friends, his employees, his students — to quivering jelly by verbally demolishing them, preferably in public. All of us who admired him and loved his family found his vituperative

Advocates for the National Seashore, including Chermayeff, argued that "greedy developers" would destroy the shoreline if the land was not protected. Wellfleet's scenic Ocean View Drive was carved out around 1960, while park legislation was tied up in Congress, for the express purpose of developing the waterfront, such as this stretch near LeCount Hollow Beach.

outbursts distressing beyond belief . . . but he was so devastatingly articulate, so elegant, so capable of enormous charm . . . so brilliant, so amusing . . . that I for one, and a few others, found it not too difficult to forgive him his monstrous temper tantrums. He simply knew more than anyone else around about the nature and essence of modern art and design, and he had a critical eye so sharp, so sure, so deadly in its accuracy, that I never stopped marveling at his visual intelligence.[30]

Even on Cape Cod, Chermayeff sometimes goaded dinner companions to tears, and he cut a fearsome figure on the beach. Kazin remembered him as "haughty," noting that he "never arrived on the beach without two enormous, restive, threatening German shepherds that frightened everyone around while his master, who had an icy Oxford accent and the majesty of a Diaghilev, could be heard knocking down everyone else's political universe. From time to time he was an advanced liberal." Edmund Wilson, meeting Chermayeff at a 1946 dinner party at the home of the transplanted Romanoff princess Nina Chavchavadze, wrote to his wife, Elena, "I became involved with the Chermaevs [sic] in one of those arguments about the Soviet Union which I am becoming extremely tired of, but which, once started, seem to have to run their course. . . . I didn't think Chermaev so bad — though he is certainly a queer product." Marian Schlesinger finished her

recollection of the Chermayeffs' quiet swims by noting that the peace didn't last:

> For when Serge got back to his deck, the stentorian roar of his commands to his dogs and his perpetual demands and complaints . . . carried undiminished across the water. . . . He was the lord of the pond and a passionate environmentalist and conservationist. One was grateful for his sensitive ears when he banished an obtrusive motorboat, offensive to the spirit of the pond, by the furious outrage of his remarks and personality. The poor owner could not stand up against it and retired his motorboat for good.[31]

In 1971, after Chermayeff retired, he and Barbara installed central heating at Slough Pond and, with Barbara's mother, spent the rest of their lives there. Ati Gropius Johansen marveled at their transformation from urbanites to woodspeople: "They lived there through thick and thin, Barbara still cutting wood — my God, they were in their seventies and eighties, I think. We were all just speechless about their ruggedness." Chermayeff died in 1996, Barbara four years later, and their ashes are buried near their home on Slough Pond. Despite terrible arthritis, Chermayeff sketched and painted until the end, telling Powers at age 93, "I do this to keep myself alive."[32]

MARCEL BREUER

One summer day in the early 1940s, Marcel Breuer, his wife, Connie, and their baby son, Tamas, drove out to Cape Cod to try to find Chermayeff, Breuer's old friend from London. Unfamilar with the area, the Breuers stopped in every town to make inquiries until someone in Wellfleet pointed them down the long dirt road to Chermayeff's piney retreat.[33] The Breuers were smitten, and in 1944, just months after Chermayeff bought his property, they bought a 19-acre plot across the road. By 1946, before a single nail had been hammered, Breuer had published, in *Interiors* magazine, a design for a colony of five nearly identical houses on his rolling land overlooking Higgins, Williams, and Gull ponds. The Bauhaus had come to Wellfleet.

Marcel Lajos Breuer — Lajko (pronouned "Loyko") to his friends — was born in 1902 to a secular Jewish family in Pécs, Hungary, a university town near the Yugoslav border. After high school, he won a scholarship to the Academy of Fine Arts in Vienna, but when he saw the traditional curriculum and "indifferent" students, he later said, "I walked into the Academy and walked out again."[34] Culturally isolated by political upheaval after World War I, Breuer was, in the words of scholar Isabelle Hyman, "looking for a revolution in art without knowing where to find it." He apprenticed briefly with a Vienna architect and cabinetmaker, but when a friend showed him a brochure for the new Bauhaus in Weimar, Germany — featuring Lyonel Feininger's famous cathedral woodcut — Breuer packed his bags. In 1920, at age 18, he became the fledgling school's youngest student.[35]

Bauhaus founder Walter Gropius, seared by combat experience in World War I, had envisioned a revolutionary school that reconciled fine art with expert craftsmanship and, later, mass production. "There is no essential difference between the artist and the artisan," he wrote in the Bauhaus manifesto. "Let us therefore create a new guild of craftsmen, free of the divisive class pretensions that endeavored to raise a prideful barrier between craftsmen and artists!" Despite the political and economic turmoil that surrounded the school throughout its short life (1919–33),

Young Breuer in his first tubular steel chair, the B3 or "Wassily" chair (1927), which combines a stiff frame with soft seating material. The chair's structural logic and mechanical connections are all plainly visible.

the Bauhaus was remarkably successful in that goal, and Breuer was arguably its most illustrious product. The Bauhaus *Vorkurs,* or Preliminary Course, centered on the peculiar natures and qualities of different materials. Students made intensive studies of paper, wood, metals, wool, glass, and so forth, and each had to become proficient in a craft, such as weaving, cabinetry, or metalworking. Though Breuer and his peers agitated for an architecture curriculum, the Bauhaus did not offer one until 1927, so he completed his training in 1924 in cabinetmaking. The following year, after a short stint in the Paris office of the architect Pierre Chareau — later known for his Maison de Verre (1932) — Breuer was invited to return to the Bauhaus as a *Jungmeister*, or young master, and named head of the cabinetmaking workshop.[36]

In this early version of the B33, or "Cesca," chair (1928), Breuer pairs a steel skeleton with hand-wrought leather bands, in keeping with the Bauhaus precept of marrying traditional craft with industrial innovations.

That same year, at age 23, Breuer developed his first piece of furniture made of bent tubular steel, the B3 chair — later dubbed the "Wassily" chair, because Breuer once made one for his friend Wassily Kandinsky — and the B9 stool. Though his earlier wooden chairs and cabinets had been praised, his steel pieces brought Breuer international recognition, and royalties from their production helped him through the subsequent lean years. His B33 chair (later called the "Cesca") is one of the most ubiquitous and copied chairs in modern history: the continuous steel tube provides structural support with the absolute minimum of bends while the back and seat are leather, fabric, or stretched wicker hung from the frame. There is absolute clarity about the functions performed by each part, the methods of fastening the parts together, and the reasons for the use of each material.[37] The inspiration for the steel designs came from a milkman who appeared every morning during Breuer's first year at the Bauhaus: "He arrived on a bicycle," Breuer told the writer Peter Blake, "and I kept admiring the elegance of those

chromium-plated tubular-steel handlebars. So that's how it began." The idea seemed so outlandish that Breuer had difficulty finding a fabricator to make the first prototype; but once it was executed, the design seemed utterly obvious. William Landsberg, who studied with Breuer at Harvard and later worked in his firm, noted this quality in Breuer's work: "He solved problems so directly, they always came out clean and sure, the inevitable thing, why didn't everyone think of it?"[38]

Breuer's fascination with the cantilever thus began in his furniture. It is hard now to imagine the shock of seeing a chair with no back legs at a time when many people were still living with Victorian settees, but Breuer would forever find ways to express the desire to float above the earth. Blake maps Breuer's designs, from chairs to buildings, as a vertical stacking of the rational and romantic: "To Breuer the framework, the weight-supporting unit in any design became a distinct entity to be expressed in structural terms. The added, non-structural portion with which the human being comes into immediate contact — this assumed an entirely different character, less abstract, less hard, less sharp-edged."[39] The multitudinous versions of each of his chairs and later furniture lines in aluminum, bent plywood, and cutout slab plywood speak to one of the trademarks of Breuer's architecture: his capacity to work and rework an idea, exploring every potential application.

Breuer's earliest building designs introduced themes that would reappear throughout his career. His 1927 proposal for Bauhaus young masters' housing, BAMBOS 1, was a clear departure from the blocky, more massive structures of the early modern movement. Each residence comprised two separate volumes: a living space on the ground, and a studio in a flying box supported by very thin columns. Breuer's drive to defy gravity appears in the floating staircases — hovering treads suspended like retractable airplane stairs — and impossibly thin structural columns. Most walls are either solid or floor-to-ceiling glass on a visible modular panel system; the solid walls are light, prefabricated cement. Instead of flat roofs, Breuer used gently pitched shed roofs, and he introduced the use of spars

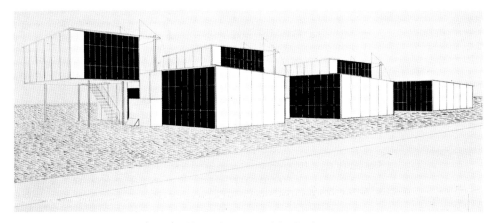

Marcel Breuer, BAMBOS 1 (1927). This early proposal for Bauhaus young masters' apartments introduces many of Breuer's enduring themes, including nautical masts and rigging and the contrast between earthbound and flying structures.

BAMBOS 1, model

and cables to support a canopy. The flying box and the idea of separating the public and private areas of a house — a dichotomy sometimes expressed as day and night, loud and quiet, children's and adults' — will return in his 1940s work on Cape Cod.

At the Bauhaus, Breuer and his mentor, Gropius, were the nucleus of a close circle of friends including the graphic designer Herbert Bayer, the artist and photographer Moholy-Nagy, and the painter and performer Xanti Schawinsky. The group took frequent trips together, skiing in the Alps or relaxing on the Swiss shores of Lake Maggiore. A love of sunshine and sports was a hallmark of Europe's early modernists, who wanted to escape what they saw as the dark, unhealthy, overupholstered trappings of the previous epoch. Many photographs of Bauhaus students and faculty show them cavorting in the sun — indeed, one reason for the school's eviction from its first home in Weimar was the students' proclivity for swimming nude in the city's Goethe Park.

Breuer would ultimately express his passion for the outdoors architecturally in a fresh context overseas. Breuer left the Bauhaus in 1928 to open an architecture firm in Berlin, after which he practiced briefly in Switzerland and Hungary; he then spent two years in London, where he, Gropius, and Moholy-Nagy were neighbors in the Lawn Road Flats, or Isokon Building (1934), an idealistic new apartment complex designed by Wells Coates. Breuer built some projects, but prewar business was depressed. In 1937, Gropius, newly installed at Harvard's rapidly modernizing Graduate School of Design, invited Breuer to join him in teaching

a modified version of the Bauhaus curriculum. Upon his arrival that spring, Gropius had sent Breuer a rhapsody:

Air clear as glass, lots of sun, and blue Roman skies. All around an unspoiled, untamed landscape, most of which has not been degraded into parks and in which one doesn't always feel like a trespasser. In addition, fine wooden houses in the Colonial style, painted white, which will delight you as much as they do me. In their simplicity, functionality, and uniformity they are completely in our line.

Gropius was not the first, and would not be the last, to see both a modern and a visceral human quality in historic New England architecture. He went on, "The inviting appearance of these houses mirrors the incredible hospitality of this country, which probably stems from old pioneer times."[40] Breuer sailed from Southampton in July 1937 and docked at New York in August.

After marveling at the modern metropolis, Breuer joined Walter and Ise Gropius at their rented house on Planting Island, at the base of Cape Cod. For the next month Breuer relaxed with the old Bauhaus inner circle, several of whom had followed Gropius to the United States in the hope that he would find them jobs.

Soon afterward, he wrote to F. R. S. Yorke, his business partner in London, to announce that he was not coming back: "I am sorry I could not fill this letter with only a good description of the beautiful bathing here, the Colonial style and the skyscrapers."[41]

Breuer joined the Harvard faculty that fall, working with Gropius to adapt the Bauhaus pedagogy to a new culture and a new generation. Himself a generation younger than Gropius (and, by way of comparison, Ludwig Mies van der Rohe and Le Corbusier), Breuer was closer in age to his students; put the two men together, and it is hard to overstate their impact on twentieth-century American architecture. Philip Johnson, Eliot Noyes, I. M. Pei, and Paul Rudolph were among those they trained, and for many, Breuer was the formative influence. Johnson said bluntly, "Breuer was my teacher, and I learned more from him than from Gropius." Landis Gores recalled the "subtly stimulating and ever thought-provoking influence Breuer cast across the whole school."[42] Thanks to his approachability and his modest, workmanlike demeanor, students remembered Breuer many decades later with deep respect and affection. In 1948, two years after he had left Harvard for New York, a group of students wrote a petition urging him to "return to the School as teacher and critic." Ninety-five students signed it, and copies

Marcel Breuer, Breuer House, Lincoln, Massachusetts (1939), from the south, as it looks today. The public, private, and screened-porch components are clearly articulated as an aggregation of parts.

were sent to Breuer and the GSD administration. Breuer framed his copy and hung it in his office.[43]

Alongside their teaching positions, Breuer and Gropius opened a firm together in Cambridge. Their output consisted mostly of competition entries for institutional works and a handful of houses, including the two iconic homes they designed for themselves in the pastoral suburb of Lincoln. These were radical for New England at the time, but they were relatives of works the pair had built in Europe. White, two-storied, and roughly cubic, their forms eroded by roof decks or extended by entries and porches, these houses carry on the lineage of European modernist villas such as Gropius's Masters' Houses at the Bauhaus in Dessau (1926) and Le Corbusier's Villa Stein (1927). The key difference is that the Lincoln houses incorporate wood siding, which Gropius and Breuer laid vertically in a break from tradition, and some wood framing. Gropius's house (1938) also has a central entry and stair hall, a subtle nod to the colonial homes that surrounded him.

Breuer's small bachelor house (1939) next door, however, shows that he was beginning to go his own way. While the Gropius House is a single volume, with room functions only hinted at by their windows, the volumes housing each function in Breuer's house seem to want to break free from one another, sliding around and jostling for position. The house gathers around a trapezoidal, two-story living room that ends in a convex stone wall containing the hearth. The kitchen, dining room, and maid's room are a few steps down, and a bedroom looks down from a mezzanine half a flight up. There is a complex spatial excitement on the journey from front door to bedrooms as you wind around, looking into and past the main space from three different levels. In the living room, a south-facing glass curtain wall makes the small footprint feel much larger. A small door in the stone wall leads to a large, sequestered screened-in porch.

Outdoors, above the recessed window wall of the living room, the roof is supported by a pair of wooden masts, pinned in place by nautical-looking steel flanges. Breuer takes pains to show how each piece of the house interlocks with those around it, both on a large scale and in small details; the connections reveal and explain themselves. The tension between transparency and solidity appears in the butting of the window wall directly into the massive stone wall: the stone continues outside and beyond the glass to emphasize their fundamental difference. Years later, in his book *Sun and Shadow*, Breuer argued lyrically:

Breuer House, view of living room from bedroom level

The real impact of any work is the extent to which it unifies contrasting notions — the opposite points of view. I mean unifies, and not compromises. This is what the Spaniards express so well with their motto from the bull fights: Sol y sombra, sun and shadow. Half the seats in the bull ring face the sun, the other half is in the shadow. They made a proverb out of it — "sun and shadow" — and they did not make it sun or shadow. For them, their whole life — its contrasts, its tensions, its excitement, its beauty — all this is contained in the proverb sol y sombra.[44]

Less than a year after he moved in, Breuer married Constance Leighton, who had been a secretary in the Cambridge office he shared with Gropius.

In 1940, after seeing Breuer's house, a Cambridge couple, the Chamberlains, commissioned the firm to design a very small weekend cottage nearby, on the wooded banks of the Sudbury River in Wayland. The Chamberlain Cottage (1941) is essentially a small wooden box balanced on a smaller stone base. Breuer's

design constitutes a complete departure from the firm's oeuvre and presents new themes that will figure prominently in his future work, particularly his Wellfleet cottages. The commission came shortly before Breuer dissolved his partnership with Gropius, but it seems clear that at this point Breuer was working with autonomy.

Breuer's interest in the possibilities of traditional American wood framing led to exterior stud walls skinned inside and out with tongue-and-groove siding, nailed on in opposing directions (vertically outside, horizontally inside) to create a stiff, continuously stressed wall panel. Since the whole main floor thus acts as a box truss, Breuer could achieve cantilevers and window openings without large beams or lintels. The Chamberlains' entry stairs and landing hang from the frame, with the bottom step and supports hovering just above the ground. In a telling break from the European white-house paradigm Breuer had maintained with Gropius (in their own homes and a handful of other commissions), he clear-stained, rather than painted, the vertical fir siding to highlight its natural texture and grain. Inside, for the first time in Breuer's work, the fireplace breaks free of the walls to become a freestanding sculptural object and room divider. The screened porch becomes its own hovering box, protruding boldly from the main volume with its girders pinned between elegant paired columns. This expression of a porch or terrace away from the main building, with its own access to the ground, has precedents in earlier modern villas, such as Breuer's unbuilt design for the Schneider House (1929), where the balcony almost resembles a diving board; Breuer's first built house, the Harnischmacher House I (1932); and Breuer and Gropius's Hagerty House (1938). Plunging directly into the elements, such porches reflect the new, post-Victorian belief in outdoor recreation.

Though only 600 square feet, the Chamberlain Cottage contains the germ of what became known as Breuer's "long house" concept: a rectangular wood-framed box suspended in the air. The form sprang from Breuer's fascination with wood-stud construction, but he drew on his cabinetmaking background to customize it: by laminating layers of wood into stiff slabs,

In the Chamberlain Cottage (1941), Breuer created a rigid exterior shell by attaching one layer of siding to another, first horizontally, then vertically, allowing for overhangs and openings with minimal use of large supporting timbers. Ultimately, whether due to shortcomings in the planning or the construction, Breuer's rigid wall system sagged and had to be substantially rebuilt.

he created, after a fashion, large-scale plywood, which at the time was used primarily in cabinetry, not for sheathing buildings. The tiny house hovers boatlike above the ground, its entry stair a gangplank — an apt device, since the house was probably raised onto its pedestal in part to keep it above the river's flood plain. Five years later, Breuer would design his first fully developed long house for the shores of a Cape Cod pond.

Although Breuer was a child of the Bauhaus — which, like a medieval guild, encouraged anonymous authorship — he took a nuanced, personal approach in his own designs. Reacting to Le Corbusier's famous slogan, Breuer once said that a house is indeed a machine for living in, "but you don't want to get greasy

if you lean against the wall. You want to have . . . something simpler, more elemental, more generous and more human than a machine."[45] The Geller House (1945), on Long Island, was Breuer's first built residential project after his split with Gropius, and it set the pattern for his other major house type: what he called the binuclear house, divided into public and private areas. This idea had been percolating in Breuer's mind at least since his entry to the 1943 *Arts and Architecture* competition, Designs for Postwar Living: an H-shaped plan that could join with a second, offset H to create cluster housing with interior courtyards.

The Geller House stretched out along the ground on a semirural site. Public spaces occupy a long, thin wing that ends in a massive stone hearth, while bedrooms form another squarish wing. Part of the rationale for the binuclear design was that veterans needed peace and quiet to recuperate from the war, so the house has a children's living room in the bedroom wing, far from the main living area. A narrow entry hall bridges the two, and a separate guest and garage wing is at a right angle. The entire assemblage sits on grade, with fieldstone walls and wood screens defining the outdoor spaces. Courtyards are created or suggested in the negative spaces, and the building's functions now break free from one another. Both roofs are early examples of the butterfly form, pitched gently to the center in an inversion of the traditional peak. Natural, native materials dominate: unpainted fir siding, fieldstone walls, and flagstone floors, suggesting the prosperous but informal lifestyles of the clients who were beginning to seek Breuer out.

In 1946, Breuer left Harvard and opened an office in New York. The Museum of Modern Art staged an exhibition of his work and asked him to design a demonstration house for its sculpture garden, a project that catapulted him into the public eye. As he joined and helped shape colonies of modern architects in New Canaan, Connecticut, as well as Wellfleet, his two house types — the light, elevated long house and the low, earthbound binuclear — now took shape for a variety of clients, budgets, and sites.

By the mid-1940s, some of the Bauhaus crew from Planting Island, and their friends from the design world, were spending summer holidays in Wellfleet and Truro. The Gropiuses, with their daughter, Ati, and Eero Saarinen and his wife, Lily, would come and stay with the Chermayeffs, who had settled into Phillips's rental cottage on Slough Pond. Schawinsky and Breuer took turns renting an old ice house on Ryder Pond in South Truro, and in 1944 the Breuers bought their own plot across the dirt road from the Chermayeffs, who had just purchased theirs. Breuer now conceived and published his group of five neighboring homes: a personal vision of community and privacy, allowing each family to escape from society and still be surrounded by friends. The plan was idealistic yet grounded in the very real potential of Breuer's property and social circle — and possibly in memories of Gropius's

Masters' Houses at the Bauhaus. (One house in the grouping was a version of the H plan he had submitted to *Arts and Architecture* in 1943; the other four were a new design.) Envisioning a utopian community of like-minded neighbors, sophisticated about design but happy with rustic amenities, Breuer tried to sell plots in his colony to friends. Schawinsky saved $5,000 for the purpose, but reportedly lent it to his friend Konrad Wachsmann, and that was the end of that.[46] The Breuers' close friends Stephen Borsody, a Hungarian diplomat, and his wife, Zsoka, considered joining the scheme, but Borsody ultimately said he didn't want to drive down that long, pitted road for the *New York Times* every morning.[47]

The long-house prototype Breuer developed for his waterfront site was thoroughly documented in preliminary construction plans and in the renderings published in *Interiors* in 1946. Though some elements, such as the entry stairs, are direct quotes from the Chamberlain Cottage, this long house is another departure: instead of resting on a stone base, the Wellfleet house floats on round cedar posts buried in the ground. These act as footings, much like the wood piers of the oyster shacks that still stood in the town's shallow harbor. Building on stilts was both a sensitive response to the Cape's undulating terrain and shifting sands, and a way to avoid the cost and craftsmanship needed for a masonry foundation. The piers allowed Breuer to customize the floor height of each house for the best views, and then helped keep the house cool, with breezes passing below and through the higher structure. This prototype is 16 by 65 feet, with five 12-foot structural bays and a short cantilever on each end. The living room is at one end and the master bedroom at the other, with the kitchen, bath, and a small bedroom in between. The siding is raw plywood, and on the pond side, an open deck and a brise-soleil hang from cables. One rendering shows the house through the windshield of a car; another two show a car parked under the house, suggesting that Breuer imagined at least 7 or 8 feet of headroom below.

While plans for a Wellfleet house were shelved for three years, Breuer's concept of the long house continued to evolve, and the first example he executed was

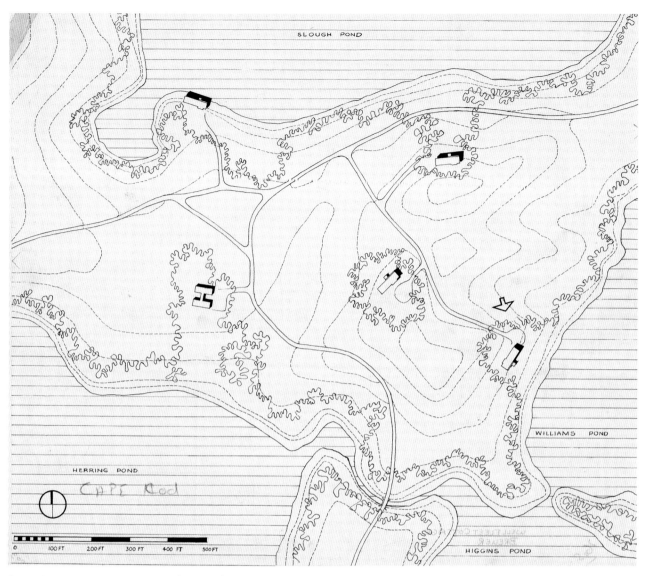

Breuer's proposed cottage colony (ca. 1945). Breuer envisioned a small colony of houses based on his prototype and populated by his friends. His own house (see arrow) was the only one ever built on the property, but his friends still found their way to Wellfleet.

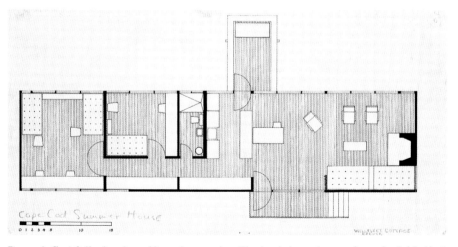

Breuer's first fully developed long-house plan. The basic layout proved so adaptable that all four of Breuer's Wellfleet houses are essentially versions of it.

Rendering of Breuer's long-house prototype from the pond side of the site. Later, in built versions, the hanging porch was roofed and screened in response to Cape Cod's weather and insect population. After the cables on the cantilevered porch at his first New Canaan house failed, Breuer reimagined the structural diagonals in timber.

Rendering of prototype as seen from downhill

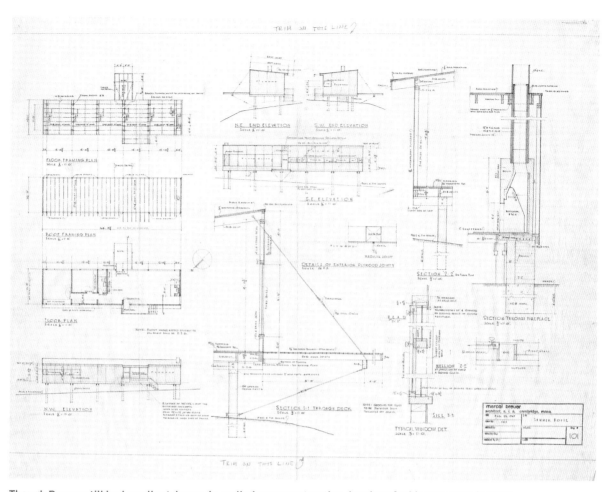

Though Breuer still had no client, he made preliminary construction drawings for his prototype in 1945.

Rendering of prototype from an approaching car, as if seen by the weary urbanite arriving for a summer weekend

his own house in New Canaan (1948). This New York City bedroom community was a hotbed of modern residential experimentation by 1947, with Breuer and many of his former students, including Philip Johnson, Eliot Noyes, John Johansen, Landis Gores, and Ulrich Franzen, building and settling there. Roughly 20 by 74 feet, Breuer's Connecticut house sits on a masonry base with ambitious 10-foot cantilevers on each end. Again testing the limits of wood-frame construction, Breuer used layered diagonal siding and hidden diagonal wall framing to brace the overhangs. On the living-room end, he added the stress of a large deck hung on cables. The double cantilever proved impossible, and the deck soon needed to be propped up by a fieldstone wall. This house was an urbane version of the long-house prototype, with partial stone flooring, painted interior finishes, and an elegant version of the stairs first seen in the BAMBOS 1 design: their structure and railing are a web of slender steel bars, while the treads hover weightlessly.

Ironically, given his published visions for Wellfleet, the first house Breuer built on Cape Cod was not a long house but a high-budget binuclear for Stuart Scott, a lawyer friend from New York, and his wife, Katie, in the mid-Cape town of Dennis. The Scott House (1948) might be called an extreme binuclear in

that the two parallel wings do not touch; the original plan resembles an equal sign. The main building holds the living areas and three bedrooms, all of which open onto a stone terrace overlooking Scargo Lake and Cape Cod Bay beyond. The secondary wing houses a garage, maid's quarters, and a so-called dormitory for the family's teenage daughter. Old fieldstone walls on the site were recycled to make a new, head-height stone wall, bisecting the dormitory (where it becomes a double-height fireplace wall) and creating a series of varied courtyard spaces. The dormitory has a large, two-story living room for "record hops," a kitchenette, a mezzanine bedroom, and separate showers and dressing rooms for boys and girls. At the mezzanine level, a powerfully geometric sun screen caps the west facade.

In the Scott residence, Breuer reworked the kit of parts he developed for the Geller House, adapting them for a new site and client. The Scott dormitory resembles the Geller guest wing, and the garages in both houses, with walls that don't reach the ground, are identical. Built a year prior to Breuer's MoMA demonstration house, the Scott House dormitory predicts some of its key elements, including the basic volume, butterfly roofline, and mezzanine bedroom overlooking a living room. The refined finishes in Scott, including

Marcel Breuer, Scott House, Dennis, Massachusetts (1948), as seen in 1950. The Scott House might be called an extreme binuclear in that the two wings of the house do not touch. The stone wall that bisects the dormitory creates courtyards with different functions and levels of privacy. *Right*: Sue Scott outside her dormitory

cypress-board ceilings, stone floors with radiant heat, built-in furniture, and birch-plywood wall paneling, make this house unique among Breuer's works on Cape Cod. The sliding-glass doors were made on-site of frameless plate glass in ball-bearing tracks; amazingly, though basic and minimalist in the extreme, they still operate. Soon after the house was finished, Breuer and his friend György Kepes used it as a way station while building their own homes in Wellfleet. The Scotts remember fondly that Breuer would come for weekends bearing buckets of mussels, which he would personally make into bouillabaisse. In 1958, Breuer designed an addition to the main building, expanding the kitchen and adding a dining room; this came close to connecting the two wings, creating a roughly U-shaped plan.

In July 1948, Breuer finally got clients for his first Cape Cod long house: his friends György and Juliet Kepes, both artists. Hungarian-born György Kepes — who, like Gropius, committed himself to the arts after serving in World War I — had worked with Moholy-Nagy on film, stage, and exhibition designs in Berlin in the early 1930s, and followed Moholy-Nagy to teach at Chicago's New Bauhaus in 1937. In the mid-1940s,

Kepes taught with Chermayeff at Brooklyn College, and in 1946 he joined the MIT faculty. He devoted much of his career to bridging the gaps between art, science, and technology, and in 1967, he founded MIT's interdisciplinary Center for Advanced Visual Studies. His own work spanned painting, photography, and other media, including stained-glass windows.[48] British-born Juliet Kepes was a painter and an acclaimed author and illustrator of children's books. In the late 1940s, she designed for the couple's daughter, Julie, a complete bedroom environment — centered on a handpainted mural — which was featured in *Life* magazine and, in 2012, partially re-created for the Museum of Modern Art exhibition *Century of the Child*.

In today's world of custom homes in resort destinations, it may seem odd that Breuer's four Wellfleet houses are minor variations on a prototype. But Breuer, the product of a design culture imbued with social conscience, was committed to the ideal of good design for the masses, and spent much of the early 1940s vainly trying to build mass-produced modular housing. When confronted with the problem of a low-budget summer cottage, he saw no reason to start from scratch each time.

A large, roofed patio runs the back length of the Scott House, overlooking Scargo Lake and Cape Cod Bay to the north.

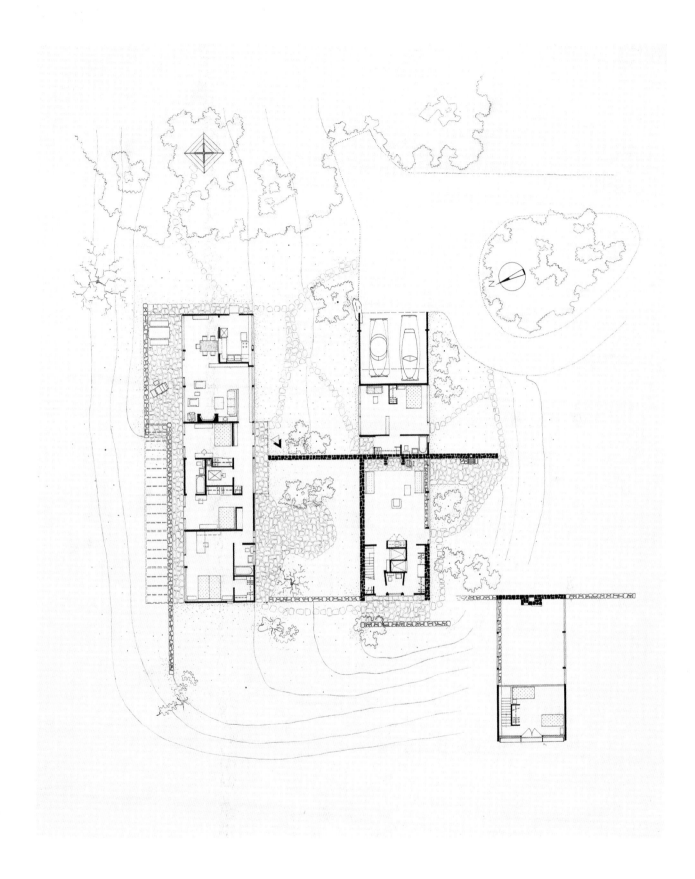

Scott House, plan (1947)

Old stones, from dry-laid walls on the site, were repurposed for the Scott House's masonry construction. Conceptually, the house seems to reoccupy a long-abandoned foundation.

Scott House, living room

Living room (top) and main bedroom (above)

Dormitory, public space with concealable kitchenette and, above, sleeping loft. *Opposite*: View from sleeping loft

Breuer's friends György and Juliet Kepes with the mural they painted in their daughter's room in Cambridge, as seen in *Life* magazine, 1949

Breuer outside his Wellfleet house, with Connie and Tamas on the porch, 1950

Kepes, left, and Breuer enliven a gathering at Kepes's plywood-skinned house on Long Pond.

THE WELLFLEET COTTAGES (1949–63)

Although Breuer's long house was designed to occupy any number of settings, his own Cape cottage is hard to imagine without its astonishing site. Ati Gropius Johansen, who began visiting Wellfleet with her parents, Walter and Ise, in the 1940s, said more than 60 years later, "Breuer's house made a big impression on me and, I think, on my parents because that was the first we had seen of that kind of rural living." But in her recollections, the house is actually secondary: That plot "is just to die for, it's so beautiful," she said. "It's grown up very much now, but in the old days you could see three ponds fully from it — my parents were impressed by that, and Lajko kept saying, 'Buy some land, buy some land,' and [my father] didn't . . . which I regretted always." The Kepes House had an equally

Breuer House (1949), as originally built. A stone's throw across Williams Pond is the oysterman's house where Thoreau stayed, as recounted in *Cape Cod*.

lovely situation, she said, because "at that time you could see all across Long Pond. . . . I think I was more impressed by the sites than anything else."[49]

After nabbing such a spot, the Kepeses had less than $5,000 left for a house. Breuer offered his *Interiors* magazine prototype, with a few modifications: instead of sitting on cedar pilings, this house is held aloft by 4-inch-wide posts, on concrete footings, which travel from grade up to the roof with in-fill stud walls between them. The structural bays are 10 feet long, with a 2-foot cantilever at each end, and the floor platform rests on girders notched into the posts, making a stiff frame something like a small railroad trestle bridge. The Kepeses wanted a master bedroom and

studio beyond the hearth, making their house one bay longer than the prototype and moving the hearth toward the middle. While construction on the Kepes House was under way, Breuer decided to build a variation of the prototype house for himself on the land he had bought in 1944. To save time and money, he hired the same contractor, Ernie Rose, to build his house as well, and the two families moved in by the summer of '49. Breuer wrote to Gropius, "We have a new little cottage with 3/8" plywood walls, and nothing else. 'Dieux [sic] me pardonnera, c'est son métier.'"[50]

Breuer sited both houses to give the porch the best water views. Screened-in and roofed, each porch hangs from its frame by a sort of truss, with two diagonal

Top: Lunch is served on the suspended porch with a view of three ponds. *Above*: Connie, Marcel, an unidentified guest, renderer D. C. Byrd, and Tamas (foreground), in their living room.

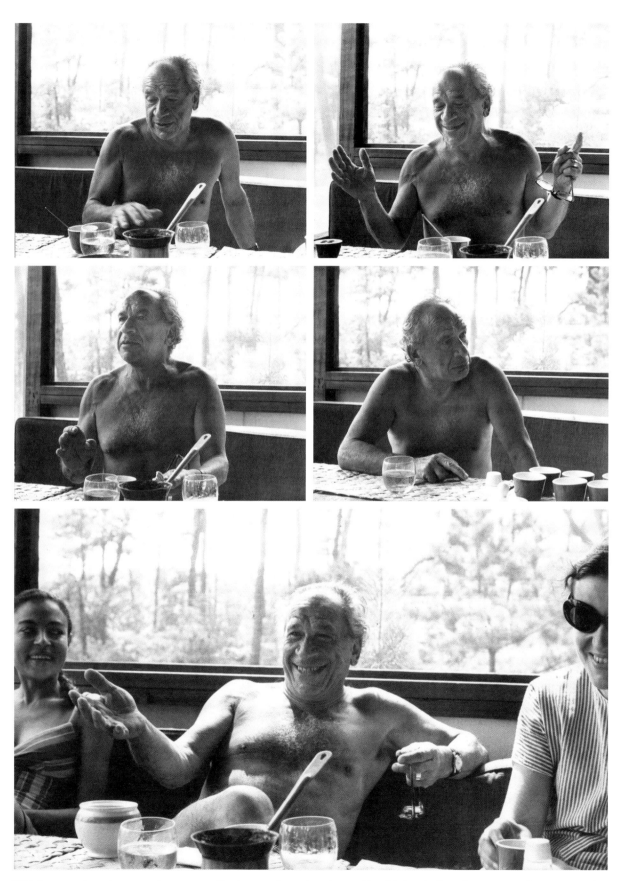

Widely remembered as an antic presence, Bauhaus artist and performer Xanti Schawinsky tells a story on Breuer's porch.
In the bottom photo, Christine Benglia Bevington is on the left and Connie Breuer is on the right.

struts attached to the roof rafters above and two bracing up from the footings below. This remarkable space, the center of activity for both families, feels like a hovering cube with a vast command of the landscape. The effect is heightened at Breuer's house, where he suspended the porch over a steep drop with a sweeping view of the woods and three ponds — Higgins, Williams, and Gull. The assembly is remarkably firm and has survived well, in contrast to the failed New Canaan cable scheme.

In 1955, Breuer wrote in *Sun and Shadow* of the virtues of spaces both anchored and aloft:

> In our modern houses the relationship to the
> landscape is a major planning element. There are
> two entirely different approaches. . . . There is
> the house that sits on the ground and permits you
> to walk out into the landscape at any point, from
> any room. . . . And then there is the house on stilts,
> that is elevated above the landscape, almost like
> a camera on a tripod. This will give you a better
> view, almost a sensation of floating above the
> landscape, or of standing on the bridge of a ship.
> It gives you a feeling of liberation, a certain élan,
> a certain daring, while the idea of being in a house
> close to the ground might . . . increase your sense
> of security.[51]

Breuer's Wellfleet porches were the ultimate cameras on tripods — and, indeed, were all "set on the bridge of a ship" overlooking bodies of water.

As a living experience, the houses were summer camps in the air. The siding was unfinished Weldtex, a plywood of striated fir, and the framing was exposed indoors — there was no interior wall finish. "The materials were all rustic," said Gropius Johansen. "Nothing was painted white, everything was just rough — the floors and the material and the space and the appointments, everything." There was no electricity and no running water. A kitchen hand pump flushed the toilets, and the stove and fridge ran on propane gas. The sliding windows were unframed pieces of plate glass in a hardwood groove, with a wood handle glued to the leading edge. Furnishings at the Breuer and Kepes

Kepes and Breuer play chess on Breuer's porch.

houses were also minimal: woven fiber mats covered the floors. The Breuers' couch was a mattress, and their porch featured his famous dining table made from a square slab of slate on a stack of concrete blocks. Sitting on that porch in 2012, Tamas Breuer remembered the house's earliest days:

> It was just a bare shell of a building . . . and it was
> very primitive. Our notion, I think, was to be kind
> of roughing it out here. . . . This is a very small
> house, really, when you think about it. And it
> shakes when you walk through it. All the glasses
> wobble and clatter.

Breuer needed a phone to stay in touch with his office, but had a hard time getting a line installed down the mile-long sand track from the main road. He finally hooked up to Jack Phillips's private poles, out toward Horseleech Pond, and the phone company agreed to bury the wire from the last pole to Breuer's house. Even so, Tamas said, the wires have always been exposed beneath the house, so mice periodically chew through them and cut the dial tone. The Kepes family faced a different logistical challenge: they did not drive. To get from Cambridge to Wellfleet, Kepes arranged for one of his MIT students to drive the family down every June and pick them up around Labor Day. To buy groceries, they walked a mile from Long Pond into Wellfleet center, pulling a small wagon.[52]

Above: Kepes House (1949), west side, facing Long Pond. *Opposite*: North wall of main bedroom/studio, and living room. The Kepes living room remains almost exactly as it was built. Woven mats cover plywood floors, and a wall section behind the fireplace slides to provide privacy for the master bedroom.

174

Breuer House, south wall of living room. Breuer continually tinkered with his summer house, adding such features as the birch plywood ceiling indoors and suspended slat ceiling on the porch.

View from the bench seat on Breuer's porch

View of main house from porch of studio building, added in 1962

All this reductivism reflected the clients' modest budgets, seasonal usage, and bohemian lifestyle. But both cottages were also, in effect, chassis that could be embellished as future funds allowed: starting with a wooden frame, the owners could hang different materials, much as one could change the seating of Breuer's bent-steel chairs. Incredibly, apart from the installation of electric lights and a water pump, the Kepes House, still in the family, remains as it was built. Books and family artwork cover the unfinished walls; colorful textiles, handmade objects, shells, and fossils adorn tables and furniture. Breuer, in contrast to Kepes, tinkered with his cottage throughout his life, adding vertical cedar siding, oak flooring, Homasote interior wallboard, and birch-plywood ceilings. At one point, he installed a slatted ceiling in the porch, which, by hiding the underside of the shed roof, enhanced the floating-cube effect. Interested in how color affected space, Breuer painted accent walls and doors the electric color that came to be known as "Breuer blue," and sometimes painted other walls bright yellow or red. In 1962, he added a squarish multipurpose wing, connected to the house by an entry deck, and in 1967 added a bedroom and a darkroom suite for Tamas to the new wing. These changes made the house, in effect, a hybrid of his long-house and binuclear types.

Although Breuer's house was the only one built in his imagined cluster, a sympathetic, mostly Hungarian community grew around him organically, including not only Kepes but Stephen and Zsoka Borsody, structural engineer Paul Weidlinger, MIT physicist László Tisza, and their families. (Despite their common heritage, they generally spoke English together.) Romanian-born cartoonist Saul Steinberg, a recent immigrant thanks to the New Yorker's sponsorship in 1942, was a summer fixture at the Borsodys' house and drew many of his cartoons in Wellfleet. Their children would splash and make fun of Steinberg as he floated in Cape Cod Bay, topped with a big hat and ensconced in an inner tube because he burned easily and never learned to swim. "It was a good mixture of interesting people and a lovely setting," Zsoka Borsody remembered almost 70 years later. "The easy-goingness of just stepping out of [the] house and being surrounded by water and sun and wind and trees — I often thought, look, how do we deserve this life? It seems to be the most luxurious way to live. It is a mental freedom. It is a physical freedom. It is a liberation. That's how we should be, but it not very often happens."[53]

In 1953, Edgar Stillman hired Breuer to build a larger version of his long house on the top of a dune on Wellfleet's Griffin Island, at the end of Chequessett Neck Road. This site had a panoramic view of the bay and was fully exposed to the wind from all directions. Stillman — brother of Breuer's friend and frequent client Rufus Stillman — wanted four bedrooms and a larger public area for his family, so Breuer widened the house to 18 feet and made it seven bays long with,

Opposite and this page: Breuer's Stillman House (1953) is a larger version of his prototype and, unlike the Breuer and Kepes houses, sat exposed to the elements on a bayside dune. Breuer painted one end of the house red orange, as if to celebrate its sunny site. The living room features a built-in dining table with a curved, boatlike shape. Accent colors on the interior and exterior walls include cobalt blue ("Breuer blue"), blue gray, and bright red orange. *Bottom right:* Edgar Stillman, ca. 1954, catches the breeze on the entrance ramp.

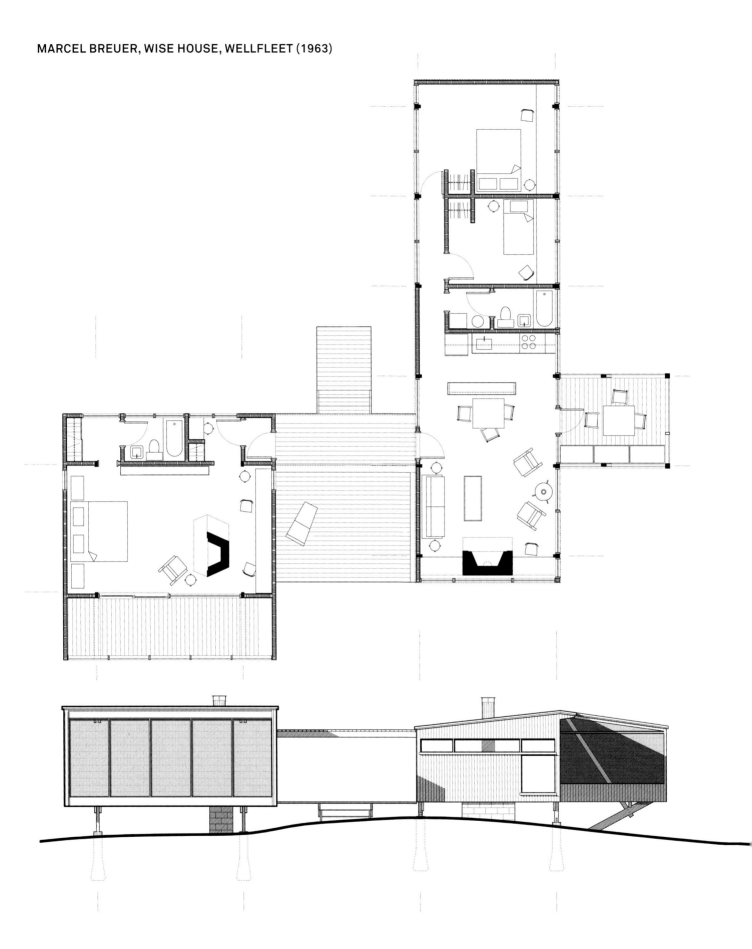

Opposite, top: The plan is a mirror image of Breuer's newly expanded (in 1962) Wellfleet house. Breuer added to both the Wise House and his own once more, to make another bedroom and bath on the far side of the studio. *Opposite, bottom*: South elevation. *Above*: View from the southeast showing main house (right) and studio building. *Right*: The house is sited on a peninsula that projects into Wellfleet Harbor and the surrounding marsh.

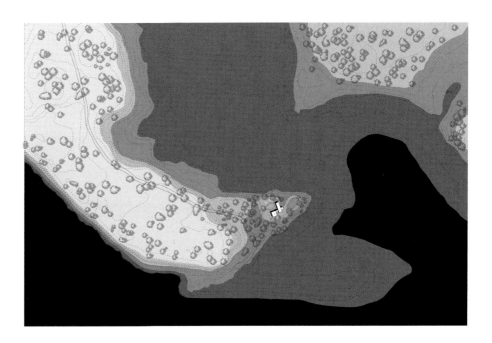

again, a 2-foot cantilever on each end. A center hallway leads to the children's narrow bedrooms and terminates, as usual, in the master bedroom. Here, the screened porch is two bays, or 20 feet, wide, with another open deck module alongside it. A bridgelike entry ramp features wood railings hung on cables stretched from the eaves, recalling the spars of a sailboat. The exposed site called for steel rods X-bracing the pilings to withstand the wind load and extended roof overhangs to block the sun's glare. Perhaps in celebration of the starkly sunny site — so different from his own wooded acres — Breuer painted an exterior end wall reddish orange, a long exterior wall deep blue, and several interior walls in other bright accent colors.

Spanning hollows scooped out by glaciers, or dunes confronted by surf, Breuer's Cape Cod houses hover on their stilts like birds in shallow water, knowing they will have to retreat when the tide comes in. The Stillman House has, in fact, been moved twice due to storm-driven erosion, losing in the process its wood stilts and diagonal struts, its entry ramp, bridge, and porch, and its intended relationship with the landscape.

In 1963, Breuer was asked by Howard Wise, an art gallerist, and his wife, Barbara, an archivist and film curator, to design a house on an unspoiled bayside peninsula. By this time, Breuer was executing large international projects such as the UNESCO headquarters in Paris and the IBM research center in La Guarda, France, and was hard at work on the Whitney Museum in New York. He took the plan of his own Wellfleet house, including its recent addition, and flipped the whole arrangement into a mirror image to exploit the new site's topography and views. Though the Wises could have afforded more extravagant amenities, they chose the same simple finishes and frameless homemade windows and sliding doors that grace the Breuer and Kepes houses. An extension in 1972 added another bedroom and bath to the Wise studio wing, which mirrored the bedroom-darkroom addition to Breuer's house. In 2012, several important elements of this house were demolished and removed.

————————————

One of Breuer's last house designs was his third home for Rufus Stillman in Litchfield, Connecticut. The Stillman House III (1974) is essentially Breuer's own Wellfleet house with a few modifications, grafted onto a small stone structure comprising a retaining wall, a basement, two bedrooms, and an enclosed sculpture garden. With it, Breuer comes full circle from his Wellfleet long house, re-creating a flying rustic cabin where his old friend might feel the liberation of floating above the landscape.

Until the end of Breuer's career, his office continued to design individual houses while also working on more-lucrative commissions. They represented, "in a way, a laboratory department of our office. We can develop ideas and details for a client, on a relatively small scale, which we could not develop in a larger project."[54] Together, Breuer's houses show the workings of a profound and methodical mind: ideas conceived, then turned this way and that, flipped, and combined with the last inspiration until their potential has been fully realized. Breuer also drew on the affinity he saw between modern and folk architecture. As early as 1934, in a lecture in Zurich titled "Where Do We Stand?" he said:

> That the type of men who are described as modern architects have the sincerest admiration and love for genuine national art, for old peasant houses as for the masterpieces of the great epochs in art, is a point which needs to be stressed. On journeys what interests us most is to find districts where the daily activity of the population has remained untouched. Nothing is such a relief as to discover a creative craftsmanship which has been developed immemorially from father to son, and is free of the pretentious pomp and empty vanity of the architecture of the last century. Here is something from which we can learn, though not with a view to imitation.[55]

When he came to Cape Cod in the 1940s, Breuer found such craftsmanship in utilitarian fishermen's buildings and the small timber bridges spanning creeks and marshes. He seemed to tap aspects of the Yankee building tradition without explicitly copying them, by adopting, for instance, the vocabulary of masts and

The Wise House (1963) spans the rolling glacial terrain like a small trestle bridge.

The Wises hired Breuer to add a bedroom and bathroom to their studio wing, left, in 1972.

Stillman House III, Litchfield, Connecticut (1974). In essence, Stillman III, one of Breuer's last house designs, combines a Cape Cod long house with the vocabulary of stone and courtyards from his binuclear concept.

rigging, much as old Cape Codders built their houses from the planks and knees of wrecked ships.

Breuer and his Wellfleet builder, Ernie Rose, developed an enduring and mutually respectful relationship: Breuer insisted that Rose build all his houses in town, and their letters show that they worked closely to build simply and expeditiously. Breuer died in New York in 1981, after a long illness, and Connie died in 2002; their ashes are buried beneath a stone in front of their Wellfleet cottage. Rose died in 2010 at the age of 100. Remembering Breuer fondly in his nineties, he said of his former client, "I didn't know that he was going to be famous for something."[56]

OLAV HAMMARSTRÖM

It is tempting to define Olav Hammarström in relation to the renowned architects for whom he worked: Alvar Aalto, Eero Saarinen, Kevin Roche, and Walter Gropius. Kind, soft-spoken, and humble perhaps to a fault, Hammarström spent decades as a workhorse in the service of big firms and bigger projects. He kept Aalto company on late-night charrettes; tagged along on Saarinen's honeymoon with his second wife, *New York Times* art critic Aline Louchheim, for the sake of a commission; and helped Gropius design a Rosenthal china pattern. Yet he always retained the right to work privately on the side, to maintain some control of every phase of a project — the creative process he had learned as a young man in Finland. In addition to his little-known contributions to larger buildings, Hammarström left a body of modest works in the United States, including five churches and more than 50 homes. Committed to the welfare of every tree on a site, he created some of his most emblematic designs, including his own longtime summer house, for small wooded lots on Cape Cod.

It was Hammarström's talent for drawing that pushed him, somewhat unexpectedly, into architecture. Born in 1906 in Heinola, Finland, to a Swedish father and a Hanseatic mother, he grew up speaking Swedish (as did about ten percent of Finland's population), German, and Finnish, and studied Latin and English in

Olav Hammarström, 1952

high school. While working on a construction job, he took night classes in drafting, was recruited as a draftsman by a local architect, and, with that architect's help, won admission to the architecture program at Helsinki University of Technology — alma mater of Alvar Aalto and Eliel Saarinen, Eero Saarinen's father. Throughout his career, he had an enduring love of drawing: "I could spend endless hours on drawings, just to get what I felt perfect," he said in 1982. When he was a student, Finnish architecture programs included two years of general architectural history plus a year of Scandinavian architectural history — far more history than comparable programs in the United States offered. Exams required students to "draw a section of Notre Dame cathedral, or draw a floor plan of such-and-such church in England! You really had to study. . . . You had to show the construction, that you really knew what you were doing. Actually, I loved it." Students also had to measure and draw a historic Scandinavian building that had never been documented. Hammarström picked a Gothic cathedral in a small town near Helsinki, and found the assignment "a marvelous experience."[57]

Like most of his Scandinavian contemporaries, Hammarström was not a Bauhaus acolyte. Wood and masonry, not glass and steel, were his chosen materials. His modern moment came when the Swedish architect Gunnar Asplund directed the design of the 1930 Stockholm Exhibition in a groundbreakingly functional style, creating a rift between traditionalists and modernists throughout Scandinavia's artistic comunities.[58] "Incredible revelation," said Hammarström, "not only to me but practically for the whole group of my [classmates]. It was the first time we made a complete protest of the history" emphasized in the curriculum, and began to agitate for instruction in modern design. Hammarström began to design in the newer idiom, and won some student competitions. Some of his professors approved, while others "didn't quite understand it . . . it didn't go to their heart."[59]

Because he worked in various architecture firms to finance his degree, Hammarström graduated after 10 years with an ample resume. In 1937, he took a job with a Helsinki firm that was designing a new factory and miners' community in Petsamo, in far-northern Lapland, for the International Nickel Company. Thanks to his rudimentary English, he was appointed the on-site architect and spent six years in the Arctic. After building a series of bland, plaster-on-wood barracks according to plan, Hammarström said, he "started humanizing things." He designed two single-family homes, using wood and fireplaces to warm the interiors; and, in response to the needs of the community, he found himself building public spaces such as schools, cultural centers, a library, and a ski jump, all planned around the area's frigid climate and dark winters. "It was to me an intrigue and social awakening to see . . . how a community starts operating," he said. "I had no idea. The city plan was just a couple of barracks!" At one point, the British modernist Maxwell Fry, who would soon partner with Gropius, was brought in to design the home of the mine's manager. Knowing Fry's glass-and-steel composition would not work in the Arctic, Hammarström persuaded him and the manager to accept a new design. Forced to build continuously, with no mentors on hand, he developed confidence and skills he would not have acquired in a Helsinki office.[60]

In fall 1939, the Soviet Union attacked Finland, and thousands of Soviet troops made a beeline for the nickel mine. Hammarström and 600 others set fire to the entire town he had built. Returning to Helsinki in 1940 with "nothing except a dirty uniform and a toothbrush," he was greeted by friends suggesting he take over Aalto's office. Aalto, having designed the Finnish Pavilion at the New York World's Fair in 1939, was back in the United States as a cultural ambassador cum fundraiser for the Finnish government, and the three remaining architects in his firm had been killed in the war. Hammarström settled into the office and ran it for two months, mainly overseeing city-planning projects and never communicating with Aalto until several years later. "I don't think he even knew I was running his office," he recalled with amusement. After his own military turn scouting Russian positions for the Germans, Hammarström spent several years rebuilding the mining town, only to see it destroyed by Germany in 1944. With Aalto's recommendation, he got a government job in regional planning, but, as one of Finland's few surviving architects, he was overworked, psychologically exhausted, and creatively unsatisfied. "All the friends that I had who had survived the war," he said, "practically all of them died, either by suicide or drinking themselves to death. And I had a choice: I could have stayed there and done the same thing, but it just was a question of survival." He was thinking of quitting architecture when doors began to open abroad.

First, Danish architect Jørn Utzon — now known for the Sydney Opera House (1973) — invited Hammarström to join him in opening a Scandinavian architecture firm in Casablanca, Morocco. Then, while plans were laid, Aalto invited Hammarström to supervise construction of his first permanent building in the United States, the undulating Baker House dormitory at MIT. "I said, 'Absolutely not!'" Hammarström recalled with a laugh. "I think it much more fun to go to Casablanca and have my own camel, and Bedouins as building supervisors!" But the Moroccan project collapsed, and he was off to Cambridge in 1948.[61]

His challenge now was to learn the American building process so that he could liaise between Aalto and the Boston firm preparing his working drawings (Perry,

Shaw & Hepburn). Hammarström found Aalto to be an excellent draftsman who made not only conceptual sketches but also drawings for the builders: "He considered working drawings beautiful things." When the American technical staff turned Aalto's artworks into maps of mechanical systems, "Alvar was so insulted, he took it as a personal thing," Hammarström said. And, like his boss, Hammarström missed the Finnish practice of collaborating with the builder in a more fluid, spontaneous process. What was lacking, he said, "was to trust the builders. If you handed [an American building] specification to a Finnish building constructor, he would take it as a personal insult: 'Don't you think I know my job? Does every little thing have to be detailed like that?'"[62]

Hammarström was inspired by Aalto's creative process, but would have found it challenging over time. "Nobody lasted long in his office," said Hammarström, not because Aalto was difficult, but because he kept ridiculous hours: He rose at 11 a.m. and worked from 4 p.m. to three the next morning. His staff, however, had to be on site in the morning, and after dinner "you had to spend the night working with him again" because he wanted company while he drew and drank. "I had hours and hours of conversation with Alvar Aalto," said Hammarström, "but the funny thing is that they were all completely one-sided, because Alvar Aalto talked like a waterfall." When Aalto had an idea, "he immediately got it down on paper, a very visual imagination; he was just as much a painter as an architect. So he drew those fine sketches, and then slowly started shaping them up into buildings, or site plans, or city plans." Hammarström would start "fooling around" with Aalto's concepts, and so went their brief collaboration. Baker House was completed in 1949, although Aalto, having returned to Finland to be with his dying wife, did not see the finished building until the 1960s.

Hammarström now rekindled relationships with a number of other Finns. He had first met Eero Saarinen in the 1930s, when the young Yale graduate had come back to stay at his childhood home, Hvitträsk, the palatial house and studio complex designed by his father, Eliel, and two colleagues on a lake near Helsinki. Eero had lived in Michigan since 1923, when Eliel had been hired to design the new Cranbrook Educational

Community and then to lead the Cranbrook Academy of Art. In 1949, Eero invited Hammarström to join the Michigan-based architecture firm he now shared with his father. Meanwhile, Eliel's faculty appointments included his old Helsinki friend and celebrated textile designer Marianne Strengell, who chaired Cranbrook's weaving department from 1942 to 1961. As it happened, Strengell and Hammarström had grown up together, first meeting as partners in a dance class when he was eleven and she was eight.[63] Both now divorced, with children (Hammarström's daughter lived in Finland), they reconnected in Boston in 1948, married the following year, and settled in the Cranbrook community.

Hammarström and Strengell were extremely close to both Saarinens — to Eliel personally and Eero, professionally. "I liked Eliel very much," said Hammarström. "He was a very humble and warm-hearted man. He was a leader and such a strength in the field of architecture. He was small in size, and extremely well dressed in pastel colors, and he had this marvelous sense of humor." On his daily rounds through the office, the semiretired Eliel relished his chats with Hammarström, who alone appreciated his bottomless supply of dirty Finnish jokes. In 1950, Eliel Saarinen died while Hammarström was out playing tennis with Eero; after a friendly chat with Strengell, Eliel had gone home to listen to the news. "Suddenly, somebody came out to the tennis club and said, 'Eero, come quickly home,'" Hammarström recounted. "And Eliel had died falling asleep in Eero's chair, in a big Womb chair, so it was an ideal death, in a way."[64]

After Eliel's passing, the tenor at the Saarinen office changed. Hammarström once admitted that he had not enjoyed skiing with Eero in Finland; the younger Saarinen was so obsessed with proper technique that outings soon grew tedious. The presence of his father in the office had relaxed him, but as Eero's visibility grew, so did his competitive instincts. Hammarström found his work habits "almost compulsive" and his projects sometimes overdesigned, as if he didn't know when to stop chasing perfection — often "he had something very good and then he started again almost from scratch," Hammarström lamented. Still, Hammarström was one of the best friends of this famously driven man with few intimates. "Eero was not an intellectual, but a brilliant designer," Hammarström said, "and that's maybe why I felt quite close to him, because he dealt very much by intuition."[65]

Hammarström worked primarily on Saarinen's massive General Motors Technical Center, spending much of his time on the Central Restaurant (1954). "Eero realized that I was more or less a loner," he said, "so he left me practically all alone in designing the restaurant building." That said, in the two-year course of the project, Hammarström spent three months arguing with Eero about "dimension and proportion and trim and so forth" on a single glass-and-steel elevation. Saarinen clearly valued his opinion. At one point, Hammarström recalled,

> We had an argument about the handrail to a short stair in the sitting area in the restaurant, and Eero had one idea and I had another idea, and I felt mine was very good so I tried to fight, and Eero finally said, "No, this is it." And when it was all built, Eero looked at the handrail and said, "How did we get this handrail?" And I said, "You insisted on it!" And he said to me: "You should have fought harder! Why didn't you fight for it?"

To soften the building's stark lines, the architects found old trees elsewhere on the site and moved them near the facade at a cost of about $1,000 each. For the interior, Hammarström oversaw the creation of a spectacular, 36-foot-long metal screen of interlocking rectangles, by the sculptor and furniture designer Harry Bertoia, to separate the lobby from the lake-view restaurant without walling it off. The restaurant "became an awfully handsome building," he said, and won the AIA Honor Award in 1955. Hammarström also worked on the Engineering, Research, and Styling buildings and made presentation drawings for General Motors, detailing the landscape even on such a flat industrial site; he sketched trees in different colors and emphasized the central reflecting pool.[66]

While these Finns were establishing themselves in the United States, they were quietly discovering the same place to relax. Aalto visited Cape Cod on at least two occasions, in 1940 and 1946. His colleague Veli Paatela, who worked on Baker House at MIT, recalled the latter trip as one of Aalto's countless sources of inspiration for architectural forms: "Once, when we were on a beach on Cape Cod, by the Atlantic, Alvar and I were going to go for a swim, [and] Alvar suddenly stopped. The waves had washed in a few coral onto the sand and Alvar stood there and said: 'I'm just filming this into my memory.' The shape was interesting to him and he stored it in his memory. You could see from his sketches that he had a large store of shapes stored in his mind."[67]

Hammarström first came to Cape Cod at the invitation of Strengell, who had visited Eliel Saarinen and his wife, Loja, when they stayed at the waterfront Belmont Hotel in West Harwich. Her third trip, in 1948, was to Wellfleet, inspired by snapshots taken by an architect at Skidmore, Owings & Merrill, New York, where she consulted on a textile project. Determined to see what looked like a "very, very nice place," she and a friend picked up Hammarström in Boston and drove out to stay in the "little, little house" she had rented. In 1949, after another academic year at Cranbrook, she and Hammarström were married in Wellfleet, and within another year they had bought land with an ocean view — a breezy, secluded site near Newcomb Hollow Beach.[68] Freed from the constraints of corporate work, and granted the kind of wooded setting so central to most Finns' identities, Hammarström now began sketching the first of the 57 houses he would design over the next 25 years.

HAMMARSTRÖM HOUSE (1952)

Hammarström was a passionate nature lover, but not until his late forties, when he and Strengell established a summer foothold on Cape Cod, did he get the chance to design a building around its landscape. The couple took to the Cape, he said, "maybe partly because we remembered certain areas in Finland where [we] had lived, with dunes and pine trees." He mapped the key trees on his Wellfleet site, made pastel topographical drawings of the land, and situated his house so that it displaced only one tree. He then wove a long dirt driveway through the woods without felling any trees at all. He later said, "I often choose the poorest space on a lot to save the most beautiful."[69]

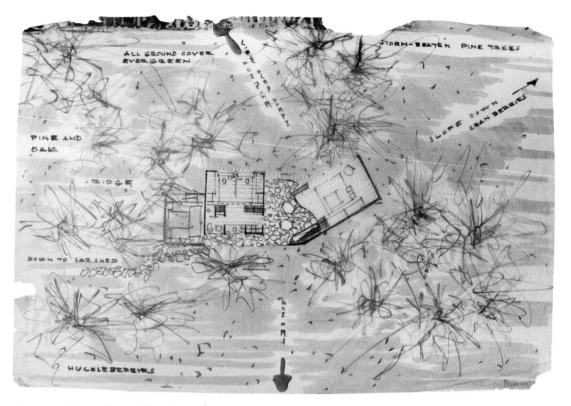

Hammarström made pencil-and-watercolor sketches of his new property, near Wellfleet's Newcomb Hollow Beach, as lovingly as he drew his plan for the house itself. He documented every natural feature, from the Atlantic sunrise to the huckleberry shrubs and "storm-beaten pine trees."

On the east side of the house, the ground slopes beneath the living room (left).

In 1962, the Hammarström House was published in *Interiors* magazine, where photographs by Ezra Stoller immortalized the brilliance of Marianne Strengell's textiles. A rarely closed set of sliding barn doors forms the main entrance, drawing back the curtain on a surprise ocean view. Another barn door opens at the back, forming a breezeway that connects the winter wing (not shown) and the oak-floored living room to the right.

Hammarström's fireplace, a triangular shell of sheet metal fashioned by an old shipbuilder, was among Wellfleet's best-looking failed design experiments—it filled the room with smoke. Burlap covers the wall behind the fireplace; the sling chairs are Hammarström's design.

OLAV HAMMARSTRÖM, HAMMARSTRÖM HOUSE, WELLFLEET (1952)

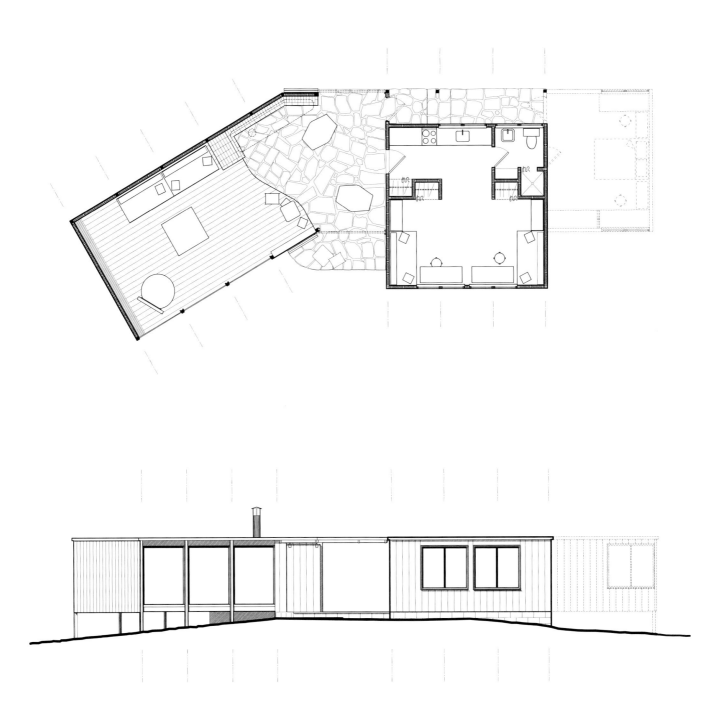

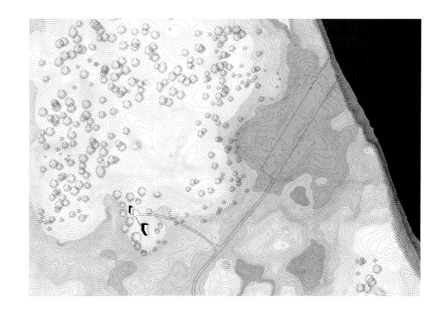

Opposite, top: The heated, off-season part of the house (center) holds all of the plumbing. The summer living area (left) is connected by the roofed breezeway. A master-bedroom addition (right) was completed soon after initial construction. *Opposite, bottom*: East elevation. *Above*: View from the southeast. *Right*: The Atlantic is to the east.

Clad in spruce stained dark with creosote, Hammarström's house blends quietly with the bark of the pitch pines around it. Although it occupies a high point for an ocean view, the house is nearly invisible on the approach, a shadowy presence amid pines, scrub oaks, and berry shrubs at the end of a long, bending flagstone path from the driveway. The house has two sections, angled at around 35 degrees to each other — in addition to saving trees, Hammarström designed the house to follow the ridge of the hilltop and grab the water view for the living room. Joining the two sections is a breezeway that became a Hammarström signature: tiled with irregular flagstones, it opens on both sides with enormous, sliding barn doors, forming a roofed outdoor room and allowing the slate to flow out the back door to form a small patio. "What we achieved was a very close relationship to the ground," he said. The breezeway floor "was level with the lingonberries and cranberries, all over on both sides, so you barely knew if you were inside or outside." The Hammarströms rarely closed the barn doors, so, according to *Interiors* magazine, "small animals and breeze-borne bees, flies, low-lying clouds, and forest scents move unimpeded" through the house.[70]

In the summer, you enter the house by wandering into the breezeway. At that moment, the ocean bursts into view through the living-room window — or, at least, it did in Hammarström's day, before trees obscured it. The breezeway wanders over to the fireplace, forming a natural hearth, and ends at a foot-high step — sinuously curved in a gentle S shape across the room — up to the oak-floored living room. Stepping up to the living room, in contrast to the breezeway, "you had your view over the ocean, [but] this was closed in," said Hammarström. "I think [it] a good feeling also to have it closed in, and not open all over the place." With the dark-stained beams exposed overhead, the room feels sheltered despite the dominant wall of glass; Hammarström compared it to a womb. At the room's far end, a floor vent pulled in air because the windows did not open (fixed windows were more affordable than sliding glass doors). When the breeze got too cold, the vent was covered with one of Strengell's thick, vividly colored shag rugs.[71]

Hammarström and Strengell called the breezeway and living room the "summer room" — set partly on stilts,

with the ground sloping gently down below, it could only be used in warm weather.[72] The other half of the house was winterized, with a concrete foundation. Like Breuer, Hammarström used his living-room stilts, on concrete footings, as posts supporting the roof. Unlike Breuer, however, he covered his interior walls with Homasote and, on the display wall behind the living-room couch, burlap. Totaling a snug 900 square feet, the house was made almost entirely of lumberyard materials.

Hammarström's fireplace, with its open brick base and dramatic, triangular sheet-metal hood — made by an old shipbuilder — is a perfect example of how the Cape Cod modernists played with ideas in their own summer homes. Opening to the slate floor while reaching up to the hardwood, it defined the transition between the breezeway and the living room, but "it was a complete gamble, because it was against all the rules how to build a fireplace," admitted Hammarström. "This . . . very broad fireplace and very short chimney didn't work too well, to put it frankly, because in the breezeway, you had to have those side doors closed, otherwise you got too much air in, so you got smoke into the room. . . . It was a thing I would never do for a client, but I could do it for myself [as an] experimental thing, and see how it worked." Another failure was the original 12-inch tongue-and-groove spruce vertical siding; the boards shrank and warped, leading to water damage indoors.[73]

In 1951, Hammarström and Strengell spent the summer in the Philippines, where a U.S. government agency had invited Strengell to help revive weaving as a cottage industry. Their Asian experience, which included study trips to Japan, shows in their Wellfleet house: they sometimes dined with friends on a low table in the living room, seated on the rug or on Strengell's cushions. Below the living room, on the ground between the stilts, Hammarström installed spotlights to illuminate the trees outside. "They had an incredible effect," he said. "For when you have stronger light outside than inside, you have no reflections in the glass window, so [there's an] even stronger feeling between indoors and outside during the night. . . . You think you're sitting right in the trees. It was just beautiful." In the living room, the couple lit only candles. *Interiors* called the scene "pleasantly eerie."

Hammarström's Saarinen House, Wellfleet (1960), **photographed by Eric Saarinen from Herring Pond**

Hammarström designed all of the furniture in the house, much of it plywood that could be assembled by the builder with a hammer and nails. To speed house-cleaning, all beds and tables are cantilevered, legless, from the wall. Hammarström liked to spend his maintenance time outdoors, where he pruned his trees and berry bushes. "I had a glorious time in a simple house," he recalled happily.[74]

Soon after the house was built, Hammarström added a small studio and guest house near the driveway, and extended the winter part of the house. But after he and Strengell — like the Chermayeffs — retired and moved permanently to the Cape in the 1970s, they sold their beloved retreat when the long, snowy driveway and other complications of rural life in the cold proved a challenge. They bought a Cape near Wellfleet center and never went back to visit, preferring to remember the house as they had made it.

Hammarström left Saarinen in 1954 to work independently. Once he became known in Wellfleet, clients all over the Cape commissioned him to design summer homes and art studios; and so, in addition to houses elsewhere in the country, he designed almost one house a year on the Cape for the next 20 years. Some themes emerged — Hammarström exposed his framing indoors for both efficiency and intimacy; exposed the rafter tails under the eaves; and kept interior lighting to a minimum, emphasizing natural and indirect lighting. One such house was for Lily Swann Saarinen, who was married to Eero Saarinen from 1939 to 1953. Swann, an award-winning sculptor, was a member of the first U.S. women's Olympic ski team, in 1936, and met Saarinen while studying at Cranbrook soon after. With the name "Saarinen" carved into the requisite wooden sign nailed to a tree on the approaching road — the same rutted sand track that leads to Breuer's and Chermayeff's properties — Hammarström's Saarinen

The breezeway frames the pond and served as an outdoor sculpture studio.

House (1960) has fooled many an enthusiast into thinking Eero Saarinen had something to do with it.

Like so many Cape modern houses, this one — built by Hayden Walling — is defined by its dramatic site, and incorporates an older structure into its design. Perched on a steep drop, it is, like Hammarström's own house, arranged for a surprise water view: as you walk downhill from the parking area toward the house, a flagstone breezeway frames a tantalizing glimpse of Herring Pond. The breezeway, which doubled as Swann Saarinen's sculpture studio, leads out to an expansive deck built of 2-by-4's set on stilts over the slope. Nestled among old

trees — and wrapped around a black locust — the deck is a deeply intimate space floating high above the pond.

"I love the *site*," said Susan Saarinen, daughter of Lily and Eero. The house "fits into this landscape gently. . . . Finns tend to be very sensitive about working with the land, siting brilliantly, so that [the house] fits whatever the lay of the land is."

Hammarström's composition is a low-slung structure attached to an old, one-room fishing cabin with a steeply pitched gable roof. (In homage to the grayish bark of the nearby locust trees, Hammarström applied an opaque driftwood stain to the siding, rather than the

Off of the unheated guest suite, Hammarström built the deck around the trees. Siding on the railings provides some visual privacy.

creosote he used when building near pines.) Inside, he removed one wall of the fishing cabin and turned it into a cozy gathering space that flows easily into the new house. Hammarström worked with "the wonderful idea of starting in the dark, solid living room and then having the house open up to the pond with the deck. That was one thing that my mother wanted," said Saarinen. Running a wall of four sliding glass doors along the pond side of the living room and kitchen, he drew the plan so that even those seated in the old cabin can see Herring Pond. "Nature is part of our everyday experience" in the house, said Saarinen. "It is so *there* and so visible."[75]

That same year, near Newcomb Hollow, not far from his own house, Hammarström designed a cottage for the Hungarian couple László and Vera Tisza — he an MIT physics professor known for his pioneering work with liquid helium, she a child psychiatrist. Here, by putting patios and walls of sliding glass doors on either side of the living room, Hammarström made the entire living space a giant breezeway. The Tisza House (1960) is now owned by the National Park Service.

Hammarström's most celebrated Cape Cod building was the first of his five churches: Wellfleet's Chapel of St. James the Fisherman (1957). Commissioned by a summer-only Episcopal congregation, it was imbued with the vision of its larger-than-life pastor, James A. Pike, the famously progressive dean of New York's Cathedral Church of St. John the Divine and owner of a house on Gull Pond. Pike, who brought the congregants around to the idea of a modern design through stirring oratory, wanted a return to the early Christian ideal of participatory worship in the round. With the right house of worship, Pike would not have to look down from an altar; he could "sit together with his family," the parishioners. Choristers would not perform as a group on stage; they would sit among their fellow worshippers and lead them in song. The altar, or Holy Table, would be at the center of the sanctuary, not at the end.[76]

Working from the inside out, Hammarström designed a 58-foot square, capped it with a gently pitched roof, floated a pyramidal steeple on stilts, and placed its tip 58 feet from the ground for a pleasing sense of proportion. He arrayed the pews diagonally across each corner, situating worshippers "in the round" within the square plan — so, while the church seats 320, no one is ever more than six pews from the altar. The church is framed with Douglas fir and clad in vertical spruce boards, all stained with creosote. The dark exposed timbers and unfinished walls recall the inside of an old ship, and a giant scallop shell — the symbol of St. James — forms a baptismal font.

Inside, muted lighting heightens the contemplative mood. Under the floating steeple, Hammarström created an enormous, invisible skylight over the altar by placing 25 Vascolite domes, each 2 feet square, at roof level and directing their light down through a white wooden grid. He then ran awning windows along the floor, another light source that would be hidden from a seated congregation. Although he was not a person

The Saarinen House was published in *Interiors* magazine featuring this photo of Marianne Strengell lounging on the expansive deck. A wall of glass creates an indoor-outdoor living room and kitchen overlooking Herring Pond, and a locust tree bursts through the 2-by-4 decking.

Nestled among pitch pines at the corner of Route 6 and Cove Road in Wellfleet, Hammarström's Chapel of St. James the Fisherman (1957) was his most acclaimed work. Nodding to local building tradition, Hammarström clad the bell tower in cedar shingles.

of faith ("I had never practically in my life been in a church. I never thought of designing a church!"), Hammarström was inspired by the way in which Gothic and Baroque churches create mystery and a sense of remove from the outside world by hiding or diffusing their light sources. Of course, the chapel's doors could always be thrown open to let in light, breezes, and glimpses of the trees.[77]

A thrilled Dean Pike wrote to his parishioners, "In being more modern than some services to which you have been accustomed, we are actually more primitive and more ancient. . . . We are hoping that we may provide a stimulus to renewal of simple, realistic and corporate liturgical worship, not only within the Episcopal Church but in the Christian Church generally." The chapel was published in *Architectural Record*,

Architectural Forum, *Interiors*, *Woman's Day*, and the *New York Times*. "I am very satisfied," Hammarström told a reporter. "It gives the right feeling. It looks as if it belongs here. That is always the first test for me. It looks as if it has been here for ages."[78]

When Eero Saarinen decided to move his office from Michigan to Hamden, Connecticut, to be closer to New York, Hammarström agreed to rejoin the practice, and he and Strengell moved east. In the late 1950s, he made the presentation drawings in Saarinen's winning competition entry for the U.S. Embassy in London (1960), and grappled with a shambolic corporate organization chart to design interior floor plans for Saarinen's 38-story CBS Building (1965). After Saarinen died of complications from brain-tumor surgery in 1961, Kevin Roche took charge of design

All interior fittings, from the pews to the baptismal font, were designed by Hammarström and built on-site by local craftsmen. Hammarström chiseled the hanging cross himself, and stained it with gold flecks to catch the light from above; György Kepes designed the stained-glass window. Natural light from 25 skylight domes flows down through a white, creosote-tipped wooden grid.

within the firm, and Hammarström did significant work on the much-loved atrium and interiors of the Ford Foundation building (1967) and on the Oakland Museum (1968). Feeling unappreciated, he left; taught some courses at MIT and Yale; and in 1968 joined The Architects' Collaborative (TAC) in Cambridge, where he worked primarily on European resorts.

Gropius, in this last year of his life, was still active in TAC, dropping in every afternoon to consult on projects. Hammarström described his contribution as "clarity, mainly clarity . . . it was like a professional purification, to leave out everything that's not necessary." He remembered Gropius's critique of TAC's plan for its new headquarters at 46 Brattle Street in Cambridge, designed by

veteran architects who had worked together for years: "The first scheme was somewhat uneven and unbalanced, and he had all the partners together and he gave them a lecture like if they had been small schoolboys, he was so strong in his critiques. And they almost sat redfaced and listened to him, and then they ripped the whole thing up and started from scratch." Hammarström worked closely with Gropius on a Bauhaus-inspired tea set for the German china company Rosenthal, and found him "extremely polite, a kind of European politeness. It was 'Mr. Hammarström' and 'Mr. Hammarström,' up and down, bowing here and bowing there." Yet there was no room for error in the work, even from a master who, famously, did not himself draw:

In a drawing, he really required the absolute perfect line. . . . Whatever you do, it has to be so sharp and crystal-clear. . . . I remember one presentation drawing, it was the edge of a coffee pot. And you could not draw it freehand, you had to use various tools to get the sharp[ness], and somehow I had made a little, little [mistake] in the line, it was not bigger than the head of a needle. And Gropius: "You must have to correct this." You couldn't believe it — you could barely see it, but it has to be exact. But then he was very pleased.[79]

Hammarström was in his sixties at that point. Not all senior creative professionals would accept such micromanagement, yet Hammarström willingly played second fiddle for the overwhelming majority of his career. Clearly, it was his easy temperament, as much as his raw skill and work ethic, that made him such a successful colleague for so many of the twentieth century's greatest architects.

In the 1960s, Hammarström told observers that he designed from the inside out: his first priority was an efficient floor plan, followed by nourishing views. Unlike Breuer and Chermayeff, he gave each new house a new design; yet his method tended, by definition, "to negate the possibility of radical or innovating forms," wrote Harvey Geiger in a 1964 Yale dissertation. Susan Saarinen agreed but praised his subtlety, saying, "Olav's buildings tended to be rich in materials and spare in form."[80] Once again, Hammarström's humility may have obscured his contributions.

Strengell died in 1998 in Wellfleet, Hammarström in 2002. He said of his career: "I never even thought of what I'm going to be paid. I design until I am happy myself. Sometimes I feel it's funny that people pay me for something I love to do — really! I think it's ridiculous [but] they do it, thank God."[81]

PAUL WEIDLINGER

In 1936, a young Hungarian structural engineer named Paul Weidlinger finished his studies in Zurich and found himself, like many Europeans in the building professions, unemployed. Following a fruitless lead to London, he sat alone and broke in a Quaker-run bed-and-breakfast, coloring in O's in the phone book with a pencil. Suddenly he found a name with a striking number of circles, and realized it was a fellow Hungarian: former Bauhaus master László Moholy-Nagy. "So I took my last pennies to spend on a tube ride to South London, where he had an art school," said Weidlinger. "I knocked on his door and he hired me." A skilled draftsman, Weidlinger helped Moholy-Nagy with hand-lettering for custom advertisements.

Within a year, Moholy-Nagy was off to Chicago (by way of Planting Island, Massachusetts) to run the New Bauhaus. He invited Weidlinger to join him, but the younger man thought the United States uncivilized and Chicago a den of gangsters. So Moholy-Nagy suggested he apprentice with Le Corbusier, in Paris, and wrote him a letter of introduction. Weidlinger protested, saying the idea was "a bit like going to work for God" as he would have no access to the master. Moholy-Nagy urged him to "just breathe in the air, look at the drawings on the wall, listen to what other people say, it will be very important."[82] So Weidlinger moved to Paris.

By this time, Le Corbusier was such a celebrity that young architects actually paid *him* to "breathe in the air" of his office. Thanks to Moholy-Nagy, Weidlinger was allowed to work as a draftsman free of charge, moonlighting as a baker, a farm hand, and a spark-plug scavenger to pay the bills. Now and then, when money was tight, he slept under a bridge. Although Weidlinger did not work closely with the master, he found the apprenticeship rewarding. Le Corbusier himself had little paid work at the time, but busied himself with his Plan Obus, an aggressive redesign of Algiers that obsessed him for years and was never built. "I was amazed by what was going on there," Weidlinger remembered. "I saw things which I never heard about. People were designing cities! They

Paul Weidlinger and his future wife, Madeleine Friedli, probably in Zurich in the 1930s

Paul Weidlinger, *Self-portrait*, pastel (ca. 1930s)

were designing countries! It was incredible. It was wonderful to be there."[83]

Born in Budapest in 1914, Weidlinger studied engineering at the Technical University in Brno, Czechoslovakia, and the Federal Polytechnic Institute in Zurich, where he lived with a young Swiss woman named Madeleine Friedli. In 1939, after his apprenticeship with Le Corbusier, Weidlinger fled Europe as the Nazis encroached — Weidlinger's background was Jewish, though he never revealed this even to his own family — and worked for several years in Bolivia. In 1943, he and Madeleine, now his wife, and their daughter made their way to the United States, and in 1949 he opened his own engineering firm in Washington, D.C., moving to New York in 1951.

Soon renowned for both structural innovation and appreciation of good design, Weidlinger, with his growing staff, served as the structural engineer for dozens

of twentieth-century landmarks, including Peter Blake's Pinwheel House on Long Island (featuring sliding walls as well as windows, 1954); Breuer's St. Francis de Sales Church in Michigan (with hyperbolic parabaloids of cast-in-place concrete, 1964), his Whitney Museum (1966), and his federal Department of Housing and Urban Development (HUD) building (1968); Eero Saarinen's CBS Building (New York's first reinforced-concrete high-rise, 1965); Pietro Belluschi's Alice Tully Hall at the Juilliard School (1969); Edward Larrabee Barnes's Walker Art Center (1972); and Pei's Javits Center (1986). He worked especially closely with Gordon Bunshaft of Skidmore, Owings & Merrill on buildings including Yale's Beinecke Rare Book and Manuscript Library (1964), the Banque Lambert in Brussels (1965), and the Smithsonian Hirshhorn Museum and Sculpture Garden (1974). Filling the room with smoke from their pipe and cigarettes, Bunshaft and Weidlinger enjoyed

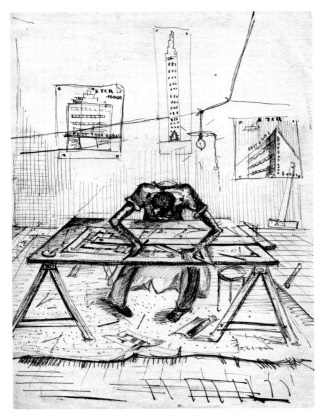

Weidlinger's sketch of a draftsman at work, New York (1940s)

Weidlinger at work in New York in the 1940s or '50s

arguing about the details of a structure in the making, overwriting each other's lines on a sketch.[84] Weidlinger also collaborated with artists such as Pablo Picasso, Isamu Noguchi, Kepes, and Moholy-Nagy on large sculptures and installations.

First renowned for his work in high-rise building and high-strength concrete, Weidlinger soon developed another specialty: structures that could withstand disasters, including nuclear explosions, earthquakes, and conventional explosives. In that vein, he consulted with the U.S. State Department on the designs of several embassies and on classified security projects in both the cold war and counterterrorist eras. And, after the most epic building collapse of our time, on September 11, 2001, Weidlinger Associates was commissioned by Silverstein Properties to analyze the buckling of the World Trade Center towers. The firm is consulting on blast-resistant security structures for several new buildings at the site.

By the 1950s, thanks in part to referrals from a network of émigrés including Breuer, Kepes, and Josep Lluís Sert, Weidlinger was commuting regularly to Cambridge to lecture at Harvard and MIT.[85] It was likely through the same group that he discovered Wellfleet and bought land on Higgins Pond, a short walk from Breuer's house. In 1953, Weidlinger built himself, Madeleine, and their daughter and son a cottage — his first realized architectural design. A few years later, he served as the structural engineer for Hammarström's Chapel of St. James the Fisherman.

WEIDLINGER HOUSE (1953)

From a boat on Higgins Pond, Weidlinger's summer house looks like a white box floating 10 feet above the ground. Like Breuer's own "camera on a tripod," it serves as a platform for viewing nature. Anchored on concrete blocks at the higher end of its gentle slope, the house quickly shoots out over stilts of increasing

The 4-foot-deep veranda wraps around three sides of the house's public wing, shaded from the hottest rays of the sun by an equally deep eave. The stilts below are X-braced for stability with steel rods, which were painted yellow. Weidlinger's living room features massive sliding-glass doors facing west (shown in top photo) and south. The fireplace, a near replica of the one in Breuer's nearby cottage, is slightly askew, giving the room an internal dynamism.

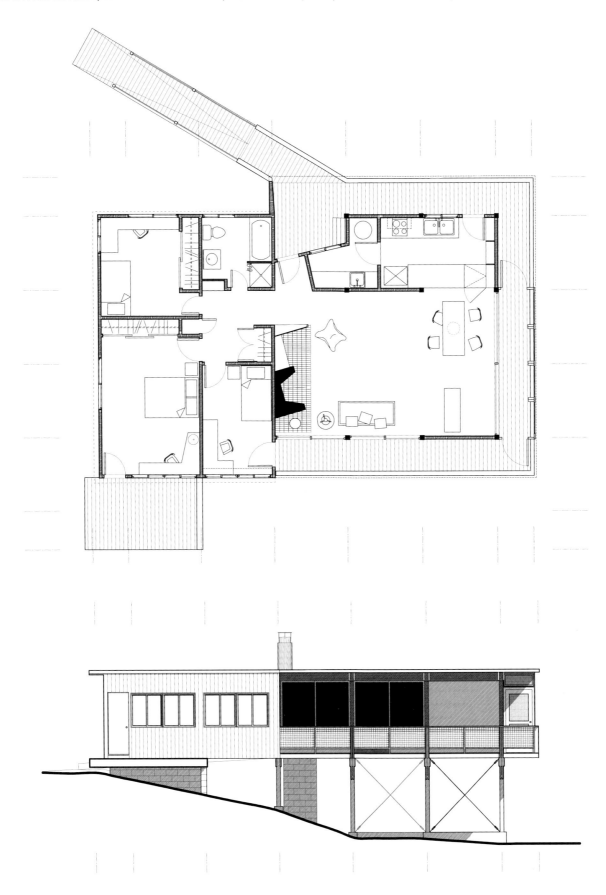

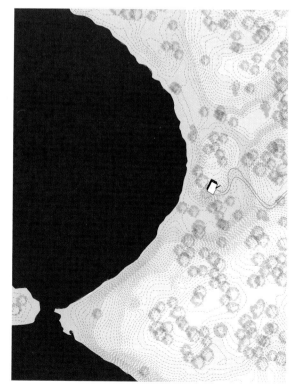

Opposite, top: The public area on the right is post-and-beam construction with a surrounding 4-foot-deep veranda. The bedroom area, left, is a more enclosed, stud-wall system. *Opposite, bottom:* West elevation. *Above:* View from the southwest. *Right:* The house overlooks Higgins Pond, near the sluiceway connecting it to Gull Pond.

Taking advantage of the slope of the waterfront site, Weidlinger anchored the bedroom zone of the house to the hillside with concrete, and suspended the living space on stilts as the ground fell away. Derelict for 15 years, the structure was restored in 2014.

Due to its elevation and a series of large glass doors, the living room has panoramic views of Higgins Pond. The door on the left in the photo above is 16 feet wide, an extraordinary free-span opening, and both sides originally slid open.

height until it appears suspended in midair, so that anyone approaching sees the pond as much as the house in front of it.

Weidlinger imported a number of Le Corbusier's and Breuer's ideas to this quiet site, including dramatic ramps, defined public and private spaces, and the use of color. The house stands pondside at the bottom of a deep natural bowl. The long, bumpy dirt driveway cuts diagonally down the sloping site in a steep but even descent, revealing partial views of the house below. The drive then twists to the left and ends in a parking spot under the house — a realization of Breuer's long-house prototype and a nod to the iconic driveway at Le Corbusier's Villa Savoye (1929). From here, a path up another slope leads to a wooden ramp that intersects the house at a 30-degree angle. This angle is echoed in the torque of both the entry wall and the hearth inside, creating a dynamic tension within the rational 8-by-8-foot grid of the overall plan.

Taking a cue from Breuer, Weidlinger visibly divided the house into public and private zones. Resting partly on grade is the three-bedroom private area, a conventional stud-wall construction wrapped in Weldtex siding. Painted light gray, this fir plywood sets off the bedrooms as a solid volume with punched window openings. The living area, in contrast, is an open post-and-beam structure with facade sections that are fully glazed or fully solid. Surrounded on three sides by a shaded, 4-foot-deep veranda for easy egress, this area is supported on posts that hold the house as much as 10 feet in the air as the ground falls away. Two 8-by-8-foot sliding glass doors face west, toward the pond, and a massive, 16-foot-wide sliding glass door faces south, protected by a screened section on the veranda. The solid portions of the facade, thick plywood painted white, act as shear walls to brace the heavily glazed assembly. Below each one, steel X bracing — originally painted yellow — carries its forces to the ground. A clear structural diagram, the house offers a glimpse into the thought process of one of the twentieth century's great engineers.

The steel mesh panels between the deck rails were originally painted yellow, while the exterior doors, metal chimney, and steel window and door frames were

As part of the restoration of the house, the steel railing mesh and X bracing were repainted their original mustard yellow and the doors, roof fascia, and chimney their original brilliant blue.

painted the brilliant blue favored by Breuer. The fire-place, too, is a direct Breuer quote: a simple brick box with an exposed terra-cotta flue.

"I loved it," said Weidlinger's older son, Tom, who spent summers in the house in the 1950s and '60s. "I think what was cool about it, for a young person, was it was like being in a ship in a forest. There was this kind of nautical feel; you almost felt you were on a voyage when you went up that ramp and into the house." Like Chermayeff's studio prototype, just two ponds away, the Weidlinger House is an unapologetic man-made object in untouched surroundings; it hovers silently in its still-pristine landscape. As Tom said, "I remember waking up early in the morning and it being really, really quiet, so you could almost hear your own heartbeat."[86]

In 1982, Weidlinger was elected to the National Academy of Engineering for his overall innovations and "outstanding contributions in the design of steel and reinforced concrete structures." Three years later, Weidlinger Associates received an Institute Honor from the American Institute of Architects for structural solutions, research, and computer applications that have "revolutionized building in America." Some of Weidlinger's creations have yet to be realized, including "super-strength" concrete; an air-supported fabric roof spanning more than 1.25 miles; and a system of submersible concrete cylinders to be built on land, floated out to sea, and anchored to the ocean floor with tension cables to support a floating airport.[87] Intellectually curious to the end, he continued to push the frontiers of engineering until shortly before he died, in 1999 — the year his American practice turned 50. His legacy is the ongoing work of his firm, which now employs more than 300 people.

Notes

1. Ati Gropius Johansen telephone interview with Christine Cipriani, Aug. 13, 2009; Guy Wolff telephone interview with Peter McMahon, Feb. 11, 2013; Hayden Herrera telephone interview with Christine Cipriani, June 10, 2013.
2. Alfred Kazin, *New York Jew* (New York: Knopf, 1978), 236–38; Edmund Wilson, *The Sixties* (New York: Farrar, Straus and Giroux, 1993), 105; Kazin, 239.
3. Powers, *Serge Chermayeff*, 7–9.
4. Ibid., 9–13.
5. Serge Chermayeff interview with Richard Plunz, quoted in Powers, 12; Powers, 12–13, 8, 15.
6. Ibid., 15–17, 32.
7. Ibid., 17, 41, 30, 25–28.
8. Chermayeff, *Design and the Public Good*, 15–16.
9. Powers, 43–44; Paul Nash, *Room and Book* (London: Soncino, 1932), 32, quoted in Powers, 44; Powers, 63–64.
10. Ibid., 103–5, 69, 71.
11. Peter Willis and Russell Stevens, "Earl De La Warr and the Competition for the Bexhill Pavilion, 1933–34," *Architectural History*, vol. 33 (1990), 139, 146; Powers, 75–81.
12. Chermayeff, *Design and the Public Good*, 19–20; Powers, 100.
13. Serge Chermayeff interview with Victoria Milne, quoted in Powers, 12; Blake, *No Place Like Utopia*, 10.
14. Henry-Russell Hitchcock, "An American in England," *Architect and Building News*, Jan. 15, 1937, 69, quoted in Powers, 91.
15. Powers, 119–120, 125, 129.
16. Ibid., 136, 138, 122, 132.
17. Ibid., 126.
18. Ibid., 145–47; Serge Chermayeff interview with Betty J. Blum, transcript, Chicago Architects Oral History Project, Department of Architecture, Art Institute of Chicago, May 24–25, 1986, 54–56.
19. Powers, 234.
20. Serge Chermayeff, *The Application of Colour in Modern Buildings* (Ardeer, Scotland: Nobel Chemical Industries, 1935), quoted in Powers, 104.
21. Norman McGrath telephone interview with Christine Cipriani, Mar. 27, 2013.
22. "Pennants, Bow Ties, and a Keg of Nails," *House & Home*, July 1954, 121.
23. Stephan Wilkinson telephone interview with Christine Cipriani, Apr. 10, 2013; Peter Chermayeff telephone interview with Christine Cipriani, Apr. 26, 2013; "Pennants, Bow Ties, and a Keg of Nails," 120–21; Ivan Chermayeff telephone interview with Christine Cipriani, Apr. 11, 2013.
24. Martin Tolchin, "From Rat Race to Quiet Art Gallery," *New York Times* News Service, Aug. 7, 1971.
25. Powers, 152, 207, 192; "Lilliputian New Yorkers Invited to View Exhibition of Tomorrow's Small House," press release, Museum of Modern Art, May 25, 1945, http://www.moma.org/learn/resources/press_archives/1940s/1945; Serge Chermayeff interview with Blum, 26–30, 37–38; Rogers quoted in Powers, 209–10; Ivan Chermayeff telephone interview with Christine Cipriani, Apr. 11, 2013.
26. Chermayeff and Alexander, *Community and Privacy*, 72, 146, 160–61.

27. Ibid., 95, 111.

28. Ibid., 67, 135, 204.

29. Serge Chermayeff, "His Studio and Cottage Involved, Yet Favors National Park on Cape," letter to the editor, *Boston Daily Globe*, Apr. 19, 1959, A2.

30. Blake, *No Place Like Utopia*, 15, 17.

31. Kazin, *New York Jew*, 237; Edmund Wilson to Elena Wilson, Sept. 0, 1946, in David Castronovo and Janet Groth, eds., *Edmund Wilson: The Man in Letters* (Athens: Ohio University Press, 2002), 147; Schlesinger, *I Remember*, 119.

32. Gropius Johansen interview with Cipriani; Powers, 10.

33. Tamas Breuer interview with Peter McMahon, Wellfleet, Mass., Aug. 24, 2012.

34. Quoted in Hyman, 40.

35. Hyman, 39–42.

36. Gropius, *Manifest und Programm des Staatliches Bauhauses*; Hyman, 47–50, 52–53.

37. Critic and architect Peter Blake, who collaborated with Breuer in the 1940s, points out that this hyperarticulation owed something to Russian Constructivism, which Breuer was known to admire. Blake, *Marcel Breuer*, 16.

38. Ibid.; Blake, *No Place Like Utopia*, 141; Hyman, 100.

39. Blake, *Marcel Breuer*, 16.

40. Walter Gropius to Marcel Breuer, Apr. 17, 1937, quoted in Hyman, 89.

41. Marcel Breuer to F. R. S. Yorke, Aug. 31, 1937, quoted in Hyman, 95.

42. Landis Gores to AIA awards program director, Oct. 8, 1980, quoted in Hyman, 100.

43. Hyman, 116; Pearlman, *Inventing American Modernism*, 115.

44. Breuer, *Sun and Shadow*, 32.

45. Marcel Breuer, lecture given at Sarah Lawrence College, Sept. 29, 1950 (Archives of American Art, Smithsonian Institution).

46. Tamas Breuer interview with McMahon.

47. Zsoka Borsody interview with Peter McMahon, Wellfleet, Mass., Nov. 11, 2011.

48. "György Kepes, Founder of CAVS, dies at 95," *MITnews*, Jan. 16, 2002, http://web.mit.edu/newsoffice/2002/kepes.html.

49. Gropius Johansen interview with Cipriani.

50. "God will forgive me, that's his job." Marcel Breuer to Walter Gropius, May 18, 1949, Bauhaus-Archiv Berlin.

51. Breuer, *Sun and Shadow*, 40.

52. Gropius Johansen interview with Cipriani; Tamas Breuer interview with McMahon.

53. Zsoka Borsody interview with Peter McMahon, Wellfleet, Mass., Aug. 25, 2012.

54. Masello, *Architecture Without Rules*, 8.

55. Blake, *Marcel Breuer*, 119.

56. Ernie Rose interview from documentary film *Built on Narrow Land*, directed by Malachi Connolly, 2013.

57. Olav Hammarström, oral history interview with Robert Brown, Oct. 21, 1982, Archives of American Art, Smithsonian Institution, tape 1.

58. David Ryan, *Scandinavian Moderne: 1900–1960*, exhibition brochure, Minneapolis Institute of Arts, http://www.artsmia.org/modernism/e_sm.html.

59. Hammarström oral history, Smithsonian, tape 1.

60. Ibid.; Marianne Strengell and Olav Hammarström, oral history interview with Mark Coir, Dec. 17, 1990, Cranbrook Archives, 11.

61. Hammarström oral history, Smithsonian, tape 1.

62. Hammarström oral history, Smithsonian, tapes 1, 2; David Fixler telephone interview with Christine Cipriani, June 6, 2013.

63. Eeva-Liisa Pelkonen and Donald Albrecht, eds., *Eero Saarinen: Shaping the Future* (New York: Finnish Cultural Institute / New Haven: Yale University Press, 2006), 324; Strengell and Hammarström oral history, Cranbrook, 66.

64. Hammarström oral history, Smithsonian, tape 2; Marianne Strengell, oral history interview with Robert Brown, Jan. 8–Dec. 16, 1982, Archives of American Art, Smithsonian Institution; Hammarström oral history, Smithsonian, tape 2.

65. Hammarström oral history, Smithsonian, tapes 2 and 3.

66. Ibid., tape 2.

67. Harry Charrington and Vezio Nava, eds., *Alvar Aalto: The Mark of the Hand* (Helsinki: Rakennustieto, 2011), 149.

68. Strengell and Hammarström oral history, Cranbrook, 67–68.

69. Hammarström oral history, Smithsonian, tape 4; Harvey Geiger, "Olav Hammarström: City Planner, Architect, Designer" (Ph.D. diss., Yale University, 1964, unpag.).

70. Hammarström oral history, Smithsonian, tape 4; "Three Houses in Wellfleet," *Interiors*, Aug. 1962, 55–67.

71. Hammarström oral history, Smithsonian, tape 4; "Three Houses in Wellfleet."

72. Hammarström oral history, Smithsonian, tape 4.

73. Ibid.; Geiger.

74. Geiger; "Three Houses in Wellfleet"; Hammarström oral history, Smithsonian, tape 4.

75. Susan Saarinen telephone interview with Christine Cipriani, June 10, 2013.

76. "Religious Buildings," *Architectural Record*, Dec. 1958, 138–39.

77. "Places of Worship," *Interiors*, Dec. 1957, 85.

78. Dean James A. Pike and Dean John Coburn, quoted in Geiger; Ivan Sandrof, "Adventure in Architecture," *Worcester Sunday Telegram*, Aug. 25, 1957.

79. Hammarström oral history, Smithsonian, tape 3.

80. Geiger; "Three Houses in Wellfleet," 58; Susan Saarinen interview with Cipriani.

81. Hammarström oral history, Smithsonian, tape 4.

82. Paul Weidlinger interview with Tom Weidlinger, June 1996; John Peter, ed., *The Oral History of Modern Architecture: Interviews with the Greatest Architects of the Twentieth Century* (New York: Abrams, 1994), 152.

83. Paul Weidlinger interview with Tom Weidlinger; Peter, 152.

84. Matthys P. Levy, "Paul Weidlinger, 1914–1999," *National Academy of Engineering Memorial Tributes*, vol. 12 (2008), 330, http://www.nap.edu/openbook.php?record_id=12473&page=330.

85. Matthys P. Levy e-mail interview with Christine Cipriani, June 22, 2013.

86. Tom Weidlinger telephone interview with Christine Cipriani, June 20, 2013.

87. Levy, "Paul Weidlinger, 1914–1999," 329, 331.

4

LATE MODERNISM ON CAPE COD

There's nothing left of what to us was Wellfleet. It was a community of kindred spirits of the avant-garde, a very genuine way of living — the best form of play for these very creative people.

— ATI GROPIUS JOHANSEN

In a sense, the project of the modern movement was to assimilate the Industrial Revolution: to make use of new materials and engineering without clothing them in historical garb. The Arts and Crafts movement, the early work of Frank Lloyd Wright, and many other proto-modern and early modern movements had struggled to come to practical and aesthetic terms with a world where the old order was being discredited and things had to be reimagined from scratch. The Bauhaus then sought to bring good, useful design to the masses by integrating industrial production with the continuum of traditional handcraft. The ideal was, as Charles and Ray Eames would later put it, "the best, for the least, for the most." Whether they drew inspiration from nature, technology, or mysticism, what all of these movements had in common was the rejection of both inherited wisdom and historical revivals.

Modernism would always contain this duality: the embrace of technology and the love of vernacular folkways. The two were famously juxtaposed in the Eameses' house (1949) in Pacific Palisades, California, a hyperrational assemblage of light, factory-made panels filled, like a toy box, with handwoven textiles and bright, playful artifacts from preindustrial cultures around the world. The steel factory window and the Inuit whalebone harpoon were both authentic, functional objects, designed without bourgeois pretense.

After its long struggle for acceptance in the United States, modern architecture was adopted most visibly after World War II by corporations, government, and universities. Though high-modern homes — such as TAC's lavish Murchison House in Provincetown (1959) — remained mostly the domain of a rarefied clientele, modern planning principles and design aesthetics trickled down to suburban developments in various forms. But by the late 1960s, modernism was the victim of its own success: it had become the new orthodoxy. Down-market Brutalist office buildings and Miesian strip malls blanketed the land, and a new generation of architects was discontent with the old Bauhaus-inspired pedagogy now ubiquitous in design schools. Technology now seemed to cause so many more problems than it solved — industrial pollution, mechanized warfare, mass consumerism — that an aesthetic born of technology seemed tainted as well.

Despite earlier attempts to homogenize the modern movement, however, the strands of its DNA were always diverse, and by the 1970s they began to unravel. Fans of the machine aesthetic built Lego-like superstructures with exposed mechanical systems, such as Renzo Piano and Richard Rogers's Pompidou Center in Paris. Back-to-the-land hippies, most famously in northern California, made rambling, handcrafted houses that looked as though they had sprung spontaneously from found materials. Firms such as Archigram and Superstudio,

Charlie Zehnder, Kugel/Gips House, Wellfleet (1970), west elevation

known for their influential but mostly unbuilt ideas, were inspired by such diverse sources as Buckminster Fuller, Airstream trailers, and megabuilding schemes, including Le Corbusier's plans for Algiers, in their proposals for conceptual, unbuildable cities and spaceship-like living pods. And the group known as the New York Five — Peter Eisenman, Michael Graves, Charles Gwathmey, John Hejduk, and Richard Meier, all enamored with aspects of Le Corbusier's early villas — designed small, complex houses, some more formal than functional, often accompanied by intensely theoretical writings. Its creators having soured on changing the world, this architecture looked in on itself; in 1973, a competing group of architects dubbed the New York Five "the Whites," denouncing their self-absorbed abstractions. Without a unifying theory, the generation coming of age in the 1960s and '70s took pieces of modernism's remnants and ran in different directions.

Remarkably, all of the strains of late modernism are represented on the Outer Cape: a neovernacular house built by MIT students, a purist gem by one of the Whites, a boldly original house by someone who had worked closely with Le Corbusier, and prismatic homes of poured concrete. Collectively, their designs made a striking shift upward, from long, low boxes to vertical towers.

MAURICE K. SMITH

Maurice K. Smith, born in New Zealand, came to the United States in 1952 on a Fulbright grant to experience the buildings of Frank Lloyd Wright and to study architecture at MIT with Fuller, Serge Chermayeff, and György Kepes. That summer, he came to Wellfleet as an intern to draft plans for Chermayeff's studio prototype. He slept in the Chermayeffs' loft bedroom with Serge's son Ivan, and drew in an unfinished work space attached to the family's rustic cabin. It was a heady experience: Kepes and the Moravian-American architect, writer, and exhibition designer Bernard Rudofsky lived nearby, and cartoonist Saul Steinberg and the Sardinian artist Costantino Nivola were frequent guests. Smith joined the group for many cocktail hours of lively debate. "Chermayeff, Kepes, and Rudofsky

Bernard Rudofsky, Serge Chermayeff, and György Kepes on Cape Cod in the 1940s

were very good friends at that time," he said. "They all grew beards in the summer, and all behaved very openly," with a notable lack of reserve around a student. Rudofsky was then writing a draft of *Behind the Picture Window: An Unconventional Book on the Conventional Modern House and the Inscrutable Ways of Its Inmates* (1955), which argued that American house design at the time was unsuited to human habitation, especially in comparison with the functional simplicity of traditional Japanese homes. "Rudofsky was the best part of that summer for me," said Smith. "A couple of times a week, I would walk over to his house, and I got to see some of the chapters of the book as he finished them." The following summer, Fuller asked Smith and two of his other MIT students (Peter Ford and Bill Wainwright) to help build one of his first commercially commissioned geodesic domes, in Woods Hole, near the base of Cape Cod.[1] For 50 years, the dome housed a popular, if leaky, restaurant; abandoned in 2002, it is now slated for preservation.

Many of the Cape's designers, artists, and writers worked in their studios until late afternoon. "Kepes had a sign that said, 'Do not disturb until 4 p.m.,'" remembered Smith. After that, people would emerge to swim, play ping-pong, and start the tea or cocktail hour. Aside from being the resident ping-pong champion, young Smith had the job of maneuvering drunk guests into a car and driving them home. Edmund Wilson, he said, was particularly hard to manage, as the portly man had to be hoisted onto a bench on his front porch.[2]

Buckminster Fuller supervises work on a geodesic dome in Woods Hole, 1953

Maurice K. Smith (holding drill) with other MIT students, 1953

Smith joined the MIT faculty in 1958 and stayed for 40 years, exploring his fascination with vernacular methods of planning and construction. By making careful drawings of the public spaces in medieval Andalusian hill towns, he discovered repeating measurements in the dimensions of streets, alleys, and plazas, and ultimately decided that they were partly dictated by the width that two fully laden donkeys needed to pass each other.[3] This exploration led to his concept of "habitable three-dimensional fields," which rejected the self-contained, sculptural works of high modernism as static and dead, arguing instead for "incomplete buildings" that are always open to growth. Feeling an affinity for the work of poet and Black Mountain College professor Charles Olson, who argued for a natural, "open form" in poetry, Smith wanted architecture to be fully participatory, free of hierarchy and restraint—to invite alteration by the user.[4] In his house

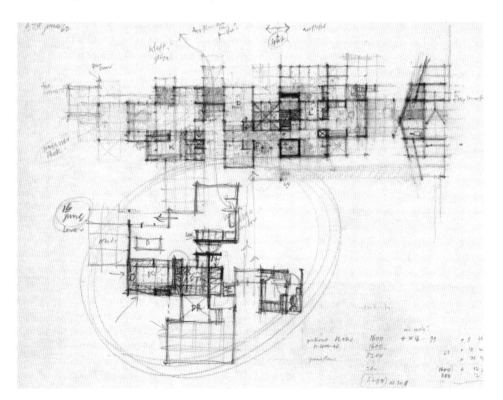

Maurice K. Smith, Blackman House, Groton, Massachusetts (1965), plan. Smith felt that buildings should be participatory and evolve with the needs of users. The plan suggests a flexible field into which the house could grow.

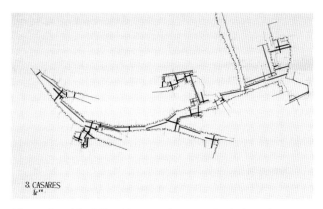

Dimensional Stability Diagram, Casares, Spain (1982). Smith scrutinized repeating units of measurement in small Andalusian villages to understand preindustrial planning strategies.

designs, this concept took the form of multiple levels, irregular perimeters, and a great variety of spatial experiences. Like Wright's Usonian houses, which were based on a repeating geometric module, Smith's were meant to grow organically, creating more space for the occupants as needed. Any visitor to MIT's architecture studios in the late 1970s could see the effects of Smith's theories: students built their drafting areas on platforms occupying multiple levels and planes, filling the high-ceilinged hall like a beehive in a hollow tree.

Smith's ideas found their way back to Cape Cod through two of his students, Steve Leff and Toby Hanks. In 1968, Smith gave the pair a set of drawings he had done for a low-cost house in Amherst, Massachusetts, "to get them started in life."[5] Hired by Brandeis philosophy professor Peter Swiggart to build a summer house for his family on a bay-side marsh in South Wellfleet, Leff and Hanks set up camp on the site and built the house entirely out of salvaged timbers, bricks, windows, doors, and fixtures. The result is a complex assemblage of cozy nooks and exciting vertical spaces. Every bedroom has its own tree-house-like balcony, set high among the leaves, and the multitude of shed roofs gives the house a chaotic profile. Some of the recycled fir beams rest on an irregular brick outcropping, while others hang precariously from another beam or platform. Although there is a consistent structural logic, each intersection of materials seems to have been invented on the spot.

Smith's design is an heir to both the colonial custom of architectural salvage and Jack Phillips's penchant for

recycled materials in the frontier days of local modern design. Despite their ad hoc appearance, neovernacular projects like the Swiggart House were serious responses to the reductive, impersonal qualities their designers saw in postwar architecture. Many students in the sixties were, of course, rejecting corporate America in general, not just corporate modernism, and for many, the formal, crystalline monuments of Mies van der Rohe and Philip Johnson seemed to combine the worst of both. But young people were, in fact, drilling down into Louis Sullivan's dictum that form follows function, trying to scientifically determine how built form is dictated by the day-to-day use of ordinary people.

Rudofsky, for his part, believed that people in the Western world had "lost their spontaneity and innate ability to design houses, clothing, and shoes that liberated, rather than restricted the body," and that "this cultural inertia had profoundly negative sociological and physical consequences," wrote the curators of an exhibition of his work in 2008.[6] Practicing what he preached, he and his wife, Berta, summered for years in a tiny cottage on Great Pond, a former Girl Scout cabin with no plumbing or electricity. Former neighbors say that he liked to sit out on his lawn and read the New York Times in the nude. As for shoes that liberated the body, Berta had been pressed into leading a class on sandal making when the Rudofskys were teaching at Black Mountain College in 1944. The resulting Bernardo sandal company still produces comfortable, elegant, handmade footwear.

Rudofsky eventually wrote a series of books on the irrationality of the modern American lifestyle, several of which inspired major exhibitions at the Museum of Modern Art. The most influential was Architecture without Architects: A Short Introduction to Non-Pedigreed Architecture (1964), a cross-cultural exploration of vernacular architectures designed and built by ordinary people. In a book that every architecture student in the country soon seemed to carry, Rudofsky argued that preindustrial cultures had found ways to make elegant buildings and towns in harmony with nature, available materials, and human needs, with no advice from professionals:

Maurice K. Smith, Smith House, Harvard, Massachusetts (begun 1966). The architect's own house, where he still lives, is a work in progress.

By invariably emphasizing the parts played by architects and their patrons [the historian] has obscured the talents and achievements of the anonymous builders, men whose concepts sometimes verge on the utopian, whose esthetics approach the sublime. The beauty of this architecture has long been dismissed as accidental, but today we should be able to recognize it as the result of rare good sense in the handling of practical problems. The shapes of the houses, sometimes transmitted through a hundred generations, seem eternally valid, like those of their tools.[7]

More than a decade later, Christopher Alexander — who had coauthored *Community and Privacy* with Chermayeff — published a book that, like Rudofsky's, became a bible of its era: *A Pattern Language* (1977). This thousand-page encyclopedia laid out what Alexander and his coauthors saw as timeless solutions to design problems at every level, positing inherently pleasing and functional solutions to, for example, the depth of a window seat, the organization of a sidewalk cafe, or the appropriate parameters for a cemetery. Among the ideals pictured are Georgian crescents and thatched Irish cottages; all images of twentieth-century designs are cautionary, such as that of a slablike apartment block with the ominous caption "Contact is impossible."[8]

It seems fitting that so many of the neovernacular modernists spent formative afternoons on Chermayeff's deck overlooking Slough Pond. Chermayeff, Kepes (who advocated for the integration of art, science, and nature), Rudofsky, and Smith were all, explicitly or implicitly, critiquing top-down formalism in favor of responsive, user-friendly design. The Outer Cape may, in fact, have been the perfect incubator for such ideas, offering a bucolic setting, a like-minded cohort, and the space to experiment with both brave new assemblies and beloved old cabins — often in the same building, as at Chermayeff's house.

Steve Leff and Toby Hanks, based on drawings
by Maurice K. Smith, Swiggart House, South
Wellfleet (1968), northeast corner

Swiggart House, living room (opposite) and dining area

CHARLES GWATHMEY

Begun the same year as the Swiggart House, but in stark contrast, stands Charles Gwathmey's waterfront Cooper House (1969) in Orleans, 13 miles south of Wellfleet. Gwathmey, on a tour of Europe following his graduate studies in architecture at Yale, was inspired by visits to Le Corbusier's villas and especially his iconic chapel of Notre-Dame du Haut at Ronchamp, France (1954). He set out to create the same kind of sculptural presence in a small building, resulting first in a 1965 vacation house for his parents in Amagansett, New York. Though it comprised only 1,200 square feet, the house's crisp, abstract form made Gwathmey, still in his twenties, famous almost overnight. The Hamptons became a proving ground for young architects, and the Gwathmey House a template for a community where, by the late 1960s, the idea was not to blend into the landscape but to stand out. The vertical reach, huge swaths of glass, and object-ness of these houses formed a refined version of Le Corbusier's 1920s machine aesthetic.

Like Le Corbusier in, for example, his Carpenter Center for the Visual Arts at Harvard (1963), the New York Five often began their houses conceptually with a cube, and then eroded, rotated, and enlarged it with extensions of the structural grid and with curved sculptural elements such as porches, ramps, and stair towers. Standing like pieces on a chessboard, they represent a clear break from the modern tradition of long, low houses resting among the trees. Gwathmey described his parents' house as "a solid block that has been carved back to its essence,"[9] and the observation also applies to the Cooper House: here was a formal language free of explicit vernacular elements except for the vertical cedar siding, standing in for Le Corbusier's concrete. These tight wrappers of unadorned wood over geometric forms harken back to Breuer's Chamberlain Cottage, but also, consciously, to the Shingle Style of the late nineteenth century. Although the Cooper House, at about 2,800 square feet, is much larger than its Long Island cousin, it, too, is roughly cubic and wrapped in vertical cedar, and fea-

Charles Gwathmey, Gwathmey House, Amagansett, New York (1965). The house Gwathmey designed for his parents is formally a cube with additive and subtractive elements.

tures a double-height living room open to a double-height porch carved from the building's volume. The master bedroom, which occupies a balcony overlooking the main living space, has roughly the same height and perspective as the osprey nests on nearby telephone poles. The living room is accessed by a ramp from the parking area and the garage below. Though the shapes employed are very simple, there is a complex interplay of interior and exterior spaces, and the house stands proudly on a fully exposed peninsula on Woods Cove, overlooking Nauset Marsh and the Atlantic just beyond, as if taunting the Cape's unforgiving elements.

Unfortunately, whether due to design or construction errors, the roof, windows, and doors in the Cooper House leaked from the start, and the house ended up foreclosed and vacant after the savings-and-loan debacles of the 1980s. During the devastating three days of the so-called Perfect Storm in 1991, windows and siding blew out and the sea flooded the ground floor. In the aftermath, a new owner enclosed the porch, boarded up windows, and painted the natural siding, making the house look less like a beautiful machine and more like the box the machine might have come in.

Charles Gwathmey, Cooper House, Orleans, Massachusetts (1969). A close relative of Gwathmey's parents' house, the Cooper House is a complex collage of simple shapes. *Right*: A view from the master bedroom of the living room, deck, and Nauset Marsh

Three early Zehnder works, photographed ca. 1960: left to right, Hesse House, Andrews House, and Cornelia House, near Ballston Beach, Truro. The Hesse and Cornelia houses were built, optimistically, after the National Seashore legislation was introduced in Congress and were later demolished.

Zehnder's Corey House, Truro (1968). Public spaces and a loft bedroom are on the right, connected to the long bedroom wing by an open deck.

An expressive sketch by Zehnder, experimenting with cantilevered trays

CHARLES ZEHNDER

Charlie Zehnder, like many Cape designers before him, never studied architecture. Yet he earned a living in the field and designed close to half of the Outer Cape's 100 or so modern houses, a body of work that chronicles a restless experimentation with form and materials. With their huge, ocean-view soaking tubs, their conversation pits, and their indoor-outdoor living rooms, his designs expressed a hedonism that often seemed at odds with New England's traditional austerity and now, in turn, seems part of a bygone age.

Raised in Newark, New Jersey, Zehnder attended the University of Virginia, where he once spent a formative evening talking with the visiting Frank Lloyd Wright. He then studied industrial design at the Rhode Island School of Design and, in 1957, after a stint in the Marine Corps, cruised up to Truro in an MG convertible. (Zehnder loved cars, boats, and planes, believing they were designed honestly.) Setting up camp on a bayside sand dune in Truro, he helped a college friend build a house, and soon he had bought some land, built himself a small cottage and studio, and found a clientele of primarily artists and writers.

Zehnder was a complex bundle of proclivities, a political libertarian and staunch proponent of property rights who surrounded himself with left-wing artists and intellectuals. He was also known for his generosity; more than once, when he had money, he spontaneously bought a car, only to turn around and give it away, just as spontaneously, to someone else who needed it. He was married for many years and had four children, but his marriage eventually ended in divorce. In 1957, he was a prime force in the creation of the Wellfleet Drive-In Theatre on what was once an asparagus field. He traveled to France to tour military fortifications; went to Norway to indulge an obsession with Vikings; and, based on his experience with aerial reconnaissance in the Korean War, searched aerially for Viking longhouses on Cape Cod. He believed he'd found one near Head of the Meadow, in Truro.

In the same vein, a cluster of diverse influences informed Zehnder's architecture. His first few houses were fairly simple boxes, and the very first — his own

home and office in Wellfleet, built in the late 1950s — was known locally as "the shoebox." Many of his subsequent designs overlap with the "modern" Shingle Style forged by Gwathmey and others: collections of wedges, cylinders, and truncated pyramids, all wrapped in cedar. But Zehnder's interests in Wright, Thomas Jefferson, and the hulking concrete bunkers of Normandy ultimately pulled him in other directions. By the mid-1960s, he began to refine a highly personal and surprising language including complex perimeters that often telescope down in area at one end of a plan; walls that lean in at a slight angle; and turretlike windows akin to those in medieval castles. Wright's influence is clear in Zehnder's use of broad cantilevers, deep overhanging eaves, butt-glazed corner windows (where glass meets glass), compressed stairways, and massive central hearths, around which his plans often pinwheel.

KUGEL/GIPS HOUSE (1970)

On the approach, Zehnder's Kugel/Gips House, in Wellfleet, looks like a collection of boxes that have been misaligned, as if jiggled by an earthquake, and then connected by a band of cedar clapboards at the roofline. Larger boxes, built of cement blocks, are connected by smaller, wood-clad boxes whose windows are butt-glazed, dematerializing them and heightening their contrast with the massive cement walls. There are glimpses of boldly projecting wooden elements, including a ramp to the ground from the larger of two decks, and a small projection of the roof that forms a canopy over the entrance. Presenting a closed face to the driveway, the house gradually opens onto tiny Northeast Pond and, beyond it, Great Pond. Around the exterior, the glass-and-cedar sections either protrude, making little bay windows, or recede, creating deep shadows. A pair of large beams travels the length of the house, shooting out beyond the eaves as if pulled by a magnetic force. Unlike most area modernists, who, starting with Jack Phillips, turned traditional cedar siding on end, Zehnder returned to horizontal clapboards to reinforce his long lines.

The house stretches out parallel to Northeast Pond to give all the rooms light, air, and water views. On entering, you get a momentary view of water before

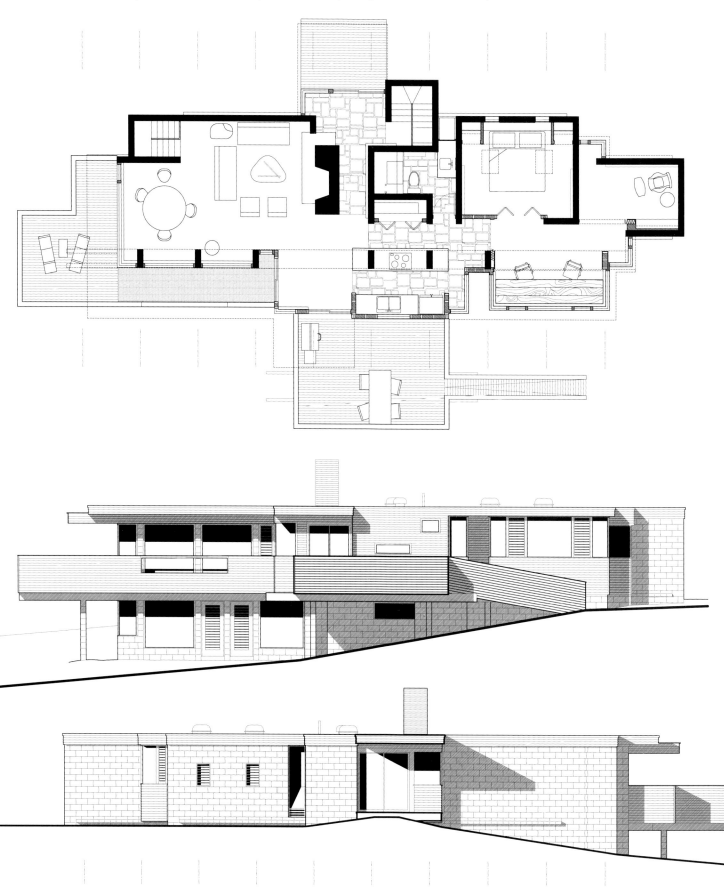

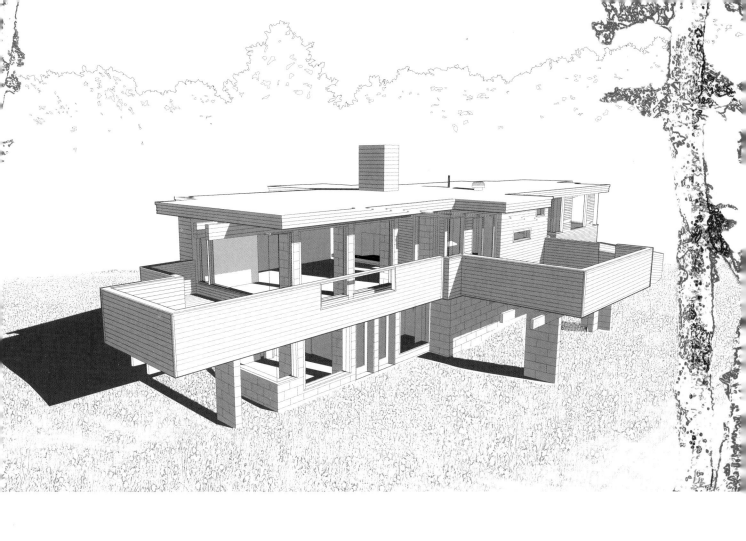

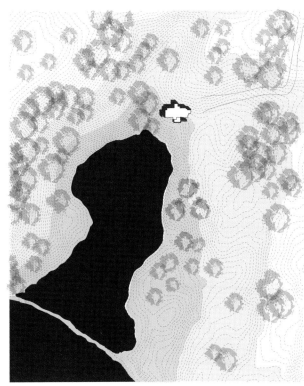

Opposite, top to bottom: Plan shows complex perimeter; south elevation; north elevation. *Above*: View from the southwest. *Right*: The house overlooks Northeast Pond and Great Pond.

Projecting cantilevers find counterbalance in heavy masonry walls dug into the hillside.

Viewed from the pond, the hovering, wood-framed volumes supported by a masonry base and piers show the influence of Frank Lloyd Wright on Zehnder's work.

Northeast Pond is reflected in a fixed window.

Living room. A long, rectangular hole in the deck rail frames a horizontal water view.

Kitchen wall, facing pond

The butt-glazed windows and enclosed railing create ambiguity about what is indoor and what is outdoor space.

The house telescopes down to a small masonry box at its eastern end, which one sees first upon arrival.
The front door is to the far right, beneath the roof projection.

The operable louvers on the nine jalousie windows continue the horizontal lines of the clapboard siding.

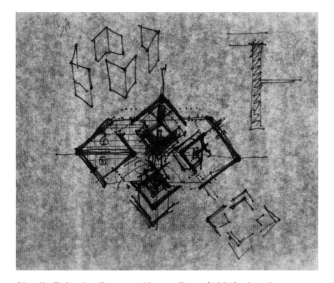

Charlie Zehnder, Pasanen House, Truro (1981), sketches

ramp very narrow — with solid railings, clad in clapboards — and both internal stairwells narrow and dark (one is only 18 inches wide), to heighten the surprise when again the view opens up. Though the structural language, the use of compression and expansion for dramatic effect, and the alternation of dark and light spaces come directly from Wright, Zehnder's subtle misalignment of walls and manipulation of views create a sophisticated experience essential to his complex and personal idiom.

Brutalism, the strain of late modernism named for its sculptural forms in raw concrete (*béton brut*), sprang from the later work of Le Corbusier and was explored intensively by Breuer and Paul Rudolph, among others. Though Boston has some famous examples, Brutalism is in short supply on Cape Cod. In 1977, Zehnder built a summer house in Truro for Paul Brodeur, a science writer and *New Yorker* staff writer, that defied all previous notions of a Cape Cod cottage: a three-story column of poured, unfinished concrete. The house is a tower with a square plan containing smaller square and cylindrical towers; in places, Zehnder carved into the sharp corners of the shell to create windows or reveal the inner volumes. The central spiral staircase leads past a series of small rooms to an open top-floor room that mushrooms out with decks that once offered views across the ocean and bay to the east and west horizons. Brodeur, who still inhabits the house every summer, his art collection covering its rough interior walls from floor to ceiling, wrote in 1986, "Living in a house by Charlie was like hanging out with Charlie himself: lots of surprises. Summer finds a shaft of light striking a wall in a way you never noticed before. A window has been angled to catch an autumn perspective you never suspected was there."[10] Zehnder's sketches for the two-story Pasanen House show a poured-concrete box exploded into four freestanding corners with wood-framed platforms bridging across, a bit like a hermit crab occupying the discarded shell of a larger animal.

passing between two masonry walls to encounter, suddenly, a panoramic view of the two ponds through a wall of glass. Perpendicular to this entry, the main path running the length of the house starts in a small, cave-like library at one end, proceeds through a series of spaces varied in their size, lighting, and materials, and ends at a huge window with a butt-glazed corner, where the interior seems to flow out to the deck and beyond to the forest. Paralleling this path is a procession of masonry piers, which support the broad planes of the projecting floors, decks, and roof. As in many of Wright's houses, including Fallingwater, the masonry mass digs into the hill, anchoring and balancing the cantilevers. In another theatrical move, Zehnder made the outdoor

The wood structure of the Pasanen House inhabits the concrete shell.

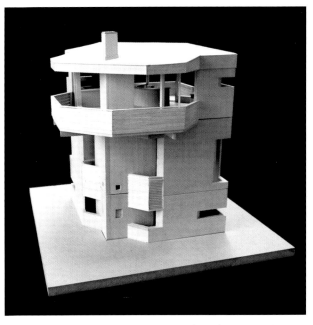

Charlie Zehnder, Brodeur House, Truro (1977), model. Slices in the outer cement tower reveal the two smaller towers inside, one housing stairs, the other the "wet" rooms (with plumbing, stacked for efficiency) and the chimney.

In his never-ending quest for inexpensive construction techniques, Zehnder worked with an off-Cape cement contractor who built parking garages; monolithic concrete structures were cheap at the time, stayed cool in the summer, and allowed for expressive details like small punched windows. Zehnder built four houses of poured concrete on the Outer Cape in the late 1970s and early '80s, a tribute to his clients' sense of adventure.

Zehnder deeply loved and understood Cape Cod, and had a unique vision of its potential as a realizable paradise. He seems to have been unconcerned with recognition outside his local circle of friends and admirers, but 50 of his carefully developed designs were built on the Outer Cape — roughly half of the area's significant modern houses. Zehnder died in a car accident in 1985. Budd Hopkins, one client with a concrete house, said movingly at Zehnder's memorial service,

> There was a pattern for many of us summer people. . . . After driving up to the Cape and unloading the car we'd turn on the water to clear the rust from the pipes, and then we'd immediately call C.Z. We'd be greeted in that warm, open-armed way he had, and then immediately we'd be invited to dinner, to one of his famous ham and hot dog and potato salad spreads. . . . One era is over but the next, historical era is beginning. In years to come people will drive to the Cape to see Zehnder houses, to study them and to envy the people who lived in them and knew their builder.[11]

Corners of the Brodeur House are cut back to allow for butt-glazed fixed windows. Beneath these, clapboards are affixed at an angle, creating space for air to pass through when an interior panel is removed.

The smaller central tower, in center of photo, was poured as a freestanding element and conceals the spiral staircase.

PAUL KRUEGER

As a student at Harvard's Graduate School of Design, Paul Krueger studied structural engineering with Paul Weidlinger and architecture with Josep Lluís Sert and Jerzy Sołtan, all three of whom had worked in the Paris office of Le Corbusier. For his only realized building in North America, Harvard's Carpenter Center for the Visual Arts (1963), Le Corbusier teamed with Sert's office to execute the plans and supervise construction. Le Corbusier asked Sert to appoint a project manager who was young, with no preconceived ideas of how things are done, and Krueger, then 28, got the job. He later described how Le Corbusier arrived with "drawings" consisting of watercolor paintings, with no dimensions and no mention of mechanical systems. Krueger was left to interpret the master's intentions, and, when questions arose, to wait three weeks between mailing his queries and receiving the answers from Paris. Krueger remembered that when Le Corbusier came to see the site, Sert and Krueger took him on a detour to show off the recently finished first phase of their Holyoke Center at Harvard. "Corbu was horrified by the concrete, which we had carefully crafted to look like his board-formed surfaces," Krueger said. "He said, 'The concrete should be as smooth as a woman's thigh' — so for the Carpenter Center we used Masonite to line the forms."[12]

Two years after the Carpenter Center was finished, Ed Mark, a young minister at the Harvard-Epworth United Methodist Church, came into Sert's office. He wanted to build a summer house on the Cape in the spirit of the Carpenter Center, he said, but he had no money. Krueger asked, "How much do you not have?" They decided that $10,000 could be found for construction, and that, in lieu of his fee, Krueger could spend a month in the house every summer.[13]

MARK HOUSE (1966)
The Mark property is a dry, heather-covered, gently sloping kettle hole in Truro. Krueger's design had two main references: fishermen's shacks in Provincetown harbor, with their rough board siding and half-submerged pilings, and Le Corbusier's Unité d'Habitation

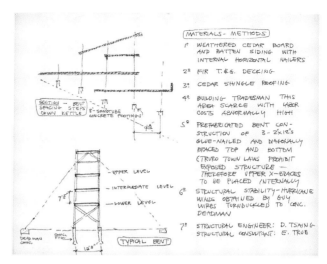

Paul Krueger, Mark House, Truro (1966), sketch showing structural concept

This model of an early version has diagonal bracing above the roofline. Since the house barely touches the land, entering it feels a bit like stepping onto a bridge.

(1952), the visionary vertical village in Marseille that stood on massive concrete *pilotis*. In that famous complex, long, narrow apartments expand to a double-height space with a balconied loft on one end — a plan that, on a Cape Cod hillside, makes the Mark House look like a freestanding slice of a much larger building.

Krueger's solution was essentially to raise a narrow pole barn (its piers continuing upward as interior posts), supporting three floor platforms and a long shed roof. Climbing vertically for exciting spatial effect

Mark House, southeast elevation. The battens on the siding visually reinforce the building's verticality. A Pullman-like sleeping box pops through the exterior wall just inside the front door (right).

and to capture distant water views, the house also creeps down into the kettle hole for privacy. (In an early version, the poles project above the roof with X bracing, but the town's building inspector thought that was going too far.) A mere 12 feet wide, the house opens toward the south for light, with nearly windowless side walls to block the winds; in addition, wind loads are counterbalanced by aircraft cables anchored to concrete deadmen on either side. You enter the main level of the house from a drawbridge-like deck, at which point you can continue into the kitchen, dining room, and living room or go upstairs to a loft space or downstairs to the bedroom.

To minimize disruption to the moor, the house barely touches the ground apart from its concrete footings. The rough board-and-batten walls, muscular timbers expressed indoors, and forceful, elevated sculptural profile make the Mark House a sort of wooden corollary to Le Corbusier's work in concrete. But Krueger also greatly admired Le Corbusier's *cabanon* on the French Riviera — a rustic but rigorously conceived one-room vacation cabin clad in rough logs — and replicated some of its details, such as unglazed windows with only bug screens and working wooden shutters. At the Mark House, he used shutters but covered the large south-facing openings with

Mark House, view from the living room toward the entrance

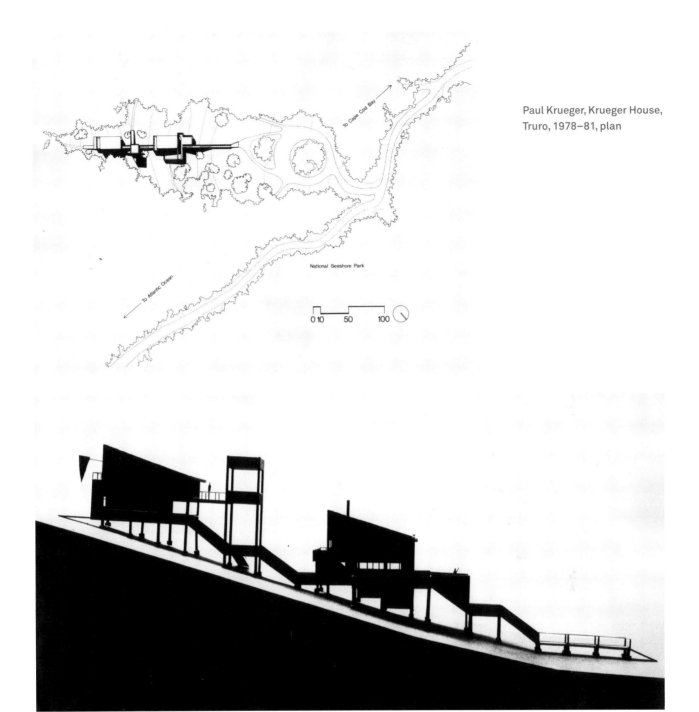

Paul Krueger, Krueger House,
Truro, 1978–81, plan

To Cape Cod Bay

To Atlantic Ocean

National Seashore Park

0 10   50   100

At the Krueger House, a circulation path connects a string of summer pavilions and living spaces.

mosquito netting, which was later replaced with bifold glass doors. Because Krueger insisted that the site have no driveway, only a narrow footpath, the two carpenters had to carry in all their materials, including heavy, 40-foot posts, by hand. They camped on the site and completed the house for $8,000.

The Mark House received an *Architectural Record* House Award in 1973, and in the late seventies, Krueger built a greatly expanded (yet still only 12-foot-wide) version of the design for himself. This narrow swath of indoor and outdoor living spaces, decks, and stairs travels more than 200 feet down a Truro hill, accommodating large summer gatherings of Krueger's family and friends.

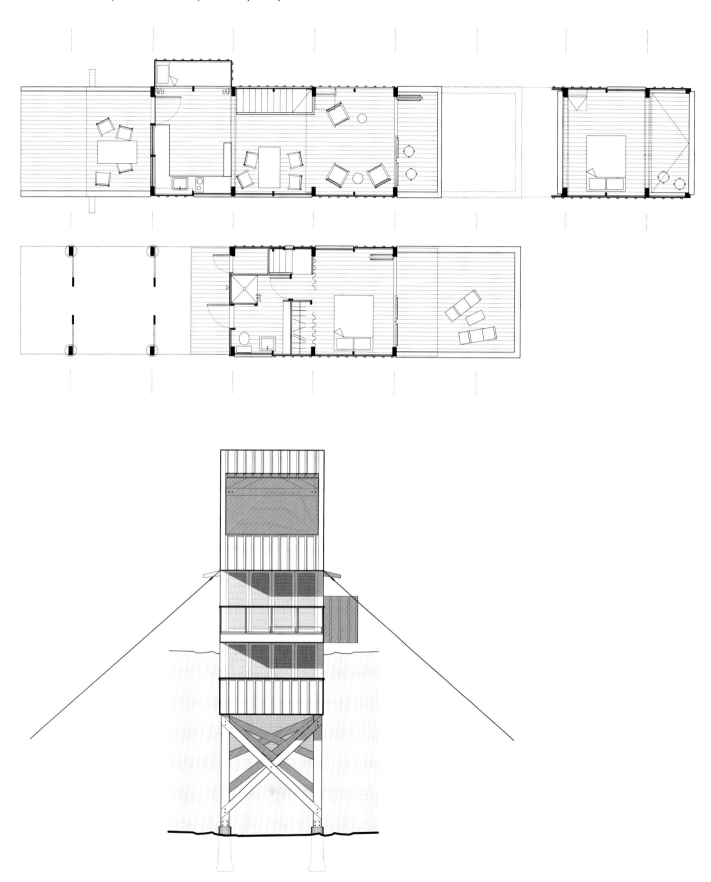

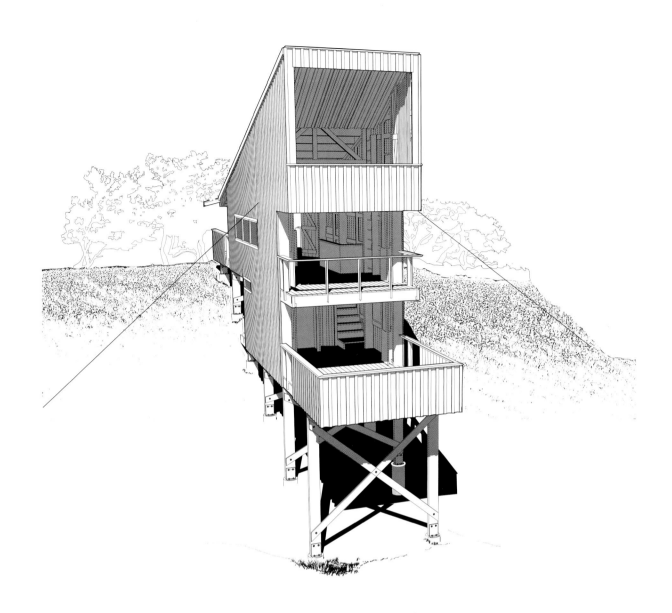

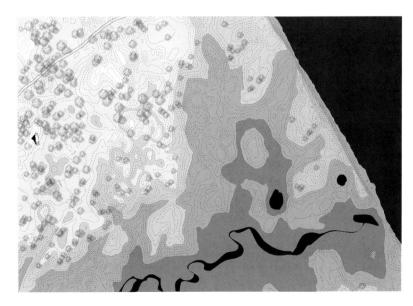

Opposite, top to bottom: Main floor plan with loft plan to right; lower-level plan; south elevation. *Above*: View from the southwest. *Right*: The house is located north of the Pamet River.

Opposite: Mark House, south side, with upper loft and balcony closed. *Above*: Ed and Joan Mark on their entry deck, 2013

The kitchen remains as built, with two burners, a sink, and an under-counter fridge. *Opposite*: The awning windows, made on site, are only closed in extreme weather and in the off-season.

CHARLES JENCKS

Postmodernism, a term used broadly today, was popularized by the theorist, critic, and designer Charles Jencks to describe the movement in architecture that sought to bury modernism — or what it had become — once and for all. In a vitriolic rejection of the Miesian idea of universal space — vast, undifferentiated enclosures of glass and steel — postmodern theory championed symbolism, irony, multiple meanings, and kitsch. Extending the idea of architecture without architects, postmodernists took great interest in casinos and roadside architecture, where a neon sign can carry more importance than the building to which it is attached; the resurrection of ornament on building facades; and the ultimate patricide, historical revivalism. The modernist ideal of the unity of form, function, and structure was thrown over in favor of applied layers of signifiers or, in the words of Robert Venturi and Denise Scott Brown, "the decorated shed."[14]

Jencks came to Wellfleet as a boy with his family, who, in 1939, built a traditional Cape overlooking the bay from Bound Brook Island. His father, Gardner, a pianist and composer of atonal classical music, and his mother, Ruth, were close to Wellfleet's literary community, so Charles spent his formative summers with the children of writers and modern architects; he even briefly attended the local elementary school. After attending Harvard, he earned a Ph.D. in architectural history at University College London, studying with Sigfried Giedion and Reyner Banham, and settled in England. In the 1970s, Jencks's name became synonymous with postmodernism in architecture when he published a series of extremely influential books including *Modern Movements in Architecture* (1973) and *The Language of Post-Modern Architecture* (1977), in which, through explanatory charts and pithy statements, Jencks framed the debate then raging between the old guard and the "pomo" insurgents.

In 1970, Jencks bought land on the ocean at the end of the long dirt road now lined with decades-old handmade signs bearing the names "Breuer," "Chermayeff," and "Saarinen." His own "new" house — an existing collection of three of Phillips's recycled army

Charles Jencks, the architectural theorist and landscape architect, owns this house made from three of Phillips's 1940s barracks units. Jencks mediated the space between the barracks and the crashing surf with multiple decks and ghost partitions—made of 2-by-2 slats, complete with "window" frames—that suggest a series of outdoor rooms.

barracks — stood so close to the shifting Atlantic that he has already had to move it inland twice. The pipe for the original well is now 100 yards out to sea.

Six years later, in the woods nearby, Jencks built the quintessential "decorated shed" as a studio. His Garagia Rotunda (1976) is an off-the-shelf, prefab garage overlaid with molding from the local lumberyard, classically inspired decoration made from cutout plywood, and a ready-made balustrade. The small, screened entry porch is surmounted by a widow's walk

Charles Jencks, Garagia Rotunda, Truro (1976), southwest elevation

View from pulpit to the rotunda

Entrance

with heavy crown molding. Another porch, this one open, has a roof of louvered lattices and a plywood oculus — the eponymous rotunda — which acts as a sundial when light beaming through it crosses the symmetrical linoleum pattern on the floor. The tiny building is a catalogue of references to Palladio, vernacular Cape architecture, and the natural world outside. Various components, indoors and out, are painted 10 different shades of blue to represent the hues found in Cape Cod's water, sky, and birds. In addition, as Jencks wrote in *The World of Interiors,* "Rhythmical harmonies are formed by the studs that support the walls. The standard 4-by-4-inch stud is used here partly decoratively and to underline the 3/9/5 rhythm of the side walls; the sides of each stud are painted in more saturated hues of blue as they approach the internal corner. This is to dramatise 'the problem of the corner' (for which there is no classically correct solution)." [15]

Jencks was, and perhaps remains, the most visible partisan of postmodernism in architecture, and his Garagia Rotunda may seem calculated to induce the maximum possible dyspepsia in the average old-guard modernist. Yet the building has much in common with its older avant-garde neighbors: like Phillips's Paper Palace and Chermayeff's polychrome Homasote cottages, it carries on the Outer Cape tradition of building one's own manifesto, giving form to big ideas using the simplest means possible.

————————

By the late 1970s, the Cape's bohemian culture had given way to an inescapable urban materialism, a subtle but fundamental shift in tone from the intellectual to the professional that began soon after Mary McCarthy published her takedown in 1955. Writer Phillip Lopate found the new summer social code stifling in an unexpected way:

> What I experienced in Wellfleet for the first time was a kind of real-estate obsession. People would get together at dinner parties and talk about who

was in whose house. . . . There was a kind of aristocracy: the people who had been coming a long time, knew Jack Phillips, et cetera, and some of it was just plain money, like you had to have a certain amount of money to be accepted in that group. . . . The bohemian ethos was celebrated, it was a legend, but in fact it was a very upper-middle-class game.

> I remember there was kind of a pond-versus-bay division, and [the bay] was considered not quite as elegant as the pond houses. It was like being in the court of Louis XIV and suddenly trying to understand what the rules were. [16]

Reuel Wilson, the son of McCarthy and Edmund Wilson, made a similar observation based on his decades of experience: "The urban intellectuals who didn't have long-standing roots in the Cape's sandy soil had, by the early seventies, gravitated to other vacation places. What then ensued was the 'richification' of our part of the Cape, with Mercedes Benzes and new luxurious houses replacing the jalopies and modest shacks of the now almost-extinct bohemians." [17] While the Outer Cape still draws urban intellectuals today, not many can truly be called bohemian. Nearly everyone wants a nice kitchen.

In architecture internationally, the colorful, stucco neoclassicism of the 1980s came and went rather quickly, but a lasting effect of the antimodern backlash was the redirection of public taste back toward historicism. The result on Cape Cod was a return to building houses that mimic traditional Capes, colonials, or Shingle Style mini-mansions. Today, the vocabulary of modernism is resurgent; but the syntax, with its emphasis on mannerism and spectacle, is a hybrid of the modern and postmodern. The decoupling of form, function, and structure, combined with the infinite possibilities of digitally enabled design and fabrication, have led to, on the one hand, unparalleled expression, and, on the other hand, uncontrolled form-making.

The problem for Cape Cod's modern houses, now historical artifacts, is that some have been a victim of their light construction. As experimental structures, designed in joy and built by a mixture of professional contractors and enthusiastic amateurs, they have not all been able to withstand the Cape's dampness or the horizontal rains thrown by nor'easters and hurricanes. Those that were not well tended gradually, and sometimes graphically, disintegrated. Those that were actually abandoned, after having been reclaimed by the National Park Service, became driftwood-gray ruins, a sight made particularly poignant by the naïve optimism of some of their designs. Like the Lewis Wharf theater, the Chequessett Inn, and so many waterfront huts and shacks before them, the houses are at risk of being reclaimed by the elements that inspired them.

Modernism is experiencing a revival in a variety of contexts — architecture, interiors, industrial design — for a number of reasons. Its social conscience and optimistic belief in progress are again relevant after decades of conspicuous consumption. The wonders of the Internet and sleek, minimalist digital devices have given people an intimate relationship with technology, for better or worse; and builders of small, affordable, environmentally sensitive, and prefabricated structures are treading a path well worn by the modernists.

It is significant that the southeast coast of Massachusetts was the beachhead for both the Pilgrims and the Bauhaus, even if encounters between their architectural progeny have sometimes been uneasy. Unlike their counterparts in Palm Springs, the Hamptons, or even New Canaan, most of the modern houses here were built not as showplaces but as hideaways, often invisible even to their neighbors, and the intervening years have caused a collective amnesia about their existence. Today, the idealistic intelligence of the Cape's modern houses has fresh appeal to a new generation of design lovers. For older visitors, too, the houses seem to rekindle memories of a time when such experiments were possible on a small salary, with few rules about what a house should or shouldn't look like. What has not changed is the appeal of Cape Cod — the dazzling light, the shifting sands, and, yes, "those damned pitch pines" — to the life of the creative mind.

Notes

1. Maurice K. Smith telephone interview with Peter McMahon, Apr. 7, 2013.
2. Ibid.
3. Maurice K. Smith, "Dimensional Self-Stability and Displacement in Field-Ordered Directional Alternations," *Places* 5:2, 1988; Maurice K. Smith telephone interview with Peter McMahon, Sept. 2010.
4. Maurice K. Smith telephone interview with Peter McMahon, Nov. 25, 2013.
5. Smith interview with McMahon, Apr. 7, 2013.
6. Brochure for the exhibition "Lessons from Bernard Rudofsky," Getty Center, Los Angeles, 2008.
7. Rudofsky, *Architecture without Architects*, preface (unpag.).
8. Christopher Alexander, Sara Ishikawa, and Murray Silverstein, *A Pattern Language: Towns, Buildings, Construction* (New York: Oxford University Press, 1977), 211.
9. Fred A. Bernstein, "Charles Gwathmey, Architect Loyal to Aesthetics of High Modernism, Dies at 71," *New York Times,* Aug. 4, 2009.
10. "Artists' Architect," *Provincetown Arts,* 2:2 (Aug. 1986), 17.
11. Remarks made at a memorial service for Zehnder, Nov. 2, 1985, courtesy of Budd Hopkins.
12. Paul Krueger telephone interview with Peter McMahon, May 8, 2013.
13. Ibid.
14. Robert Venturi, Denise Scott Brown, and Stephen Izenour, *Learning from Las Vegas: The Forgotten Symbolism of Architectural Form,* rev. ed. (Cambridge, Mass.: MIT Press, 1977), 87.
15. Charles Jencks, "Garagia Rotunda," *The World of Interiors,* Mar. 1983, 92.
16. Phillip Lopate telephone interview with Christine Cipriani, Nov. 6, 2012.
17. Wilson, *To the Life of the Silver Harbor*, 84–85.

EPILOGUE

The freezing, thawing, dampness, and frequent violent storms of outer Cape Cod are hard on human-made structures. Decay sets in quickly: wood rots, metal rusts, and everything else grows a layer of mold. Houses built in hollows never dry out, and those up on hills get blasted like moths in a wind tunnel. Some, such as the Hatch House, have survived remarkably well in spite of their very light construction, even after years of vacancy. The age-old strategy of letting wind and water pass around and through structures kept them relatively dry and sound, but many modern houses, including several owned by the National Park Service, have not been so lucky: they are deteriorating, and some are already beyond repair.

The Cape Cod Modern House Trust grew out of discussions with Cape Cod National Seashore officials — historian Bill Burke, in particular — concerning the fate of those modern houses that now belong to the U.S. government. Seven of them can be described as significant, and of these, five are listed on the National Register of Historic Places. Yet the government has no mandate or budget to protect them. The only route to preservation is for a nonprofit organization to apply to lease the vacant houses from the National Park Service and raise funds to restore and repurpose them.

Seeing a crying need, the trust first launched an ongoing project to collect and archive all available material on the Outer Cape's modern architecture, which meant scouring libraries and archives, driving down old fire roads on a tip, and interviewing the few surviving architects or their families and friends. Since only a handful of the buildings had been published, period photos existed mostly in personal albums. Research was complicated by the destruction of most local records when Wellfleet's town hall burned down during a blizzard in 1960, and by the fact that building permits and plans were often not required at all until the late 1960s.

The trust then took the plunge and applied to the National Park Service for a long-term lease on the Kugel/Gips House, which had been vacant and neglected for 11 years. Though there was no town record identifying the architect, trust founder Peter McMahon, having grown up in a house designed by Charlie Zehnder, recognized Zehnder's hand. The roof had failed, the decks had rotted through, and the interior was flooded and moldy, but the house was structurally sound and remained one of the designer's best works.

The major source of available funding was the Wellfleet Community Preservation Act, which awards grants for historic preservation. To win a grant, and then a lease from the National Park Service, the trust had to demonstrate to both federal officials and Wellfleet residents that the houses were architecturally and culturally significant. At town meetings, someone would reliably stand up and say, "I am older than these buildings! They are not historic!" Still, Wellfleet has been the major funder of the Kugel/Gips and Hatch restorations, followed by donations, trust memberships,

Porter House, Wellfleet (1961). A derelict structure, whose designer remains anonymous, owned by the National Park Service

The Kugel/Gips House during restoration, 2009

and public events such as an annual modern-house tour, lectures, and symposiums. Restoration work has been carried out by volunteers and local tradespeople, often with donated or discounted labor and materials.

The trust now holds long-term leases on three buildings: Zehnder's Kugel/Gips House, Jack Hall's Hatch House, and Paul Weidlinger's own house. Since these structures were laboratories for their designers and studios for their occupants, they were restored not as house museums but as functioning homes for artist and scholar residencies. Since 2010, the trust has awarded residencies to architects, visual artists, composers, and researchers. The residents of 2013 were six teams of finalists in a competition, initiated by the trust, to design affordable housing for Wellfleet. Donations from trust members help sustain the residency program, and, in exchange for their support, members may stay in one of the restored houses on a weekly or even monthly basis in the summer.

Central to the trust's mission is the notion that buildings and landscapes bear cultural memories. Standing in the modern houses today, you can still feel their designers' passion and intelligence. The trust has sought to make an impact by physically restoring a few of these derelict buildings, catalyzing a wide range of people to see the value of their local modernist legacy, and reintroducing the ideas embodied in the work of the ecologically sensitive visionaries who built these houses. As a result, most stakeholders have come to feel pride in their connection to the story. Many private owners of modern houses in the area now have a renewed interest in maintaining and restoring them.

Foresight has preserved many of the extraordinary landscapes that inspired Cape Cod's modernists. The goal now is to extend the lives of the buildings they designed, and to carry on the tradition of freethinking problem solving to nurture new creativity.

View of Cape Cod Bay and Provincetown
from the Hatch House deck

ABOUT THE AUTHORS

Christine Cipriani has written about architecture, design, and culture for *Architectural Record*, *Dwell*, *ArchitectureBoston*, *Modernism*, and other publications. Previously, she edited nonfiction at publishers including Beacon Press and Penguin India. She has vacationed in Wellfleet since early childhood, and lives near Boston with her husband and daughter.

Kenneth Frampton is a British architect, critic, historian, and the Ware Professor of Architecture at the Graduate School of Architecture, Planning, and Preservation at Columbia University. He is recognized internationally for his writing on twentieth-century architecture; key publications include *Modern Architecture: A Critical History* and *Studies in Tectonic Culture: The Poetics of Construction in Nineteenth and Twentieth Century Architecture*.

Peter McMahon is the principal of PM Design, a firm focused on sustainable design and the restoration of mid-twentieth-century buildings. His own summer house in Wellfleet has been published in *House Beautiful* magazine. In 2006, McMahon co-curated the exhibition *A Chain of Events: Modern Architecture on the Outer Cape, from Marcel Breuer to Charles Jencks*. In 2007, he founded the Cape Cod Modern House Trust to document, preserve, and revitalize modern architecture on the Outer Cape, where he lives year round.

SELECTED BIBLIOGRAPHY

Christopher Alexander, Sara Ishikawa, and Murray Silverstein, *A Pattern Language: Towns, Buildings, Construction* (New York: Oxford University Press, 1977)

Henry Beston, *The Outermost House: A Year of Life on the Great Beach of Cape Cod* (New York: Doubleday, 1928. Reprint, New York: Henry Holt, 1988)

Peter Blake, *Marcel Breuer: Architect and Designer* (New York: Museum of Modern Art, 1949)

———, *No Place Like Utopia: Modern Architecture and the Company We Kept* (New York: Knopf, 1993)

Marcel Breuer, *Sun and Shadow: The Philosophy of an Architect*, ed. Peter Blake (New York: Dodd, Mead, 1955)

Serge Chermayeff, *Design and the Public Good: Selected Writings 1930–1980*, ed. Richard Plunz (Cambridge, Mass.: MIT Press, 1982)

Serge Chermayeff, interviewed by Betty J. Blum, May 24–25, 1986. Chicago Architects Oral History Project, Department of Architecture, Art Institute of Chicago

Serge Chermayeff and Christopher Alexander, *Community and Privacy: Toward a New Architecture of Humanism* (Garden City, N.Y.: Doubleday, 1963)

Abbott Lowell Cummings, *The Framed Houses of Massachusetts Bay, 1625–1725* (Cambridge, Mass.: Harvard University Press, 1979)

Joachim Driller, *Breuer Houses* (London: Phaidon, 2000)

David Dunlap, Building Provincetown, http://buildingprovincetown.wordpress.com

Leona Rust Egan, *Provincetown as a Stage: Provincetown, The Provincetown Players, and the Discovery of Eugene O'Neill* (Orleans, Mass.: Parnassus Imprints, 1994)

Walter Gropius, *Manifest und Programm des Staatliches Bauhauses in Weimar*, 1919, http://bauhaus-online.de/en/atlas/das-bauhaus/idee/manifest

Olav Hammarström, interviewed by Robert Brown, Oct. 21, 1982. Washington, D.C.: Archives of American Art, Smithsonian Institution

Olav Hammarström and Marianne Strengell, interviewed by Mark Coir, Dec. 17, 1990. Bloomfield Hills, Mich.: Oral History Collection, Cranbrook Archives

Cynthia Huntington, *The Salt House: A Summer on the Dunes of Cape Cod* (Hanover, N.H.: University Press of New England, 1999)

Isabelle Hyman, *Marcel Breuer, Architect: The Career and the Buildings* (New York: Abrams, 2001)

Henry C. Kittredge, *Cape Cod: Its People and Their History* (New York: Houghton Mifflin, 1930. Reprint, Hyannis, Mass.: Parnassus, 1987)

Daniel Lombardo, *Cape Cod National Seashore: The First 50 Years* (Charleston, S.C.: Arcadia, 2010)

———, *Wellfleet: A Cape Cod Village* (Charleston, S.C.: Arcadia, 2000)

———, *Wellfleet: Then and Now* (Charleston, S.C.: Arcadia, 2007)

Joan Marks, "The Seacoast of Bohemia," *Provincetown Arts*, 1994, 39–44

David Masello, *Architecture Without Rules: The Houses of Marcel Breuer and Herbert Beckhard* (New York: Norton, 1993)

Mary McCarthy, *A Charmed Life* (New York: Harcourt, Brace, 1955. Reprint, New York: Harvest, 1992)

A Member of the Humane Society [James Freeman], *A Description of the Eastern Coast of the County of Barnstable from Cape Cod, or Race Point, in Latitude 42° 5', to Cape Mallebarre, or the Sandy Point of Chatham, in Latitude 41° 33', Pointing Out the Spots, on Which the Trustees of the Humane Society Have Erected Huts, and Other Places Where Shipwrecked Seamen May Look for Shelter* (Boston: Hosea Sprague, 1802)

William Morgan, *The Cape Cod Cottage* (New York: Princeton Architectural Press, 2006)

Hugh Morrison, *Early American Architecture: From the First Colonial Settlements to the National Period* (New York: Oxford University Press, 1952. Reprint, Mineola, N.Y.: Dover, 1987)

James C. O'Connell, *Becoming Cape Cod: Creating a Seaside Resort* (Hanover, N.H.: University Press of New England, 2003)

Jill Pearlman, *Inventing American Modernism: Joseph Hudnut, Walter Gropius, and the Bauhaus Legacy at Harvard* (Charlottesville: University of Virginia Press, 2007)

Alan Powers, *Serge Chermayeff: Designer, Architect, Teacher* (London: RIBA, 2001)

William Herbert Rollins, *Journal of Last Years: 1918–1929* (Topsfield, Mass.: Perkins, 1933)

Bernard Rudofsky, *Architecture Without Architects: A Short Introduction to Non-Pedigreed Architecture* (New York: Museum of Modern Art, 1964. Reprint, Albuquerque: University of New Mexico Press, 1987)

Marian Cannon Schlesinger, *I Remember: A Life of Politics, Painting and People* (Cambridge, Mass.: TidePool, 2012)

Arthur N. Strahler, *A Geologist's View of Cape Cod* (Garden City, N.Y.: Natural History Press, 1966)

Henry David Thoreau, *Cape Cod* (Boston: Ticknor and Fields, 1865. Reprint, Princeton: Princeton University Press, 2004)

University of Massachusetts and National Park Service, *People and Places on the Outer Cape: A Landscape Character Study* (Amherst: University of Massachusetts, 2004)

Mary Heaton Vorse, *Time and the Town: A Provincetown Chronicle* (New York: Dial, 1942. Reprint, New Brunswick: Rutgers University Press, 1991)

Edmund Wilson, *The Twenties* (New York: Farrar, Straus and Giroux, 1975)

Reuel K. Wilson, *To the Life of the Silver Harbor: Edmund Wilson and Mary McCarthy on Cape Cod* (Hanover, N.H.: University Press of New England, 2008)

INDEX

Project director: Diana Murphy
Design and production: Rita Jules
Editor: Anne Thompson
Separations and printing: Oceanic Graphic International,
    Hong Kong, China

Cover: Hayden Walling, Halprin House (see page 92); Marcel Breuer,
rendering of long-house prototype (see page 156)
Page 2: Connie and Marcel Breuer on the suspended porch of their
Wellfleet house, with Breuer's favorite personally assembled table, 1950
Page 4: Breuer House
Page 8: Early morning in a kettle hole on Bound Brook Island, Wellfleet
Page 262: At the Weidlinger House

Library of Congress Cataloging-in-Publication Data
is available upon request.
ISBN 978-1-935202-16-5
Fourth printing

Metropolis Books
ARTBOOK | D.A.P.
75 Broad Street Suite 630
New York, N.Y. 10004
tel 212 627 1999
fax 212 627 9484
www.artbook.com

ILLUSTRATION CREDITS

The authors have made their best efforts to locate and credit the sources and
copyright holders of all of the illustrations in this book.

Architectural Press Archive/RIBA Library Photographs Collection, 122; Avery
Architectural and Fine Arts Library, Columbia University, © Ivan and Peter
Chermayeff, 123, 124 top, 126 top, 220; courtesy Sara Barrett and Wilkinson
family, 134, 136 top, 137; Blend Interiors, Los Angeles, 148; courtesy Richard
Boonisar, 30 top; Tamas Breuer, 51, 118, 133, 172–73; Cape Cod National Seashore,
endsheets, 20, 21, 24, 27, 28 bottom, 29, 31–33, 42, 45, 146.
    Courtesy Ivan and Peter Chermayeff, 10; Cooper-Hewitt, National Design
Museum, Smithsonian Institution/Art Resource, N.Y., 136; Joan Hopkins Coughlin,
courtesy Wellfleet Historical Society, 35; © Cranbrook Archives, Olav Hammarström
Papers, 191, 193; H. K. Cummings, courtesy Snow Library, Orleans, Mass., 28 top;
Thomas Dalmas, 68–69, 100–101, 140–41, 182–83, 194–95, 208–9, 232–33,
252–53; Kent Dayton, 212–15, 230 middle; collection Leona Egan, Provincetown,
Mass., 38.
    Frances Loeb Library, Harvard Graduate School of Design, © Ivan and Peter
Chermayeff, 128–29; Yukio Futugawa, courtesy Marcel Breuer Papers, Archives of
American Art, Smithsonian Institution, 186 bottom; courtesy Nathaniel Gardiner,
95; Alexandre Georges, courtesy Susan Saarinen, 200–201; courtesy Noa Hall, 22,
47 bottom left, 53–59, 61–65, 80–81; Olav Hammarström Papers, Archives of
American Art, Smithsonian Institution, 187; courtesy Harrod family, 108; Harvard
Art Museums/Busch-Reisinger Museum, Gift of Walter Gropius, BRGA.82.135, 150.
    Henry Beston Society, 30 bottom; Nathaniel Hesse, 230 top; *House Beautiful*
©1948, reprinted with permission, 97; Uwe Jacobshagen, courtesy Bauhaus
Dessau Foundation, 149 bottom; courtesy Ati Gropius Johansen, 15; David
Kennedy, 83; courtesy Julie Kepes, 168 bottom; Raimund Koch, front cover, 4, 6,
8, 12, 18, 40, 70–79, 84–94, 102–7, 109–13, 116, 130–31, 135, 162–67, 174–79,
198–99, 210–11, 218, 224–27, 234–43, 246–47, 254–57, 262, 264, 266–67; Paul
Krueger, 248, 251.
    Library of Congress, Prints & Photographs Division, Historic American
Buildings Survey, 23, 25 (by Arthur C. Haskell); Bill Lyons, 186 top, 245 left, 259;
Marcel Breuer Papers, Special Collections Research Center, Syracuse University
Libraries, © Tamas Breuer, 147, 149 top, 155–58, 160–61, 180, 181 top and middle;
Bill Maris, courtesy Julie Maris Semel, 229; Massachusetts Cultural Resource
Information System, Massachusetts Historical Commission, 96; © Massachusetts
Institute of Technology, 221 (by Tunney Lee), 222, 223 (both by Maurice K. Smith).
    © Kevin Matthews/Artifice Images, 151; Norman McGrath, 132, 143, 144, 228;
Ellen McMahon, 265; Peter McMahon, 258; László Moholy-Nagy, courtesy Hattula
Moholy-Nagy, 14 top; courtesy Hattula Moholy-Nagy 14 bottom; Joseph W.
Molitor, courtesy Avery Architectural and Fine Arts Library, Columbia University,
124 bottom, 126 bottom, 127, 185 bottom, 202–3; Molitor, courtesy Syracuse
University Libraries, 185 top; Ralph Morse, Time & Life Pictures, Getty Images,
168 top left.
    John C. Phillips, courtesy Florence Phillips, 43–44, 46, 47 top and bottom
right, 48, 50 left; Pilgrim Monument and Provincetown Museum, 26; courtesy Sue
Porter, 159 right; Blair Resika, 52; RIBA Library Drawings & Archives Collections,
125; RIBA Library Photographs Collection, 121; Steve Rosenthal, 249–50; Eric
Saarinen, 197; Walter Sanders, Time & Life Pictures, Getty Images, 2, 159 top left,
168 top right, 170–71; courtesy Ben Schawinsky, 17; courtesy Andrew Schlesinger,
50 right; Ben Schnall, courtesy Sara Barrett and Wilkinson family, 138–39;
courtesy Eleanor Stefani, 98–99; courtesy Catherine Stillman, 181 bottom right.
    © Ezra Stoller/Esto, 152–53, 192; model by Ben Stracco, photograph by Mark
Walker, courtesy Cape Cod Modern House Trust, 245 right; © David Sundberg/
Esto, 181 bottom left; Vitra Design Museum archive, 60; courtesy Christopher
Walling, 82; courtesy Tom Weidlinger, 205–7 (photos by Madeleine Weidlinger-
Friedli, 206–7); courtesy Wellfleet Historical Society, 34, 37; Peter Zander, 66–67;
courtesy Zehnder family, 230 bottom, 244.